LEARNING
BY BREWING

LEARNING BY BREWING

THE EASY WAY TO BETTER TEA

SUGGESTIONS FOR SELECTING, PURCHASING, STORING AND
PREPARING THE WORLD'S BEST TEAS WITH A SPECIAL
EMPHASIS ON CHINA AND JAPAN

JENS DENNIG

Learning by brewing - The easy way to better tea
*Suggestions for selecting, purchasing, storing and preparing
the world's best teas with a special emphasis on China and Japan*

Jens Dennig
Pfingstrosenstr. 54
81377 Munich
Germany

Copyright © 2020 Jens Dennig

All rights reserved.

ISBN 13: 9798631582682

Preface	**15**
The road so far - my tea journey	**17**
Types of tea	**21**
Oxidation and Fermentation	**22**
Tea processing	**22**
White tea	**24**
Yellow tea	**25**
Green tea	**26**
Oolong	**27**
Red (black) tea	**28**
Dark (post-fermented) tea	**29**
Where to begin	**31**
Varieties And Cultivars	**33**
Varieties	**33**
Cultivars	**34**
Taiwan	35
China	36
Japan	38
India	39
Picking standards and leaf qualities	**39**
Deciphering tea names	**44**
Chinese tea names	**46**
Romanization	**55**
Sourcing tea	**58**
The form of the tea	**58**
The teabag	59
Loose leaf tea	59
Powder tea	60
Pressed tea	60
Sourcing options	**60**
Supermarkets	60
Large tea retailers and your local small tea business	61
Specialty tea shop	62

Teahouses	64
Online	65
Domestic or international sourcing?	66
Tea masters	67
Friends	68

The fair price of tea — 69
Quality criteria	69
Competition tea	70
Some thoughts on pricing	70
Fake tea	71

Storing tea — 73
Storage periods — 76

Preparing tea — 79
Dishes and other accessories — 79
The brewing vessel	80
Kyusu	82
Cha Hu	83
Western Teapot	90
Cooling and serving vessels	90
Tea cups and bowls	91
Tea cutlery and other tools	92
Water collection tanks	95
Kettles and water heaters	96

The right water — 97
Tap water	98
Filtered tap water	98
The mineral water you trust	99
Water comparison	100
Conclusion	101

The brewing process — 101
Western style	102
GongFu Style	104
Grandpa style	108
The wash	108
White tea	109
Yellow tea	109
Green tea	110

Chinese green tea	110
Japanese (steamed) green tea	110
Matcha	111
Oolong	113
Red (black) tea	113
Postfermented (dark) tea	113
Cold brew vs. cooled tea	114
Mizudashi　水出し	114
Korimizudashi　氷水出し	115
Gurin Ti　グリーンティー	115
ISO 3103	115
Travelling with tea	116
Water	117
Brewing vessel	117
Sieve	118
Tea	118
Conclusion	118
The perfect tea	**120**
Tea tasting	**121**
Food Pairing	**130**
Health	**133**
Organic and pesticide free tea	**133**
Active Substances in tea	**134**
GABA	135
Caffeine	135
Diet	**136**
China　中国　and Taiwan　台湾	**138**
Harvest time	**138**
Picking method and leaf quality	**139**
The best teas from China	**140**
White tea (Bai Cha)　白茶	**140**
Bai Hao Yinzhen　白毫银针	142
Bai MuDan　白牡丹	143
Gong Mei　贡眉	144
Gushu Cha Ya　古树茶芽	144

Lao Bai Cha　老白茶	146
Shou Mei　贡眉	147
Ya Bao Cha　芽苞	148
Yue Guang Bai　月光白	149
Yellow tea (Huang Cha)　黄茶	**152**
Junshan Yinzhen　君山银针	154
Huang Ya　黃芽	155
Kekecha　可可茶	156
Green tea (Lü Cha)　绿茶	**157**
Anji Baicha　安吉白茶	157
Bai Long Jing　白龙井	159
Bi Luo Chun　碧螺春	159
Guzhu Zi Sun　顾渚紫笋	161
Long Jing　龙井	163
Mao Feng　毛峰	166
Mao Jian　毛尖	168
Tai Ping Hou Kui　太平猴魁	170
Zhu Cha　珠茶	171
Blue tea (Oolong)　烏龍茶	**172**
The four leading oolong regions	173
Anxi oolong　安溪乌龙	176
Bai Ya Qi Lan　白芽奇兰	176
Ben Shan　本山	177
Huang Jin Gui　黄金桂	177
Jin Guan Yin　金观音	178
Tie Guan Yin　铁观音	179
Zhang Ping Shui Xian　漳平水仙	181
Wuyi Yancha　武夷岩茶　Rock tea	182
Bai Ji Guan　白鸡冠	185
Bu Zhi Chun　不知春	186
Da Hong Pao　大红袍	187
Fo Shou　佛手	188
Huang Guan Yin　黃觀音	190
Huang Mei Gui　黃玫瑰	190

Lao Zhong Shui Xian 老种水仙	191
Qi Lan 奇兰	192
Rou Gui Xiang 肉桂香	192
Shui Jin Gui 水金龟	194
Shui Xian 水仙	194
Tie Luo Han 铁罗汉	195
Yan Xiang Fei 岩香妃	196
Zi Hong Pao 紫红袍	197
Fenghuang Dancong 凤凰单丛 Phoenix Oolong	197
Ba Xian 八仙	198
Gui Hua Xiang 桂花香	198
Huang Zhi Xiang 黄枝香	199
Mi Lan Xiang 蜜兰香	199
Mo Li Xiang 茉莉香	200
Po Tou Xiang 姜花香	200
Shui Xian 水仙	201
Xing Ren Xiang 杏仁香	201
Ya Shi Xiang 鸭屎香	201
You Hua Xiang 柚花香	203
Zhi Lan Xiang 芝兰香	203
Taiwan oolong	203
Alishan 阿里山	204
Cui Yu 翠玉	204
Dong Ding 凍頂	205
Dong Fang Mei Ren 東方美人	206
Gui Fei 贵妃	207
Jin Xuan 金萱 Nai Xiang 奶香	207
Milk oolong	207
Lishan 梨山	208
Mi Xiang 蜜香	209
Muzha Tie Guan Yin 木栅铁观音	210
Pouchong 包种	211
Qing Xin 青心	212
Si Ji Chun 四季春	212
Other regions	213

Aged oolong 陳年烏龍	213
Red tea (Hong Cha) 红茶	**216**
Dian Hong 云南滇紅	217
Hong Yu 红玉	218
Jin Jun Mei 金骏眉	219
Jiuqu Hong Mei 九曲紅梅	220
Qi Men 祁门	221
Zheng Shan Xiao Zhong 正山小种	222
Dark Tea (Heicha) 黑茶	**224**
Shapes of tea	224
Yunnan heicha 云南 黑茶	229
Sheng 生 or Shu 熟, a question of personal preference	229
Packaging and trademarks	231
Quality and ancient trees	232
Two ways to get started	234
Regions	234
Tea factories	239
Number teas	241
Cha Gao 茶膏	249
Huang Pian 黄片 Yellow leaves	250
Lao Cha Tuo 老茶头 Old tea nugget	251
Pang Xie Jiao 螃蟹脚 Crab legs	253
Anhui heicha 安徽 黑茶	254
Liu'an heicha 六安黑茶	254
Guangxi heicha 广西黑茶	255
Liu Bao Cha 六堡茶	255
Chong Shi Cha 虫屎茶	258
Hubei heicha 湖北黑茶	259
Hunan heicha 湖南黑茶	260
Fu Zhuan 茯砖 Fu brick	261
Hua Juan Cha 花卷茶	263
Sichuan heicha 四川黑茶	264
Lu Bian Cha 路边茶 Border tea	264
Kang Zhuan 康砖 Kang brick	265
Purple tea (Zi Cha) 紫茶	**267**

Flavored teas	**268**
Bamboo	269
Bitter melon	271
Chrysanthemum	272
Jasmine tea	273
Rose Oolong	274
Citrus fruit	276
Earl and Lady Grey	276
Orange, Tangerine, et al	276
Pomelo	278
Gong Yi Cha　工艺茶	280
Japan　日本	**282**
Growing method	**282**
Shaded tea - Japan's unique cultivation method	283
Time and type of harvest	**283**
White tea (Shirocha)　白茶	**285**
Green tea (Ryokucha)　緑茶	**285**
Aracha　荒茶	287
Bancha　番茶	288
Aki Bancha　秋番茶	288
Hakuta Bancha　伯太番茶	289
Kageboshi Bancha　陰干し番茶	289
Kancha　寒茶	289
Kyobancha　京番茶	289
Yoshino Nikkan Bancha　吉野日干番茶	290
Demono　出物	290
Genmaicha　玄米茶	291
Gyokuro　玉露	292
Houjicha　焙じ茶	294
Kabusecha　被せ茶	294
Kamairicha　釜炒り茶	295
Karigane　雁音	295
Konacha　粉茶	295
Funmatsucha　粉末茶	296
Kokeicha　固形茶	296

Kukicha 茎茶	297
Matcha 抹茶	298
Mecha 芽茶	301
Sencha 煎茶	301
Variations of the steaming process	302
Shiraore 白折	303
Shincha 新茶	303
Tamacha 玉茶	304
Tamaryokucha 玉緑茶	304
Tencha 碾茶	305
Yanagicha 柳茶	305
Oolong (Uron-cha) 烏竜茶	**305**
Red (black) tea (Kocha) 紅茶	**306**
Post-fermented tea	**307**
Awabancha 阿波番茶	307
Batabatacha バタバタ茶	308
Goishicha 碁石茶	308
Mimasakacha 美作番茶	309
Korea 한국	**311**
Green tea (Nokcha) 녹차	**311**
Yellow tea (Hwangcha) 황차	**313**
Red (black) tea (Hongcha) 홍차	**313**
Yuja-cha (Yuzu tea) 유자차	**314**
Conclusion	**314**
Indian subcontinent	**316**
India भारत	**316**
Assam असम	317
Darjeeling दार्जिलिंग	318
Masala Chai मसाला चाय	321
Nepal नेपाल	**323**
Sri Lanka ශ්‍රී ලංකා இலங்கை	**324**
Other Asian countries	**326**

Georgia საქართველო	326
Indonesia	327
Laos ປະເທດລາວ	328
Myanmar မြန်မာ	329
Thailand ประเทศไทย	331
Nang Ngam นาง งาม	331
Cha Khao Hom ชา ข้าว หอม Sticky rice tea	331
Turkey	332
Vietnam Việt Nam	334
Africa	337
Ethiopia ኢትዮጵያ	338
Tanzania	339
Kenya	340
Malawi	341
Satemwa Antlers	341
Bvumbwe Peony	342
Zomba Pearls	343
Rwanda	343
Australia and New Zealand	345
Arakai Summer Green	345
Zealong	345
Colombia	346
Epilogue	348
References	349
Internet	349
Books	350
Credits	352
Photo credits	352
End marks	353

PREFACE

A very warm (or rather hot[1]) welcome! You are just about to read a book I have been looking for during the past 40 years - to no avail. So I finally decided to simply write it myself.

What is that supposed to mean? Put simply: I have now reached a point I would have preferred to have arrived at earlier, because for too long I have had to satisfy my thirst for knowledge painstakingly from fragments. This resulted in drinking tea of often only mediocre quality. I almost only drink tea and by now I am very happy about its taste most of the time. I would like to share this joy and my personal experiences with you.

My aim is to shorten the path to tea enjoyment for everyone and to help avoid disappointment.

So how do you find the path to good tea, and are there really shortcuts to it? Well, ideally, this book itself is this shortcut, but please judge for yourself. It summarizes the most important information so that you can find your way to increased tea pleasure without detours and follow your own tea path.

There are many tea books, and I have read but a small part of them. But despite my voracious reading and abundant tasting, it took much too long to get upscale and top quality into my shopping cart and, eventually, into a tasty cup of tea.

Perhaps you know the saying "Life is too short for bad wine"? No doubt you can agree with it and also replace the word wine with another one. I prefer to replace it with tea or chocolate.

But here I am focussing solely on tea, a beverage which is similar to the above-mentioned wine in many ways. Although wine is made from grapes and tea from leaves, buds and/or stems, the variety of tea is in no way inferior to that of wine.

Although originally from Asia, tea, like wine, is being cultivated on many continents and thus in a wide variety of climates, altitudes and soils. It inevitably develops special individual characteristics. The growing area becomes tastable and tangible. Tea, like wine, is harvested cheaply by machine or picked laboriously by hand and after the harvest is treated fleetingly or lovingly, with haste or with care. Simple wines can be enough for less spoiled palates, just as simple teas from huge plantations are usually at least drinkable.

But then neither of them would possess the complex aromas that connoisseurs love so much and for which they are prepared to make many a financial sacrifice. And just as some wines are matured in barriques or improve with age, high-quality teas are also carefully aged, sometimes for decades after the harvest, and thus become even richer in body and aroma. With the effort of planting, growing, harvesting, post-harvest treatment and storing, the price of these liquid stimulants naturally also increases.

I would like to underline that I do not consider myself Buddha's gift to the tea world, a professional, a tea sommelier, etc. Over the years, however, I have had the opportunity to gain manyfold experiences which I would like to share with you. I have no claim to infallibility and neither have I imbibed wisdom by the cupful. This is a book about my personal experiences and therefore cannot and will not always be fully impartial. I am sharing my knowledge to the best of my ability and I am trying to be honest and fair. I am humbly grateful to nature for allowing plants to grow that allow me to enjoy this much pleasure.

So what are the important steps on the way to enjoying tea? First of all, I will start with some basics. What is tea, what sorts are there and how are they made? With tens of thousands of different teas in the world, I will not even attempt to provide an exhaustive resource, but will instead put a deliberate focus on keeping things brief. Whether a tea is roasted for twenty or thirty seconds or is rolled to the left instead of right is irrelevant to me. Always faithful to the goal of increasing enjoyment, I will aim to provide basic knowledge that will enable the esteemed reader to move more confidently through the abundant offerings and find quality in a targeted manner. Each production method has countless variations, but only the basic commonalities shall be presented here.

Then I will continue with an examination and evaluation of the various types of suppliers and also offer recommendations for the best possible storage. Once these treasures have landed safely in the vault, we will look at the most common steeping practices. What good is it to have purchased fine teas and then not to extract the maximum out of them?

The second part of this book offers an overview of selected teas of our world. The majority of the teas mentioned in this book originate from China. This is hardly surprising for a number of reasons - after all, the Chinese tea culture is thousands of years old and the variety of terroirs, cultivars and processing techniques is unrivaled anywhere in the world. In terms of production volume, other countries are growing massively, but even if the conditions there were similar, a young plant would need 100 years or more to be allowed to call itself an old tree and be sought after accordingly. China's lead in terms of variety and quality is therefore hard to catch up with in the medium term, and consequently Chinese teas are predominant here, followed by mostly green teas of Japanese origin. However, teas from the Indian subcontinent, and even Africa and Oceania, are also considered briefly, but with much less intensity.

Sometimes I might be repeating myself in certain chapters. This is to ensure that you do not necessarily have to read this book from start to finish, but rather to allow you to jump straight into individual chapters according to your current cravings, without having read all the previous ones. I make every effort to write only about teas that I know and have bought and drunk myself at least several times. Only if a tea belongs to the tea worlds cultural heritage will I include it here even if I do not know it personally, but then I will point it out.

But now enough with the preface. May the tea be with you. Or, if you prefer, may this Chinese one-liner accompany you on your path of tea: 茶道清韵[2]

THE ROAD SO FAR

MY TEA JOURNEY

My first memories of tea are from the distant past, that is, since childhood. At home, there was always a pot of "tea" in the kitchen, usually already cooled down, which I always made use of. But this drink was made from peppermint dust collected in bags and therefore had nothing to do with real tea. Even today I still enjoy the occasional herbal infusion, preferably made from fresh material, especially sage from my own garden. As a primary school pupil I spent many Easter holidays in East Frisia, frequently drinking the so-called East Frisian tea, appropriately sweetened with cream and rock candy.

But my personal tea path really only started as a teenager in youth tea rooms and on several trips to England. At that time, such tea rooms were a useful way to make new acquaintances with representatives of one's preferred sex. They were organized by religious institutions, political youth organizations, trade unions or schools, i.e. organizations that wanted to get their future voters, believers or consumers on the path of virtue as early as possible. Unfortunately none of these tea rooms wanted to show me the path to teaology. The most disturbing thing I will always remember is "black tea with strawberry cream flavor". Even back then I wondered where the fruit and dairy products might be hidden between those leaves. Although they were often loose leaf teas, the brewing time of anything between five minutes and five hours (kept warm by means of a teapot warmer or a tea light) meant that it was not really possible to spark off a firework of pleasure. To swallow the concoction, sugar came in handy. At least the music was generally good, but that's not really surprising. After all, it was the 80s.

I got to know England on several extensive language trips and during visits to relatives and friends. Unfortunately this did not expand my tea horizon noticeably. The ancestors of today's Englishmen may have contributed a great deal to the fact that tea became socially acceptable in Europe, but the average Briton at that time did not seem to be particularly interested in variety. So, as a young guy in search of his preferred adult beverage to be, I was under the impression that there were basically two kinds of tea in England: English Breakfast in a bag (for the quick cup at any time) and English Breakfast as loose leaf tea (for the pot). For the sake of completeness, the omnipresent Earl Grey deserves to be mentioned. Only a few decades later I even got to know him in quite a drinkable quality.

To be able to consume this kind of tea at that time, sugar helped again. Milk straight from the fridge was also very welcome, as it at least brought the drink down to a pleasant drinking temperature and also helped against the goose bumps on the forearms caused by the bitterness.

Only much later did I learn that English (Irish/Scottish/Welsh) Breakfast Teas are always blends, i.e. mixtures of different black teas of varying qualities and growing areas. This was and still is similar to the East Frisian blend, which I was allowed to enjoy every year in the area around Emden, as mentioned above. This was actually the most delicious version, because sugar and fat combined nicely complement the maltiness of the tea and make it look like caramelized. Note: Cream is always preferable to milk, because of the higher fat content.

Then I came up with the idea of tasting the main ingredient undiluted, and I started asking the local tea shop not only for the raspberry-mango-coconut blend, but also for pure Darjeeling or Assam. From where exactly in Assam, Darjeeling or even Ceylon the tea originated was often not very interesting to me. For me it basically came out of the five pound tin can that the dealer had opened in front of me. And this merchant was buying mostly from his distributor, he did not hitchhike to Asia on his own two feet.

Very early, I also started to satisfy my elevated calorie needs in Chinese restaurants. For my school buddies and myself, this was a cheap way to supply our bodies with plenty of glutamate and we also started to slurp the omnipresent jasmine tea. For us teenagers and young adults with tight budgets it was especially interesting that water was refilled free of charge time and again. Sugar or milk or even cream were not served and were not missed. The light astringency suited the hearty food quite well. Moreover, the tea was always brewed for only a short time and then quickly poured into the cups. In addition, the jasmine aroma concealed the poor quality of the leaves.

As an Asian food aficionado since childhood, I quickly discovered Thai, Japanese and Indian restaurants and as a trainee, civil servant and later student I was grateful for the cheap and tasty Turkish and Kurdish restaurants in my hometown. None of them, except the Japanese restaurants, brought me any new knowledge about tea.

The descendants of the Ottomans prepared tea in a different way, but the taste (often thinner, rarely bitter) did not differ much from the British breakfast tea. Remember? Anything goes down with sugar. Only milk was not added there.

What the Ottomans did not (add), the Indians overdid. They cooked the tea (instead of brewing it) for hours, together with spices and milk and then added sugar. Great idea, because spices can not only cover up missing flavors (tea does not really taste better after hours of cooking), but also replace missing ones. Although I occasionally enjoy a good masala chai, I never really liked the chai you get after the Indian meal. Often, I would have preferred a simple black tea without milk and sugar. But mostly there was none. Or I hadn't asked for it because I did not think of it.

The Japanese teas, on the other hand, did not correspond with my preferences at first. Green tea? Green tea usually tastes bitter, or so they said. If only it had tasted bitter, unfortunately it often tasted rather thin and arbitrary, but with time I got used to it and learned to appreciate it, but honestly I only wanted to make sure that the sushi was accompanied appropriately. I did not know any good Matcha at that time either.

I went to Morocco for the first time in my early 20s and regarded the local mint tea or Thé à la Menthe as a black tea mixture with mint. The huge amounts of sugar and the abundant caffeine gave a pleasant taste and a relaxed alertness, complemented by the freshness of mint. At that time, however, domestic attempts to imitate it on my own tended to go badly. I simply did not know that the basics were mostly cheap Chinese gunpowder green tea and the dried leaves of Nana mint. The latter is often added in fresh form as well during the preparation and then it may taste almost like it tastes in Morocco. Nowadays you can also buy the mixture as Moroccan mint tea, but it still does not come close to the real deal. A recent trip to Marrakech has confirmed this once again impressively. No wonder, because the exact mixture is always a little different. Furthermore, in Central Europe we have a different water quality (minerals, degree of hardness, etc.), use different dishes and prepare the tea differently than in North Africa.

More than a decade ago, I decided to go on a meatless diet for various reasons, I also removed fish from the menu. And since I was already changing to meat-free food, I decided to also become a teetotaler, so I have not drunk any alcohol since then. As someone who liked to drink good wines and who did not spurn the occasional single malt, I was very quickly looking for a new drug or comfort food. As a self-confessed chocoholic I felt the urge to find a second enjoyable treat, which I could consume anytime and anywhere, easily and in large quantities.

Then tea came right on cue. As already mentioned, I had made some good and some less-than-great experiences with teas up to this point. At home I already had a decent tea selection, most of them from the Indian subcontinent. Now I decided to approach the topic in a more structured way and to have a closer look at teas from other Asian countries and to taste them, of course. Initially, I bought my first sample sets mainly from online suppliers. In the beginning I often decided on the big suppliers who could run prominent advertisements and later on (after I had found out that Oolongs were worth drinking) I started looking for the specialists who offered not only one or two Oolongs but 20 or more different varieties and were able to describe them in detail.

A little later I had my first Pu'er[3], and it was just horrible. It looked like a simple Ceylon tea, only with a musty taste. At that time my interest in Pu'er was almost over, but today I am glad that I have persevered. The second attempt was an old Huang Pian[4]. Also not the real thing in the eyes of many connoisseurs, but for me it was a revelation. I continued my journey with genuine Sheng and Shu and my drinking and collecting mania has had no end until today.

"I've travelled each and every highway..."

Admittedly, not really. Of the Asian tea-growing countries, I have only visited Japan, Thailand and Indonesia, and I have been to some places in Africa, but did not visit tea plantations. Fortunately, in these modern times you can have the treasures and information delivered conveniently to your home. Why crawl through the jungles of Southeast Asia when you could spend that time drinking tea instead?

"Regrets, I've had a few, but then again, too few to mention..."

In retrospect, the most regrettable thing for me is the fact that I drank inferior tea for too long and sometimes skimped in the wrong place. In other words, parsimony is not the best thing when it comes to tea, but thriftiness combined with knowledge can't hurt.

"And now, the end is near..."

Hopefully my last infusion will not come soon, but I have already made provisions for my retirement, and my Pu'er darlings will certainly mature and improve in taste over the next few decades.

But enough about my tea journey, now let's see how we can support yours.

TYPES OF TEA

Watery extracts made of herbs, dried fruits, mushrooms, bushes, grasses or shrubs may be called tea in many languages, but they are actually not tea. Some languages distinguish more precisely than others and speak of infusions or tisanes.

Infusions made from rooibos, honeybush, yerba mate or lapacho bark may be tasty or even therapeutic, but they play no role in this book.

Strictly speaking, tea is exclusively a beverage based on a plant species belonging to the Camellia family (Theaceae): Camellia sinensis. In the following, we will discuss this plant and its variants.[5]

Many tea books and online publications speak of tea varieties. However, in common language use this refers to two different ways of looking at tea. The first is the botanical view and refers to the varieties of the plant Camellia sinensis. At the same time, this refers to the different colors that stand for the different production methods and characterize the distinction at the highest level. Personally, I prefer using the terms type, sort, or kind for the latter.

Even nowadays one far too often reads that there are basically just two types of tea: black and green. But the world of tea is colorful. Not quite like the rainbow, but it does come pretty close.

Things are similar with wine, the occasional buyer distinguishes between red and white wine, and is often satisfied with that.[6] It is not much different with tea. While most non-asian people often distinguish tea only in terms of black or green, the differentiations in China are much more sophisticated, and for this reason we want to use the Chinese color theory here. After all, the mother country of tea also offers the richest selection of teas, and so we will mostly be following this color scheme.

The following table compares the Chinese names of the tea types with the rest of the world. The left column shows the English translation and then the Chinese characters, the third column then shows the spelling in Pinyin[7], and the right column shows the average oxidation level of the tea. More about oxidation and its meaning to follow further below.

The table is sorted according to my personal preference, i.e. not according to the average degree of oxidation of the tea, but from light (white) to dark, post-fermented tea. The color names refer to the typical color of the infusion in the cup[8], i.e. from very clear, light, almost white to slightly yellowish, greenish, blue-greenish[9], reddish to dark, brownish, almost black. However, sorting by degree of oxidation would also be possible and likewise logical.

OXIDATION AND FERMENTATION

In tea literature the terms oxidation and fermentation are often confused. When distinguishing tea colors, it is always about oxidation, with the exception of so-called post-fermented tea, which is produced from unfinished green tea.

Oxidation always refers to the air's oxygen reacting with the enzymes in the freshly picked tea. Depending on the variety (color) to be produced, the producer will sooner or later stop the oxidation, usually by heating. The degree of oxidation causes the typical taste and names the finished tea.

Fermentation is what usually happens after[10] completion and fixation of a tea, i.e. the microbial decomposition and transformation of leaf material, which may then lead to further typical taste results.

Overview of types and colors of tea

English	中国	Pinyin	Typical level of oxidation
White Tea	白茶	Baicha	20-30%
Yellow Tea	黄茶	Huangcha	10-20%
Green Tea	绿茶	Lücha	0-2%
Blue Tea	蓝茶	Lancha	30-60%
	清茶	Qingcha	
Wulong	乌龙茶	Wulongcha	
Red or Black Tea	红茶	Hongcha	80-90%
Dark Tea	黑茶	Heicha	100%
Flower Tea	花茶	Huacha	Not relevant
Art Tea, Crafted Tea	工艺茶	Gongyicha	Depending on the type of tea

TEA PROCESSING

The process of tea production varies from extremely simple to hugely complex. Always starting from the Camellia sinensis and its varieties, the processing and thus the knowledge and experience of the tea farmer and the tea factory make a big difference.

The processing begins with the harvest, and this is where the material is already separated into cheap and expensive quality. Depending on whether a plantation is harvested from bushes of all the same height or the picking is done from large and sometimes wild trees, with the motor scythe or laboriously picked by hand, prices can be higher or lower and the ideal leaf qualities are selected more or less carefully. Virtually only hand picking can ensure that you get exactly what you need for a particular quality level; this usually depends on the number of leaves per branch, which are harvested together with the uppermost leaf bud. In general, teas made from pure buds or from the bud with one or two leaves are the most expensive, because while snapping off a twig always takes about the same time, omitting leaves number three and four significantly reduces the amount of tea harvested per time unit. Of course, the harvest time is a factor here as well, since the older leaves are larger in autumn than the younger ones in spring, thus more leaf material is then harvested at the same labour costs.

Therefore it does not come as a surprise that spring tea is often more expensive than tea harvested later in the year. Spring harvests are also considered to be more subtle in taste, as their leaves have not been exposed to the sun for so long. They are also considered more nutritious, as the plant has been able to replenish its strength sufficiently in winter, whereas it is supposed to be more exhausted by the end of summer. The difference between the different harvest times can also be tasted in teas of the same origin and processing. Nevertheless, there are quite a few enthusiasts who prefer the autumn harvests of certain teas because they appreciate their specific nuances. Autumn harvests are usually less sweet and fruity, but more mature and yet more modest and unagitated.

Directly after harvesting, further processing of the tea leaves determines which type of tea is produced and how the desired taste is achieved.

In the paragraphs that follow, the general processing principle is described in each case, but there are always stronger or less strong deviations, which are at the discretion of the producer. Here, however, it is only a matter of a general differentiation, as the aim is not scientific depth, but taste heights.

But no matter which tea variety is to be produced, there is always the same first step, the withering directly after the harvest. This theoretically also applies to green teas, but producers mostly try to keep this as scant as possible.

As soon as the tea leaf is plucked, it begins to wilt because of the loss of water. Unlike in the wild, this wilting is controlled by the tea producer depending on the desired production goal, by determining the location (sun, shade, mats, bamboo baskets, etc.) and often also by regulating the ventilation, which can involve purposefully heating the air. When the leaves have reached the desired amount of residual moisture, this step is complete. Some tea producers are said to recognize the ideal moment by the changed scent. One can only hope that they will be spared from colds and sniffles. Chemically speaking, chlorophyll ("the green") is broken down in this step and the amount of caffeine increases. The degradation or transformation of chlorophyll reduces the grassy, vegetal taste and more complex aromas develop, which have a stronger scent and more variable taste.

So let's take a closer look at the different types of tea, their oxidation and their production processes.

WHITE TEA

Although originally from Fujian, white tea is now produced in almost all tea regions. In China, the provinces of Zhejiang and Yunnan are especially worth mentioning. Each region differs in character due to the different growing conditions and the cultivars used. Common among them are the rather large, white buds and delicate hairs on the underside of the youngest leaves, which in combination with the very light, clear infusion give white tea its name. Some infusions, especially of large leaf teas such as White Moonlight, nevertheless tend to be more orange-yellowish, but this does not change how they are to be categorized. So, orange ain't the new white here.

White tea is as diverse as the regions it is grown in. One of the most exclusive and also most expensive is ones Bai Hao Yinzhen from China, also known as Silver Needle tea. Similar teas from Sri Lanka are also called Silver Tips and sometimes Golden Tips. For this tea, only those leaf buds are used which have not yet started to open. They are covered with a silver-white fluff (that is the tiny hairs underside the developed leaf), which gives the tea its distinctive name.

If the crop is not processed promptly, it begins to wilt and dry out after harvesting, losing up to 25% of its weight in water while reacting with the oxygen in the ambient air. Depending on whether the leaf crop is dried quickly in the sun or more slowly in the shade or in sheds, it oxidizes to some degree. Due to the hot sun, the water from the leaves evaporates faster and so the oxidation can be lighter than by slow drying. During this time (usually one to three days) the leaf ingredients are chemically converted, which changes the taste significantly compared to fresh leaves.

Historically, for the production of white tea, the tea leaves are first wilted in the sun before being heated to stop oxidation once and for all. During withering, the leaves oxidize only slightly and at the same time chlorophyll is broken down by the sun's UV light. The latter leads to the incomparable aroma of white tea. Scent and taste are light and gentle like a hint of perfume, without ever being obtrusive.

There is a disagreement between the Chinese and the rest of the world's tea industry about the exact definition of white tea. While the other countries also define white tea according to the production process described above, i.e. only dried leaf material, they also demand intact white hairs under the leaf, so the definition should preferably be based on this. However, this would mean that low leaf grades from China such as Shou Mei would often no longer be considered white tea, as they do not show these tiny hairs.

"The" tea nation China has a slightly different opinion: for them, white tea is also defined by the production process, but may only consist of material that has been bred from the cultivar (C. Sinensis var. Sinensis) Bai Hao and harvested in the first spring picking. Then again, a Yunnan white tea would not be considered a white tea by that definition, since it is made from the large-leaf species (C. Sinensis var. assamica).

Why do we not simply agree on the process definition of the minimum post-harvest steps that make up white tea? Therefore, the minimum steps that should be expected from the white tea production process are:

- Withering in the sun
- Drying

So white tea is made from wilted and then merely dried leaves. Various degrees of withering take place in all types except green tea. This process prolongs the tea's shelf life among other things. Unlike all other teas, white tea does not undergo intentionally prolonged oxidation, heating, roasting etc. Oxidation stops when most of the water has evaporated, usually between 20 and 30%.

The tea does not have to look white, but often has a light grey or silvery shimmer, which is caused by the fine hairs on the underside of the leaf. Since the tea producer basically does no more post-processing[11] on the raw product, he has little choice but to use high-quality material. With teas of different colors or types, the finishing process may sometimes conceal mediocre quality; this is hardly possible with white tea. To put it simple, one can expect better average quality from most white teas than from other types of tea. However, this knowledge only helps to the extent that one should also like the taste of white tea. After all, the finest white truffles make little sense if you are not fond of fungi. White tea usually produces a very light cup and a mild aroma.

White tea is considered to be the most natural of all teas, because apart from drying and a light, short heating to preserve it, it goes through no further processing steps. However, this also deprives the leaves of the possibility of being transformed into even more complex teas by further processing. But particularly fine white tea can also mature wonderfully for several years.

YELLOW TEA

According to the sorting of the above tea color table, the color yellow follows now. This type of tea can be found almost exclusively in China. Yellow tea is a variant of green tea in terms of production technology, so if necessary you may want to briefly skip ahead to the green tea section and then return back here.

Now and then you might still read that yellow tea is equated with white tea due to its slight oxidation of 10-20%, but this is incorrect. It really is more a variation of green tea in terms of taste and has little in common with white tea.

There are several kinds of yellow teas, but they all are not well known in the West. One of the better-known ones, Junshan Yinzhen, is one of the most famous teas in China. In the infusion you immediately recognize the origin of the name yellow tea, because that's exactly what it looks like.

Yellow tea is processed in a similar way to green tea, with the difference being that it is oxidized somewhat more strongly. This process of becoming yellow sounds quite interesting, but is fairly straightforward. In Chinese it is called Men Huang 闷黄. The fixed tea is wrapped in cloths or paper and then allowed to rest one or more times. This takes between a couple hours and a few days at 25 to 35°C (77 to 95°F) which makes it oxidize more strongly than green tea. It is only by this oxidation that the tea gets its typical yellow color (caused by the decomposition of chlorophyll in the leaf) and its mild aroma. Sometimes this phase is also called a short fermentation, but it is questionable whether much microbial fermentation can take place within three days (at best) at such low temperatures. In any case, oxidation does take place, whether caused by the residual moisture in the tea or the air in the tea pile. Thus, yellow tea is, in terms of the degree of oxidation, between green and white tea.

The minimum steps that make up yellow tea are therefore:

- Withering
- Fixing (through strong heating)
- Yellowing (by moist heat)
- Drying

Sometimes yellow tea is disrespectfully referred to as an unintentional factory accident in the production of green tea; the assumption being that it turned yellow after the workers either let the tea sit for too long between the fixing step and the final drying or that they forgot about it altogether. This legend persists, but can be considered nonsense. Yellow tea has been produced for about 2,000 years and may have been created by chance. But nowadays, this time-consuming and labour-intensive step of yellowing is usually only applied specifically to high-quality, young spring buds. Unfortunately, there are suppliers in the tea industry who do not or only poorly perform this yellowing step. However, this does not prevent them from marketing some of their green tea as more expensive yellow tea.

GREEN TEA

China, Japan and Korea are the main green tea-producing countries. While China also produces many other types of tea, Japan is mainly defined and dominated by green tea. Korea lies in between - both in green tea taste and geographically.

In contrast to white tea, green tea does not undergo targeted withering. While white tea wilts after harvesting and then continues to do so until it is dry, this wilting only occurs very briefly in green tea. Green tea is often heated or fixed very shortly after harvesting, which stops any enzymatic cell activity. In Chinese, this step bears the imposing name of Sha Qing 杀青

or kill-green. This early fixing leads to an oxidation level of usually less than 2%. This is why green tea is also called non-oxidized tea.

Fixation is handled quite differently from country to country and from green tea to green tea. Japanese green teas, for example, are often steamed in hot and humid air. In contrast, most Chinese teas are baked in ovens or roasted in pans or woks.

The longer it takes to reach the required temperature of around 80°C (176°F) for fixation, the more time there is for the tea leaves to denature their contents, and the more diverse aromas can develop. Therefore, although steamed teas develop beautiful grassy notes, their aroma spectrum is a far cry from the richness of baked teas, just as the same meat tastes completely different when cooked rather than roasted or grilled.

In a nut(ty)shell, roasted Chinese green teas often offer a floral to nutty taste, while steamed Japanese green teas give a rather grassy-fresh to bitterish taste. Korean green tea, with a few exceptions, is steamed as well as roasted and thus combines the taste nuances of the two neighboring countries.

The minimum steps that make up green tea are therefore:
- Fixing (in wok, electric oven or with superheated steam)
- Drying

Unlike with yellow tea, there is no yellowing between fixing and final drying. In both yellow and green teas, the leaves are often rolled or twisted or shaped in some other way before drying.[12]

The final process of drying gives the various types of tea a longer or shorter shelf life, with green tea having a shorter shelf life than all other types.

OOLONG

Blue tea can practically only be found under the name oolong in worldwide trade (Chinese 乌龙 - black dragon). It is seldom found in international trade as blue tea (Lancha or Qingcha), but this can be neglected. In the English-American cultural area, the Taiwanese spelling wulong 烏龍 is also used. The name Black Dragon probably comes from the dark appearance of the finished leaves, but is also derived from creatures and stories of the Chinese mythical world.

The most likely reason for the naming "blue tea" is the partial green-blue color perception of the infusion. Accordingly, people in China mostly speak of it as Qingcha.

In retail, this tea is often wrongly called and offered as semi-fermented tea. The correct term would be semi- or partially-oxidized tea. If the oxidation time is either too short or too long, oolong tends to taste either like green or black tea, but a good middle ground will result in a unique taste.

If you are after a large selection of good oolong, you only need to look into China and Taiwan. Even if there are nice products coming from other countries, for me personally, there is nothing that comes close to China and Taiwan by a fair margin. No other nations can keep up even halfway - neither in quality, nor in diversity. There are three leading regions in mainland China, two of them are in Fujian and one in Guangdong. Accordingly, these regions take up a lot of space in the later chapter on China. Challengers come from countries like India, Thailand, Malawi, Indonesia and even New Zealand, but they still have a lot of catching up to do.

No matter what approach is taken to describe and structure the production process, from the minimal basic steps required, oolong is probably the most complex tea to produce, as one must complete the following steps:

- Withering
- Rolling/squeezing (for strong oxidation)
- Fixing (briefly under high heat and often under continuous rolling)
- Baking (for several hours)

In Fenghuang Dancong and Wuyi Yancha, rolling is usually replaced by squeezing and/or twisting, which already provides a way to visually distinguish them from the mostly rolled Anxi and Taiwan oolongs.

After withering and before fixation, many more steps can be executed, almost always including rubbing and shaking, often supplemented by airing or throwing the leaves in bamboo baskets or a machine. This is when the leaf juice reacts with the oxygen in the air.

This results in the usual oxidation of 30 to 60%, but there are also exceptions: teas whose degree of oxidation can reach just under 20% and up to 80%.

Depending on the strength of the oxidation and the final baking[13], one also speaks of green (approx. 15 to 40%), or red or black oolong. These colors have no relation to the colors of the different types of tea, but only serve to distinguish between the different styles of oolong. Nevertheless, some "black" oolong tastes reminiscent of black (red) tea, which is not surprising, as it might have been oxidized almost as much. Conversely, green oolong is still quite close to green tea.

The additional descriptors green or black/red for oolong is usually only used when the oxidation is extremely low (green) or unusually strong. Instead of the color distinction, sometimes (especially with Tie Guan Yin in recent times) one also refers to the classic method or style (more strongly oxidized and/or roasted), whilst the greener version may be called modern style in an analogue manner.

RED (BLACK) TEA

What we call black tea around the world is called red tea in East Asia. The reddish amber to dark red cup supports this name. This might be confusing when you talk to Chinese people or want to shop in Asia, because often traders have already adapted to the western way of using the term. Dictionaries sometimes do not help either. No matter whether you search for "black tea" or "red tea", the result is always Hongcha 紅茶 in Chinese. However, Hong 紅 is the word for red.

The finished, dry tea is almost always black, but there are also red teas that are colored like turmeric. Such red teas may also be called golden, but they are and remain red teas because of the way they are produced.[14]

Red tea is a so-called fully oxidized tea, because the oxidation process (mainly by rolling the leaves) takes so long that almost all the substances in the leaves (about 85 to 95%) react with the oxygen in the air.

The minimum steps that make up red tea are:

- Withering
- Rolling (until complete oxidation)
- Fixing
- Drying

Although red tea is cultivated throughout the world nowadays, the most famous ones still hail from Asia. If China, Japan and Korea are historically known as THE green tea countries, Japan almost exclusively so, the Indian subcontinent is likely to offer the most popular black teas.[15]

Darjeeling in India is famous for its high-altitude tea gardens. The first harvest of the year is a particular highlight there. Some of its first flush is even sent by airfreight[16], as this makes it available quickly and especially fresh. Some eager consumers just cannot wait to rip open the bags and put the leaves to the test.

Black tea from Assam is usually obtained from the Assamica variety of the tea plant and tends to be stronger and malty in aroma. Assam is often found in bagged teas and blends to give them body and depth. Ceylon tea comes from Sri Lanka and can be at least as good in quality as the teas from Assam.

Keemun (Qimen), which comes from Anhui in China, is one of the most famous red teas and is also a component of many blends[17]. In contrast, red tea from Yunnan is marketed under the generic term Dian Hong (also known as Yunnan Black in the West).

Black tea is also being produced in large quantities in the "rest of the world", for example in East Africa, Indonesia, Georgia or Turkey.

DARK (POST-FERMENTED) TEA

The word Hei 黑 in Chinese stands for either dark or black. Native Chinese speakers translate heicha 黑茶 as dark tea and the rest of the world usually calls it (post-)fermented tea, because this best describes what makes it so special. Let's have a look at what fermentation means here.

The minimum steps that make up dark tea are:
- Withering
- Fixing
- Rolling
- Drying
- Fermentation

This is very reminiscent of green tea production, but there the last step is the vigorous drying. If this is skipped[18] (for the time being), the leaves not only oxidize completely over time, but after some time microorganisms (fungi, bacteria, yeasts) start their fermentation work, similar to sauerkraut (in case you are German), kimchi (for the Koreans), wine, beer or many other fermented foods, where the producers create a whole new variety of flavors by this means. This process may last for years and decades and is often artificially accelerated by moisture, heat and even starter cultures. Roughly simplified, heicha is therefore incompletely dried green tea, which finally undergoes natural or artificial fermentation, accompanied by full oxidation.

Although heicha is produced in many Chinese tea-growing regions, this term is hardly known in the West. There are two reasons for this, firstly because the category is correctly called post-fermented tea (after all, post-fermented tea is also produced outside of China) and secondly because the term Pu'er is quite (although incorrectly) synonymous with heicha worldwide. However, Pu'er is only one type of heicha, and it always comes from the area around the city of the same name in Yunnan province.

Many Europeans only know Pu'er tea as a cheap product in loose form for less than five bucks per 100g, if at all. Visually, it resembles a simple black tea. While the latter can at least be used in samovars (if "enriched" with sugar), I can only describe such cheap Pu'er as unpalatable. No wonder that the industry desperately promotes health benefits ("the weight-loss tea") in order to get this stuff into our cups.

That being said, this section is not titled Pu'er Tea, but Dark Tea instead. And it is not only worth a separate chapter later on in this book, but besides oolong, it is also the most interesting type of tea to me, not only because of the sheer endless bandwidth of aroma on offer.

Another remarkable aspect of post-fermented tea is the diversity of shapes in which it is pressed, but more about that later.

Increasingly often it is also to be found in good quality as loose leaf tea, which then stands in no comparison to the above-mentioned abomination, which can still all too often be found in supermarkets or with clueless tea dealers.

WHERE TO BEGIN

So what is so complex or complicated about tea? One plant, six types, that sounds quite manageable, does it not? Especially since I have limited the level of detail to only mentioning the most important production steps.

From here on, however, things can get a bit more complicated, because each growing area has a unique location and thus a unique altitude and (micro-)climate and a unique soil condition (terroir); and each producer may use different cultivars of the tea plant, harvest at different times and with different methods, and modify the processing as desired.

So if you are serious about making your tea intake more palatable, it is all too easy to get lost in a vast labyrinth of details. If you are still at the very beginning of your tea journey, I would like to suggest a simple procedure to expand your horizons in the most time- and resource-efficient way possible:

1. Visit a local tea merchant and purchase one loose leaf green and one loose leaf black tea. A minimum of 25g or 1oz is recommended, which allows for several tastings.
2. Prepare the tea according to the vendor's instructions. Does it taste well? If not, prepare it differently. You will find suggestions in the chapter Preparing Tea. If it still does not taste right, then it is probably not your cup of tea.
3. If it tastes good, but still not outstanding, then at least you have found an entry point.
   a. Review what you have purchased. What country does the tea originate from? Teas from Japan, China or India can taste completely different. Now you can decide whether you want to try a tea from another country or stay within the same country. If you decide to go for another country, start from the beginning, i.e. from step 1.
   b. If you like the tea and feel that the country is an interesting one, then proceed to step 6.
4. Neither green nor black appear to be the real deal[19], but somehow you do like tea or at least want to give it another try? Return to step 1 and choose an oolong if you want something strong with a bigger bang or a white tea if everything else seems a bit too strong, or even bitter, despite the fact that you have kept the dosage quite low. Yellow tea should be tried at the earliest when you are certain that you like and tolerate Chinese green tea, also heicha is not necessarily advisable to begin your tea journey with (at least not unsupervised).
5. Now examine the tea that you already like quite well. What did you learn from the dealer? When and how was the tea picked? Is it a spring or an autumn harvest? A spring tea, or at least tea picked earlier by the same tea farmer will usually appear aromatic and sweet. But is it a little short of body and power? In that case you may try an autumn harvest[20] of the same vintage as an alternative. Or are there teas available from the same growing area, but from older tea trees

instead of shrubs? Is more selective hand picking offered instead of machine harvesting? How many leaves have been picked together with the bud? Is there a similar tea from another year for comparison? Does the store offer a higher leaf quality with less broken leaves?

6. After you have examined the quality and finer details in step 5, you will probably make one of two decisions:
    a. You are content and the next time you buy a slightly different type of tea from the same country, thus broadening your tea knowledge horizontally[21].
    b. You buy a higher quality tea of the same type and origin and broaden your knowledge vertically.
7. Only when you are >90% satisfied I suggest you buy larger portions of a certain tea. It would be a waste of tea if you bought it thoughtlessly in too large quantities and cannot enjoy it later (because its quality has deteriorated) or do not want to (because you have found better alternatives in the meantime).

VARIETIES AND CULTIVARS

After having looked at the six tea types and their essential characteristics, we should deepen our understanding of tea just a little bit more. Besides the tea type (or color) I would like to introduce you to the terms variety and cultivar. However, we will not delve too deeply into botany, because our goal is not to study hybrids or genetics in detail, but only to understand what we want to buy and enjoy. Camellia sinensis, commonly called tea, is the botanical name of a plant species[22]. Naturally occurring variants that are genetically different are called **varieties**. Artificially produced (cultivated) variants are respectively called **cultivars** (short for cultivated varieties).

A tea **type** can be produced from different varieties or cultivars and still have the same name, because the type is determined by the production method, not by the genetics of the tea plant.

VARIETIES

Many tea drinkers already know, at least by name, two tea varieties, Sinensis and Assamica. Back in my youth, in the 80s (a.k.a. "long ago"), people only spoke of China tea and Assam to distinguish between them, and that was it. What was meant by that were these two varieties:

- Camellia sinensis var. assamica
- Camellia sinensis var. sinensis

Sinensis translates as "from China" and Assamica as "from Assam", i.e. northeast India. Sinensis is a typical small leaf tea and originally grew in China, hence the name. Nevertheless, the large leaf tea Assamica is also being cultivated in China[23], especially in the southwest for the Pu'er production of Yunnan. There are less than 1,000km (620 miles) as the crow flies between the provincial capitals Assam and Kunming, and only about 300km (185 miles) from the provincial border of Assam to the provincial border of Yunnan. In between lies Myanmar (Burma), where the Assamica variety dominates in cultivation.

The large leaf variety Assamica not only produces large leaves, the plant itself can, under ideal circumstances, grow into a tree up to 20 meters (66 feet) high, unlike Sinensis, which has a limit of about eight meters (26 feet). These two varieties also differ in the maximum age they can live to. The small Sinensis is assumed to reach a maximum age of 100 to 200 years, whereas Assamica trees are in some rare cases said to be over 3,000 years old and have grown correspondingly mighty. I do not know if this is due to Allen's rule[24], but the little ones (like the Sinensis) often appear to be better able to cope with cold. It grows in higher altitudes and can also tolerate frost better than Assamica.

Now and then you can find other varieties in the shops, for example:
- Camellia sinensis var. assamica cambodiensis
- Camellia sinensis var. assamica dehongensis
- Camellia sinensis var. assamica taliensis
- Camellia sinensis var. formosensis

Taliensis is endemic to Yunnan's south and the bordering areas of Laos, Myanmar and Thailand and is considered wild tea. Taliensis is named after the Dai ethnic group. Single trees are often to be found within forests. Their characteristics and leaf sizes are more similar to Assamica than Sinensis. This variety is often used for the production of well-known teas, for example for the Yue Guang Bai 月光白 (Moonlight White) and many Pu'er, but sometimes for red teas as well.

Cambodiensis plants are somewhat smaller in growth than pure Assamica and are mainly being cultivated in India.

Dehongensis was first found and documented in the area surrounding the city of Dehong in Yunnan and is also very similar to Assamica. It is characterized by a special taste profile and almost always shows a more or less distinct red or purple coloration of leaf or stem parts. It is best known in the market as purple tea, but it is not another type (color) of tea, but merely a variety of which in principle any type of tea could be produced. Especially white and Pu'er teas from this variety are known, but also red teas are being offered on the basis of Dehongensis.

Unlike Taliensis and Dehongensis, **Formosensis**[25] is hardly found in the trade or is at least not declared as such. Formosensis is the original variety of Taiwan, and there has been so much experimentation with cultivars that the declaration of the variety can be neglected. Which finally brings us to cultivars.

CULTIVARS

For tea drinkers, the topic of cultivars is particularly interesting, as they often offer typical taste characteristics that one would like to find again when buying similar tea. Just as someone who does not like heavily tannic red wines will probably not buy a pure Merlot, someone who loves a milky, lactose-like fragrance and taste of his oolong will probably want to make sure that it was produced with the cultivar Jin Xuan. If you are looking for the real Long Jing, only accept the cultivar Long Jing No. 43 and do not choose a tea that has been produced in the Long Jing style, possibly even in another region than the true original. For example, in Taiwan a Long Jing is being manufactured using a modification of the cultivar Qing Xin, which does not have much in common with the original. I would like to compare this with the Wiener schnitzel, which is only allowed to be made of veal and should be baked in clarified butter. A cheap breaded escalope of pork from the deep fryer has to be called Viennese style schnitzel by European law.[26]

The attentive tea drinker will soon notice that Sinensis produces a light, delicately aromatic tea and Assamica rather brings forth a strong and malty tea. It is not surprising that farmers and botanists have repeatedly tried to crossbreed the different varieties in such a way that they either achieved more taste, offered higher yields, became more resistant to pests or were better suited to different terroirs[27] and climates. However, cultivars do not have to be crossed at great expense. If tea farmers continue to selectively breed naturally mutated plants, a unique cultivar may also emerge.

TAIWAN

Taiwanese tea farmers offer a good example of the latter. Many have migrated over from mainland China to the island together with their knowledge and skills, as well as their seeds or seedlings, and have optimized their plants for taste and thus commercial success over the last decades.

Taiwan is famous for breeding oolong cultivars, and some of the world's finest oolongs hail from there. The former Taiwan Tea Experiment Station (TTES, now called Tea Research and Extension Station, TRES for short) usually numbers its new breeds by TTES # ...

Some but not all cultivars also receive an additional common name, for example the following:

- TTES #12 Jin Xuan[28]
- TTES #13 Cui Yu[29] (Green Jade), also to be found as Ying Zhi Hong Xin (Hard stem red heart)
- TTES #14 Bai Wen[30]
- TTES #15 Bai Yian[31]
- TTES #16 Bai He[32]
- TTES #17 Bai Lu (also called Ruan Zhi or Qing Xin[33])
- TTES #18 Hong Yu (Ruby)[34]
- TTES #19 Bi Yu (Green jade)
- TTES #20 Ying Xiang
- TTES #21 Hong Yun[35]
- TTES #22 still unnamed cultivar, cross of Qing Xin and TTES #12
- TTES #23 still unnamed cultivar for red tea, cross of several Keemun-cultivars
- TTES #24 allegedly endemic cultivar from Taiwan

The first eleven authentic Taiwanese cultivars have not been widely spread and therefore have not been given catchy names. In the beginning, many Assamica were crossed in, e.g. TTES #2 originates from an Indian plant from Jaipur, #7 is half Thai and #8 was simply called Assamica. #24, but also #23, which was only released in 2018, will probably not appear in the trade soon, because the plantations require several years for reproduction and plant growth. Whether the dazzling name Oncorhynuhas masou (Taiwanese Masu Salmon)[36], which was given to #24 by TRES, will prevail, remains to be seen. But #22 and #23 must also first prove themselves on the market.

Other cultivars often have names under which the tea is traded, and this is not only true for Taiwan. Here you can find for example

- Si Ji Chun (Four Seasons of spring or evergreen)
- Qing Xin (Green heart, better known as Ruan Zhi (Soft stem))
- Da Ye (Large leaf)

Whether these cultivars are always entirely new crosses, re-established old varieties or brazen product counterfeits can only be conclusively answered by DNA analyses. Qing Xin is a good example here, because this is an old cultivar from the mainland being marketed under a new name.

Well, let's give the tea producers the benefit of the doubt. Nowadays, mozzarella also often comes from Northern Europe and camembert is not only from Normandy anymore. Accordingly, these replicas often taste quite pitiful, but that is another matter. It is important for us drinkers to know these details and to be able to make our buying decisions in a somewhat informed way.

In this context TTES #17 is also worth mentioning. This cultivar, called Ruan Zhi in everyday life, is especially tasty and resistant to cold and thus predestined for the highlands. Especially the popular varieties Dong Ding, Dong Fang Mei Ren and Pouchongs are based on it, but also the mainland relies on it in Anxi. Thailand appreciates it very much, not least because the Dong Fang Mei Ren is being copied there.

CHINA

Of course, the motherland of tea has also and in particular developed special cultivars over the millennia. Representatives of the most original and mostly legendary cultivars, which were selected decades or even centuries ago from a few mother plants and then propagated further, are certainly the Tie Guan Yin or the Da Hong Pao, to name only two examples from the oolong group.

But also for other varieties certain cultivars have proven and established themselves, for white tea for example

- Fuding Da Bai[37]
- Fu Ding Da Hao[38]
- Fu Xuan Nr. 9
- Fu Yun #6[39]
- Ming Shan Bai Hao
- Xiao Cai Cha[40]
- Zhenghe Da Bai[41]
- Xiao Zhong (called Souchong when made into red tea)

The names already reveal a lot in this respect. The syllable Da 大 means big, Bai 白 is white, and Fuding is a district town. But the syllable Da also indicates that it is a large leaf tea (Da

Ye Zhong 大叶种), i.e. Assamica. Xiao Zhong 小种 (small type) on the other hand indicates a Sinensis origin and is similar to the term Xiao Ye Zhong 小叶种 (small leaf type). Perhaps you know this term also under the common name Souchong[42], in that case as a name component of the well-known Lapsang Souchong[43].

For the sake of completeness, the term for the wild species (mostly Taliensis or Dehongensis) should be mentioned, it is Ye Sheng 野生. This means a large leaf tea which is not part of the Da Ye Zhong, e.g. a Taliensis. Although this variety is often found in Pu'er, the term is hardly ever found in cultivar names, but that would be quite strange in the case of a wild tea anyway.

Knowing cultivars and being able to distinguish between them is often helpful, but you shouldn't go crazy here either. Also and especially in the field of green teas there are a lot of cultivars in China. In addition to the already mentioned Long Jing No. 43, for example:

- Bai Ye Nr. 1[44]
- Bi Yun (jade cloud)
- Jiu Keng Zhong[45]
- Shi Da Cha[46]
- Meng Shan Nr. 9
- Meng Shan Nr. 11

And of course, the Chinese oolongs also do not lack a wealth of cultivars, e.g. besides the already mentioned Tie Guan Yin or Da Hong Pao there are also

- Fo Shou (Buddha's hand)
- Huang Guan Yin
- Huang Jin Gui
- Jin Guan Yin
- Qi Lan
- Shui Xian

to mention. As with the above so with the following short lists of (Japanese and Indian) cultivars I have made an arbitrary selection. Especially in China, the trade names of the teas are very often synonymous with the name of their cultivar, so lists with thousands of entries would not make much sense at this point. But it makes sense to develop a feeling for which tea is made from which original cultivar and which name components of teas indicate the variety, the origin or even the cultivar used.

In the above list Shui Xian is certainly worth mentioning. The reason why this is the case will be revealed in the chapter about Chinese oolongs, just keep reading.

Let's not get any further into the Chinese cultivars here. The lists would be endless, difficult to read, and would offer little in the way of knowledge, especially since we will never get our hands on the vast majority of cultivars. However, I would advise you to pay attention to the cultivar of your favorite teas or those of which you are looking for higher qualities. Serious traders in the high quality (and sometimes pricy) segment often indicate the names of the cultivars. Teas without this information need not be of inferior quality per se, but the information demonstrates confidence in the product and helps the well-informed consumer.

Which now brings us to Japan, because here almost always the cultivar names are given.

JAPAN

For the reasons mentioned above, I have decided not to provide long cultivar lists for Japan either. This might help to quickly recognize which part of the name indicates the cultivar, in general one can easily recognize it oneself. For example, if a tea is offered as Gyokuro Asagiri, then it is obvious that Asagiri is the cultivar. Other popular cultivars for Gyukuro are for example

- Asahi
- Asatsuyu
- Okumidori
- Saemidori
- Yamakai

Other than that, most Sencha and and other Japanese teas are being produced from the cultivar Yabukita. With 75% of the total production volume this cultivar is absolutely dominant. It is also one of the oldest registered[47] Japanese cultivars and since 1953 it has had a competitive edge over more modern competitors such as Saemidori which was introduced in 1990. Yutaka Midori follows far behind with only about 6%, Saemidori and Okumidori are only just ahead of Sayama Kaori and Zairai with 2% each and Kanaya Midori and Asatsuyu with only about 1%.

Can we now ignore everything except Yabukita? Not at all! Even though Yabukita is an all-round successful cultivar, there are at least two reasons for exploring some of the others. On the one hand, those who are happy with Yabukita can go even deeper and explore a cultivar crossed with another. Kurusawa, Saemidori, or Yamakai would be examples. On the other hand, by switching to other cultivars, a significantly different range of aromas and tastes may be discovered.

Since oolong and red tea only play very small roles in Japan, we will leave it at these few details here. Personally, I have often been able to enjoy an oolong from the Minamisayaka cultivar, and they also produce decent red tea with the Taiwanese TTES #21 Hong Yun.

Since historically only green tea was produced in Japan, the traditional cultivars are all Camellia sinensis var. sinensis. In order to produce black tea or fine oolong, native tea varieties were therefore crossed with Assam or Chinese black tea varieties at an early stage.

The best known of these is probably Benifuuki, which is also being used for green tea production. Due to its large quantities of allegedly positive ingredients, it is repeatedly attributed with therapeutic promises of all kinds, and this makes it particularly popular in the media.

However, it was not officially registered until 1993, while the Yabukita and the Hatsumomiji (preferred for oolongs) were documented as early as 1953.

INDIA

The lists of Indian cultivars are at least as exhaustive as those of their East Asian relatives. Since Indian (mostly black) teas are almost never marketed with the indication of the cultivar, we mention them here only very briefly. Indian cultivars are for example called

- Ambari Vegetative 2
- Bannockburn 68 oder Bannockburn 157
- Phoobsering 312
- Tukdah 323

or are abbreviated like B68, B157 and so on.

As tea on the Indian subcontinent, a relic from colonial times, was and is often being grown on huge plantations, it is only natural that these same plantations have developed their own cultivars to obtain weather-hardened and resistant plants for their soils. And so the cultivars listed above are actually the names of the plantations. The Ambari Tea Garden is located in West Bengal, the other three in Darjeeling. Nevertheless, in the tea trade the exact cultivar is practically never shown, because often blends are involved, and therefore our interest is waning here.

PICKING STANDARDS AND LEAF QUALITIES

It may come as a surprise that the quality of the leaves is coming up only now, since especially in India, many tea trade names start with cryptic letter combinations. But in the rest of East Asia this is rather unusual, and frankly I do not miss them much either. Nevertheless, the mostly Indian system is mentioned below.

Picking standards

English	Meaning
Buds only, Single bud	Only the uppermost, still unopened leaf (the bud) is picked
One Leaf and a bud (Imperial pluck)	The name speaks for itself, doesn't it?
Two leafs and a bud (Fine pluck)	Most common picking method
Coarse Pluck	Harvesting up to the third leaf
Souchong	Named after the historical picking method of Lapsang Souchong; whole branches with up to eight leaves

In China the leaf is carefully examined and classified both dry and after the infusions by the worshippers. If at all, Chinese factory teas provide information on the leaf quality rather unnoticeably and preferably in the wholesale trade only, and the end consumer receives very little information here. However, I do not miss these details most of the time, I prefer to notice them while drinking.

The picking standards are uniform and clearly summarized worldwide, no matter in which region the tea is harvested.

Sometimes the tea trade is even more precise in sorting and categorizing, but mainly with Indian teas. The topmost leaves are named from the tip (bud) downwards as follows:

- Flowery Orange Pekoe
- Orange Pekoe
- Pekoe
- Pekoe Souchong
- Souchong[48]
- Congou
- Bohea

This is only to be mentioned for the sake of completeness, as a consumer one will seldom be able to buy one's tea exactly according to which leaves were used in detail, but in the following we will talk a little more about the Indian quality grades.

While the tea quality (and especially its sweetness) is strongly influenced by the buds, sweetness is not always desired. For a number of oolongs, for example, one dispenses with buds completely and starts with the first leaf already opened, followed by a number of additional leaves, depending on the desired quality of the finished tea. Older leaves do not necessarily mean poorer quality, sometimes they also provide volume and balance to the tea.

A prerequisite for certain picking standards is of course hand picking[49], because if you harvest with machines, it is very difficult to distinguish individual leaves. If necessary, the leaves are then sorted by machine according to leaf grade or size and even by color. Recently, however, the machines have also learned to pick more accurately. While mechanical harvesting used to resemble the use of hedge clippers, the use of cameras and robot technology has already begun, especially in Japan. However, the absolute top qualities such as competition teas are still hand-picked.

Tea harvested and sorted by machines can therefore be of almost the same high quality and taste as purely handmade tea; but if only machines are used (and vintage ones in particular), then one quickly arrives at the very bottom of the tea chain. In the lowest position of the pecking order of tea leaves, the CTC teas are to be ranked. CTC is short for **C**rush, **T**ear and **C**url[50]. Here, mechanically harvested leaves are roughly de-stemmed at most and then torn by rolling. This is how the small broken leaves (fannings[51] and dust), which are used to fill miserable bags, are mainly produced in India and Kenya. These tortured, destroyed leaf remains are suitable for tea bags, as they release color and aroma into the water faster than whole leaf tea, but unfortunately the aroma is of very limited quality. These grades also taste much harsher and bitter, but luckily nature has grown sugar beets and cows to mitigate this.

As black tea for the masses has conquered the international market mainly from India, the Indian or English classification system was also established. It distinguishes between whole leaves, broken leafs, fannings and dust. Fannings are small and tiny fragments of leaves or buds (without stems), but larger than dust.

The further distinction between whole leaf down to dust is then made by means of the letter combinations mentioned above, which at first seem incomprehensible, but are nevertheless quite easy to identify. The table at the end of this chapter lists the most relevant terms in descending order of quality.

I deliberately refrained from listing all possible combinations and from here you should be able to easily identify additional abbreviations. It goes without saying that the path to enlightenment - pardon me, refreshment - goes in the direction of the whole leaf tea. When it comes to high quality tea, you do not need to be able to distinguish between any further Dust grades, even if they bear impressive name prefixes like Golden or Super Fine.

Close-up of young shrub growing in Austria (sic!)

Perhaps more interesting are additions such as CL for clonal plants grown from seedlings instead of seeds, but the table below should cover 90% or more of the teas on the market.

Enough now with the standards, let's keep it like the Chinese and give preference to whole leaves. Uniform size of leaves is a crucial factor, which is achieved by careful picking and sorting. Equally important is uniform oxidation and the optional roasting. This is the only way to ensure that the tea is of even quality. At least visually, the leaf already reveals many details, though often not until after a few steeping cycles, once the leaves have fully expanded.

Leaf qualities

Abbreviation	Full name	Quality
Whole Leaf Tea		
FTGFOP	Finest Tippy Golden Flowery Orange Pekoe	Generally highest quality grade with approx. 25% bud content. Sometimes for top quality even increased by the prefix S for "Special".
TGFOP	Tippy Golden Flowery Orange Pekoe	Slightly less buds, but still the highest quality material, usual standard for Single Estate Darjeelings or Assams.
GFOP	Golden Flowery Orange Pekoe	"Golden" indicates more of the light buds and very young leaves compared to FOP. Less buds/leaf tips than TGFOP, mostly from Kenya.
FOP	Flowery Orange Pekoe	"Flowery" indicates a small number of buds, but fewer than GFOP, by definition actually one bud and two leaves. Mostly simple Indian teas.
OP	Orange Pekoe	Lowest whole leaf standard, larger (and therefore older) leaves, hardly any buds, mostly simple teas from Sri Lanka. In Indonesia sometimes suffixed with S for "Superior".
Broken Leaf Tea		
TGBOP	Tippy Golden Flowery Broken Orange Pekoe	Highest Broken quality in Darjeeling and partly Assam
FBOP	Flowery Broken Orange Pekoe	Broken version of FOP with some buds, usual Broken quality from Assam (often with prefix G), Sri Lanka, Indonesia etc.
BOP	Broken Orange Pekoe	Average Broken quality in Assam, South India, Sri Lanka, Indonesia

Abbreviation	Full name	Quality
FP	Flowery Pekoe	Broken with slightly younger leaves
BP(S)	Broken Pekoe (Souchong)	Common Broken from Indonesia, Sri Lanka and South India, partly with stems (with addition Souchong mostly in Assam and Darjeeling and then produced from the fourth to sixth leaf and mostly rolled).
BT	Broken Tea	Lowest Broken quality level, mostly from South India, Sri Lanka or Indonesia
Fannings		
TGFOF	Tippy Golden Flowery Orange Fannings	Highest quality fanning, if one may speak of value at all when talking about fannings
GFOF	Golden Flowery Orange Fannings	Just above the average bag quality level
BOPF	Broken Orange Pekoe Fannings	Highest grade of fannings for bags from Darjeeling
FOF	Flowery Orange Fannings	Standard quality in Assam
OF	Pekoe Fannings	Second lowest grade of fannings, stems and ribs were sifted out, mainly from North India and Africa
PF	Pekoe Fannings	Lowest fannings grade
Dust		
PD	Pekoe Dust	Lousy dust
D	Dust	Lousiest dust

Sometimes the following characters are added to the above abbreviations, either without or after a blank:

Suffix	Full name	Quality
1 oder FF	First flush	Top
2 oder SF	Second flush	Cheaper
AUT	Autumnal flush	Often much cheaper, but depending on preferences not necessarily tasting worse

DECIPHERING TEA NAMES

In Mandarin the word for tea is cha 茶. In countries that came into contact with tea early on, the local name is based on this word. Tea has its English name from the southern Chinese Min dialect. There, the character for cha is pronounced more like thek, other dialects pronounce it like te or tay. By how the tea is named in different countries, one can see how it first arrived in these countries. Countries where the name for tea resembles the word cha were supplied by land (via the Silk Road and such). Countries where the name for tea is similar to the word thek were supplied by sea.[52]

Many languages therefore still show us the historical tea transport routes to this day. The first table in this chapter lists the translations of the word tea in a selection of significant languages. Significant in this context refers to several factors: the language is spoken by many people, or tea is an important commodity in this region, or the name of tea is completely different from the rest of the world.

Those who wish to purchase tea from new and unknown sources, catalogue their holdings or even consider starting a more or less extensive collection will soon find that knowledge of Chinese or Japanese would not be a disadvantage.

Hindi is not needed that much, as the trade on the Indian subcontinent is mainly conducted in English. Japan is a much smaller country and does not produce as many (different) teas as China.

The challenges are manifold, as the foreign language names have to be translated in a meaningful way. While this would be nice, it is not that easy. So what to do? How to approach Chinese tea wisely? The latter is quite simple. I do not approach teas at all that are being called, for example, "Chinese green tea". This already sounds rather off-putting to me, suspiciously like "cheaply bought and mixed blend of unknown provenance", which hopefully will somehow match the taste of a badly teaducated customer. The respective tea should have a name that is known or understood in China. Just as most Chinese do not know what to do with the dishes chop suey or General Tso's chicken, as those are western inventions or variations, for example Lapsang Souchong is not known there, even if the name may sound authentic to us.

Therefore you will not find such tea in the book, at least not in the headline of the respective section. It would rather appear with its Chinese name (in simplified Pinyin transcription and Latin letters), especially if the tea trade uses the same name.

The plant's name

Language	Name	Script
Amhari	Shayi	ሻይ
Arabic	Shay	شَاي
Bengalese	Ca	চা
Belorussian	Garbata	гарбата
Bulgarian, Croatian, Mongolian, Russian, Ukrainian	Caj, Tsai	чай
French	Thé	
Georgian	Chai	ჩაი
German	Tee	
Greek	Tsai	τσάι
Hebrew	Te	תה
Hindi	Chaay	चाय
Indonesian	Teh	
Italian	Tè	
Japanese	O-Cha	お茶
Korean	Cha	차
Latin	Thea	
Marathi	Caha	चहा
Persian	Cay	چَای
Polish	Herbata	
Sanskrit	Ca	चा
Spanish	Té	
Thai	Chā	ชา
Turkish, Kurdish	Çay	
Urdu	Chai	چائے

CHINESE TEA NAMES

Chinese teas are quite a challenge. Not because you can't decipher[53] their names, but because sometimes that doesn't help much. The myriads of tea farmers often call their products as the shrub has grown, and even the larger factories are not always stringent in their nomenclature.

The following name components may be included in any quantity and combination in a Chinese tea name or on a package of tea:

- Cultivar
- Size and appearance of the fresh or processed leaf
- Packaging or form (loose, pressed, wrapped, boxed, etc.)
- Production method, level of oxidation and/or roasting
- Province, region, county, town, village
- Quality level
- Age of the bush or tree
- Time of Harvest
- Flavoring (flowers, smoke, etc.)
- Manufacturer name (tea factory) or tea master name
- Marketing or fantasy names

As this is not yet sufficiently confusing, wholesalers, importers or international mail order companies sometimes try to "improve" transparency and make teas even more difficult to sort out by adding their own quality features. Quality levels such as "Super", "High", "Premium", "Special AAA", "Imperial", or "Ceremonial" are frequently applied. This sounds almost like at the gas pump, with the difference that you can probably get a better idea of what gasoline, super and diesel are.

In most cases, the specialized trade can be credited with the fact that they somehow have to communicate the differences in quality, and probably no dealer will want to advertise their goods with "bad - medium - good - super". However, it is quite tricky that many of the above qualitative classifications are mostly unknown in China in this form. I still remember very well how I once tried to reason with a Chinese tea friend about the differences between an Imperial Grade and a Competition Grade. Heads shaking all around. Sure, there are Chinese who might be able to relate to it, but most of the time these people are probably close to the tea industry.

The term Ji Pin 極品 for premium quality is still most commonly used in China. Historically, it referred to the typical export quality, i.e. the minimum standard for the international market.

What I consider particularly irritating, especially (but not exclusively) in the Pu'er sector, are the marketing-pretty teas with graphically sophisticated wrappers and imaginative artistic titles that do not provide any decent information. A positive aspect of this modern marketing is certainly that it tries to appeal to completely new (and often younger) groups of buyers. But I do not really enjoy if more information is given about the designer of the wrapper than about the tea itself. This leads to the assumption that material of uncertain origin was made prettier in order to optimize the margin. Of course this is legitimate, everyone can buy half-finished raw tea (Mao Cha) and press it into cakes and then market it under their own name. The tea may even be of high quality and taste good, but you will not learn much about tea that way.

Here are some examples of namings, I have highlighted in **bold** the name that the trader gave in the shop or on the Internet, and below that is the description of what it really was:

Muzha Tie Guan Yin Original 2002
Tie Guan Yin, strongly roasted in the classic style, from Muzha, Taiwan from the year 2002

Tie Guan Yin
Anxi Tie Guan Yin produced in autumn 2017

Premium Oolong
Tie Guan Yin

Pu Li 1972
High mountain oolong from Pu Li, Nantou, Taiwan of 1972

Yunnan Black
Dian Hong

8582
2013 Sheng Pu'er of the Dayi Company (TAETEA) after a recipe from 1985, leaf grade 8, from the Menghai factory, pressed in 2013

If the previous examples make you a little skeptical about how to find good tea under these circumstances, I can give the all-clear. I was merely trying to explain the situation, but there is no reason to panic. With some basic knowledge and research you can find good quality teas, no matter what they are called. There is often, although not always a certain order for the construction of the names. Ideally, Chinese tea names are composed of two components, namely the origin and the descriptive name, each with two to three characters.

The first part of the name often refers to the place (village, city, district, region) or mountain where the tea is grown, for example

- Xi Hu
- An Xi
- Lu An
- Jun Shan

followed by the description, i.e. the proper name of the tea as

- Long Jing
- Tie Guan Yin
- Gua Pian
- Yin Zhen

These proper names can describe how the tea looks in color or how it is shaped. Combined, this results in the quite well-known teas

- Xihu Longjing
- Anxi Tie Guan Yin
- Lu'an Gua Pian
- Junshan Yinzhen

It is also quite helpful to know that a tea sold solely as Long Jing or Tie Guan Yin probably does not originate from the famous region. A tea that is only offered as Long Jing will often not come from Lake Xihu, and will sometimes even be made from a different cultivar, but its appearance and taste will probably come close to the original. Taiwan can be rightly proud of its oolongs, so Tie Guan Yin from the island does not shamefully conceal its origin, but is also proudly marketed as Muzha Tie Guan Yin, provided it comes from Muzha.

In the context of this book, I regularly use Asian characters, although I have no expert knowledge in this matter. Even though I was allowed to indulge in an Asian martial art for a quarter of a century, I am only able to speak about 10 sentences in Chinese and Japanese in a halfway understandable way and only recognize about 50 to 100 characters. But even such rudimentary knowledge makes the tea journey much more pleasant.

The Chinese characters (hanzi) have also been adopted by the Japanese (here they are called kanji), so that one has to learn many characters only once, in case you intend to study them at all. I would like to, as far as they are related to tea. Oftentimes you find something on the Internet or stand in front of a sack or pack of unknown contents, which possibly contains what you are looking for or even a pleasant surprise, and then there is no smartphone at hand to get a rough idea of what it is. It is nice when you can at least get a rudimentary orientation. Also, many terms in romanized form may bear different meanings, so only the knowledge of the Asian signs will reveal what is really meant.

So it should be clear why I use these characters here and even dedicate an extra chapter to them.[54] Knowing the (tea) colors, the cardinal points, sun, moon and terrain names as well as some famous tea names or quality levels as signs can be really helpful in some situations.

The Chinese language already does its best to confuse the ignorant Westerners. From a rather limited vocabulary of a little more than 400 syllables, but each with up to four[55] different ways of accentuation, about 1,500 unique sounding words can be created. Limited to only this amount of words no millennia old advanced culture can develop and prosper, so the learner will also have the pleasure to study the innumerable binomials, i.e. the combinations of two of these 400 basic syllables. Soon the vocabulary has multiplied, and if that is not enough, then there are still the multiple meanings[56] of the individual syllables.

So if you do not know the hanzi or even better the binomial that is meant in each case, you can at best deduce the meaning from the spoken context. But even that is not always easy, and so in China you can certainly see people who, in the middle of a verbal communication, draw one or more hanzi in the air or even with one finger on the inner surface of the other hand, in order to make themselves understood pictographically to the other person. Of course, this is also useful if Chinese people from different parts of the country do not have a perfect command of the other person's native language. Here it pays off that the characters always have the same meaning in every Chinese language, even if they are spoken differently in Mandarin than in Cantonese or Hakka, for example.

Hakka (one of the regional languages of the indigenous peoples of Taiwan) also brings us to the next challenge in orientation within the Chinese characters.

The fact that the characters on the mainland have been simplified - in principle a welcome development - adds to the complexity. So the majority of Chinese people write in the simplified Chinese script. Unfortunately, this did not happen in Taiwan, where the traditional Chinese script is used.

So the tea called Tie Guan Yin is written 铁观音 in Simplified Chinese but in Taiwan it is 鐵觀音. In other words, wherever possible, the number of strokes has been reduced. To what extent this is really a simplification for the Chinese I cannot judge, but the old German script Sütterlin, which I was able to learn from my grandmother, also wrote much slower than the modern writing. However, all Taiwanese people I asked about it were capable of reading both variants and could tell whether it was the traditional or the simplified variant. Apparently they do not have to learn twice, because many characters were left unchanged in the mainland spelling and whoever can read Sütterlin has no real problems with the modern German fonts.

In addition, the hanzi do not consist of arbitrary strokes, but are mostly composed of so-called radicals.

The character 荼, spoken tu, should not be confused with the character cha 茶. It is generally assumed that tu is an old southern Chinese character for a bitter tasting plant. The word tu has probably evolved into the word tea, as it was shipped to Europe from South Chinese ports. On the other hand, in those countries to which tea was transported by land, the more northern cha became chai, usually via the old Silk Road.

In this book I use the simplified notation, because the mainland has much more relevance in the tea world and the characters are indeed simpler. However, I mostly avoid the accentuation as it is customary in the Latin Pinyin transcription. Whether it would really enable the majority of readers to pronounce e.g. Tie Guan Yin correctly and understandably if spelled here as Tiěguānyīn I think is quite doubtful. The readability for English speakers will not be improved by the many accents, so I abstain from using it with a few exceptions. If you want to learn more, you might want to study the Chinese language.

The Japanese language has mostly adopted the Chinese script, but doing just that did not suffice, two additional alphabets had to be added, katakana and hiragana. Both alphabets were and are necessary to represent all the words and grammatical forms of the Japanese language that the Chinese script could not provide. In addition, most Japanese only learn a good 2,000 Chinese characters correctly and replace rarely used or difficult kanji by hiragana. Sometimes, especially in children's books, above a rare kanji, the pronunciation is given in hiragana.

On the packaging of Japanese teas, the names of the products are usually written in Chinese characters, but the reading is additionally indicated in katakana. For convenience, the kanji characters are often omitted and these words are only written in katakana, i.e. ウーロン茶, which is pronounced uroncha. This refers to oolong tea 烏龍茶.

The most readable transcription of Chinese in Latin letters for us Westerners is (as already mentioned) Pinyin, for Japanese, however, the so-called Hepburn transcription is used.

Although I also use the Asian characters wherever helpful and useful in this book, I would like to summarize the most important ones right here in order to provide a first impression. Perhaps you will experience aha-effects or joyful recognition in the further course of reading.

Tea names often contain the place of origin, and these are probably the best known signs that will catch your eye on the packaging. Since sometimes tea from Korea is also sold via China or Japan or vice versa, I have added some Korean terms as well. The spelling in hanzi and kanji is essentially identical[57].

Countries of origin

Country	Hanzi/Kanji	Chinese	Japanese	Korean	
China	中国	Zhongguo	Chugoku	Jung Gug	중국
Taiwan	台湾	Taiwan		Daeman	대만
Japan	日本	Riben	Nihon	Ilbon	일본
Korea	韩国	Hanguo	Kankoku	Hang Gug	한국

Cardinal points are often used in tea names, if only because they are included in the names of the respective places of origin. For example, Bei is the first syllable of Beijing 北京, translated it means Northern Capital. Xi is part of the location name Xi Hu (Westlake) and Dong is also part of well known tea names.

Numbers also appear in tea names frequently, for example, the digit 4 is part of the tea name Si Ji Chun (Four Seasons) and the digit 8 is part of the name Ba Xian (Eight Immortals).

Cardinal points

Term	Hanzi/Kanji	Chinese	Japanese
North	北	Bei	Kita
South	南	Nan	Minami
East	東	Dong	Higashi
West	西	Xi	Nishi

Whilst the natural numbers used may differ in the Japanese language depending on the context and type of combined noun, the kanji are the same as the Chinese hanzi.

Natural numbers

Number	Hanzi/Kanji	Chinese	Japanese
One	一	Yi	Ichi
Two	两	Liang	Ni
Three	三	San	San
Four	四	Si	Yon
Five	五	Wu	Go
Six	六	Liu	Roku
Seven	七	Qi	Nana
Eight	八	Ba	Hachi
Nine	九	Jiu	Kyu
Ten	十	Shi	Ju
Hundred	百	Bai	Hyaku
Thousand	千	Qian	Sen

In addition, seasons regularly appear in tea names. In comparison with the cardinal points, it should be noted that in Chinese the syllable Dong stands for both east and winter, but with a different Hanzi.

Seasons

Term	Hanzi/Kanji	Chinese	Japanese
Spring	春	Chun	Haru
Summer	夏	Xia	Natsu
Autumn	秋	Qiu	Aki
Winter	冬	Dong	Fuyu
Season	季	Jijie	Ki

Other words from nature are more likely to be found in Chinese than in Japanese tea names. Japanese tea names follow a more simple structure and almost always only indicate the type of tea, the name of the place of origin or the producer and sometimes the cultivar, so the following table does not provide Japanese naming.

Nature

Term		Chinese
Bamboo	竹	Zhu
Bud	芽	Ya
Dragon	龙	Long
Flower	花	Hua
Fragrance	香	Xiang
Hair (young leaf), coarse/raw	毛	Mao
Lake	湖	Hu
Leaf	叶	Ye
Light	光	Guang

Term		Chinese
Moon	月亮	Yue Liang
Mountain	山	Shan
Peak	峰	Feng
Phoenix	凤	Feng
Rock	岩	Yan
Snail/Spiral	螺	Luo
Snow	雪	Xue
Stone	石	Shi
Sun	太阳	Tai Yang
Tip	尖	Jian
Tree	树	Shu
Well	井	Jing
Water	水	Shui

Xiang 香 (fragrance) is probably one of the most widely used suffixes in many oolong names. I already mentioned the colors which also belong to nature in the chapter about tea types, but especially for green besides Lu 绿 other terms like Bi 碧 or Cui 翠 or Yu 玉 (all three syllables mean jade green) and Qing 青[58] (blue or dark green) are used.

In addition, there are also a lot of adjectives that indicate quality, such as Hao 好 for "good", which are often, but not only, used for Pu'er. This is where the greatest effort is made to mark the age and quality of the tea trees and their foliage.

The following table shows typical terms used on product packaging. Over time, one memorizes the most important hanzi for one's personal everyday tea almost automatically, even if one does not plan to learn Mandarin.

Quality indications for Chinese teas

Chinesise	中国	English	Details
Dashu	大树	Big tree	100 to 300 year old tea trees.
Guan Mu	灌木	Shrub	Shrub variant of a tea plant, in contrast to Qiao Mu cultivated with a lot of effort and work.
Gushu	古树	Old tree	300+ year old tea trees.
Lao Zhong (Cong)	老丛	Old bush	Shrubs or trees of particularly high but not exactly specified age.
Lao Shu	老树	Old tree	Designation for high quality Pu'er leaves without a specific age given.
Mao Cha	毛茶	Raw, still unfinished tea	Pre-product of the Hei Cha production (practically a green tea), but is also sold and drunk in this form already.
Mu Shu	母树	Mother tree	Original shrub or tree from which a breeding series has developed, e.g. Da Hong Pao.
Qiao Mu	乔木	Tall wood	Unpruned tea trees growing wild and often singly in the forest, which had to reach for the sun and therefore grew especially high and less wide. Often also called Ye Shu.
Sheng	生	Raw, fresh	Called "raw" in English, this is the "normal" Pu'er, classically pressed from Mao Cha, which can ripen for many decades after completion and can continually change and develop.
Shengtai	生态	Bio	Ecologically grown Pu'er tea, which is not grown wild, but comes from plantations that have gone wild and where no chemicals have been used for a long time. Not to be equated with western organic certification, but clearly a quality feature.
Shu	熟	Cooked	Also called ripe.

Taidi	台地	Terrace tea, hillside	Pu'er from tea plantations, i.e. young and often average quality plants used for mass production.
Tong	筒	Tube	A tong typically consists of seven and sometimes only five bamboo wrapped bings. Seven bings of 357g each make 2.5kg of tea.
Xiao Shu	小树	Small tree or shrub	Low-growing cultivar, sometimes also a term for trees cut in height or tea trees under 70 years old.
Ye Shu	野树	Wild tree	Wild non-cultivated large-leaved plants (Assamica), often scattered in forests. Typical for indigenous, simple Pu'er teas. Also harvested in Thailand for oolong production.

Dashu and Gushu are not defined very precisely. Rather strictly speaking, Gushu starts with material that is more than 300 years old, but many exporters and traders try their best to put the label Gushu on their teas (instead of Taidi or Dashu) and most consumers who buy from certain vendors might be deceived. Currently, the bad habit of advertising tea as being from over 1,000 or in extreme cases even 1,600 year old trees is decreasing, as consumers are becoming better teaducated. Material from trees that are more than 500 years old is practically not exported, and if it is, then not in such quantities and at such prices that the common drinker would want to order. However, some ignorant merchants, who might have been ripped off themselves while sourcing, still spread the myth that they have gained exclusive access to ancient trees or the like. In the end, terms like Dashu or Gushu are quite irrelevant, top material may as well come from "only" 100 year old trees.

ROMANIZATION

On the previous pages I have written Asian names in the Latin alphabet as a matter of course, this is also known as romanization. There are several romanization systems in existence for the most important tea countries, and this explains why tea names are sometimes written in different ways. While the Hanyu Pinyin system is becoming more and more popular for Chinese, some importers, dealers and authors still stick to the older Wade-Giles system, especially in Taiwan.

The following table shows some examples of the different spellings.

Comparative romanization

Pinyin	Wade-Giles
Bao Zhong	Pouchong
Bi Luo Chun	Pi Lo Chun
Dan Cong	Dan Chung
Dong Ding	Tung Ting
Gong Fu	Kung Fu
Long Jing	Lung Ching
Pu'er	Pu-erh
Shui Xian	Shui Hsien

It is easily apparent that there are no major acoustic differences between them, so in general there should be little confusion.

The situation might be different when translations were established in the West before the establishment of a romanization system, then there were larger deviations as in the case of Lapsang Souchong (more on this later) or the oolong (wulong) and Qimen (Keemun).

You will notice a certain inconsistency in my way of writing Chinese names in the further course. A word consisting of several hanzi syllables might be written consistently in single romanized syllables (example: Tie Guan Yin) or together in one word (Tieguanyin). In individual cases it may even happen that I write one and the same romanized name differently. Readability is the most important thing for me. I also prefer to follow the spelling that I personally find most often.

Not exactly legible, despite some Hindu-Arabic numerals are used

SOURCING TEA

No matter where and how you purchase your tea, there is one thing I would like to recommend in advance when approaching a new tea: resist the impulse to obtain quantity discounts by purchasing bulk packs. Only when you have tested a tea extensively should you buy a larger quantity. Almost all tea traders offer samples weighing between five and 25 grams[59]. Some retailers even include additional small samples free of charge with orders, but in most shops consumers can also choose freely what they want to try (provided they pay for it).

Of course, you decide for yourself what exactly "extensive testing" means. If the sample already tastes excellent at the first tasting of five grams then it is advisable to purchase a decent quantity which will suffice for the next couple of weeks or months. However, as one often does not get all the parameters right at the first infusion, I personally tend to obtain samples of at least 25 grams. Ten grams can be quite scarce, as they are sometimes only sufficient for one infusion.

Many suppliers even offer so-called break-offs of pressed teas and the well-known bings[60] (Pu'er in disc or cake form), i.e. pieces of 25 or 50 grams. If it is an unknown tea, one does not necessarily want to buy a whole bing immediately. The dealers' offer to buy segments therefore offers a nice alternative. With an investment per bing from as little as 30 Euros[61] up to several thousands, this procedure can only be highly recommended.

I tend to ignore the famous words of a tea friend, "A single bing is what I call a sample. A real purchase starts with a tong!", unless I already know the tea from the previous year and trust the seller.

THE FORM OF THE TEA

Tea is usually sold in three different forms:
- Tea bags
- Loose leaf tea
- Pressed tea

In terms of quantities to be purchased, the tea form also plays a role, but the tea color is a greater factor. In general, green tea should be drunk when it is very fresh, especially if it has been processed under steam (mainly Japanese teas), so only small quantities should be purchased as they can be consumed quickly. This applies even more to Matcha which has a particularly short shelf life due to its pulverized form.

Let's have a closer look at these different forms of tea and afterwards we promptly continue to the shopping experience.

THE TEABAG

Although the classic double-chamber paper bag is still the most popular, there are now numerous new shapes such as paper bags for DIY filling, tea pyramids, plastic tea diamonds and many more playful variations to be found. Some are more or less biodegradable and some are manufactured in greater or lesser quality.

Tea bags are a practical way to prepare tea quickly and almost anywhere. A bag, hot water and a cup are all it takes. On the other hand, tea bags are frowned upon by tea connoisseurs, sometimes they are even hated. The stigma of a cheap, industrial mass-produced article is attached to them. But is this really the case and can this be claimed in general? Well, tea bags may contain (please note the subjunctive) just as good qualities as those found in loose leaf tea and there certainly is plenty of inferior loose leaf tea on the market. Moreover, the expensive tea bags of today allow more room for the tea to develop. However, small leaf grades or even dust are mostly used in tea bags, as the tea ingredients dissolve particularly quickly from these materials and pass into the infusion.

- Those who produce high quality tea also want to achieve a high price.
- In bags, tea does not appear very tempting.
- Ergo, top-quality teas are hardly ever to be expected in a bag.

Herein lies the first problem for the connoisseur and enthusiast: it is precisely this release of aromas that one needs to control! This requires controlling the infusion times and multiple steepings - practically impossible with sachets. Even if the bags contain high-quality teas and not just mediocre products, the limited space is often not enough to fully release the substances of the tea.

- Large marine mammals want to swim freely.
- So do great teas.

Some manufacturers of bagged tea are trying to achieve better quality, e.g. by sorting out stems and using larger leaf parts or even leaf tips and buds. Nevertheless, it remains a fact that the bags are usually filled with machine-harvested plantation tea and not the hand-picked and elaborately selected premium products.

The demanding tea lover prefers to be able to measure out and inspect their tea as they please. My personal conclusion therefore is to avoid bagged tea as much as possible.

LOOSE LEAF TEA

Loose or loose leaf tea is the most common form of tea which the ordinary tea connoisseur is looking for and buying.

Loose tea can develop better in water than the one trapped in the bag. It also allows for much better assessment of the leaf color and quality both when dry and after infusions.

POWDER TEA

The one most famous among the powdered teas is the Japanese Matcha. For its highest quality grades, the stems or damaged parts of the leaves are carefully removed from the individual leaves, and sometimes even the central leaf veins. Afterwards these leaves are completely ground and thus consumed by the drinker, ergo powdered tea also contains by far the greatest caffeine and nutrient content of all teas. Other teas are only brewed (several times) and in the end the exhausted leaves are thrown away. While Matcha usually stands for quality and great tastiness, especially in Japan simple powdered teas are also offered, which may taste somewhat like green tea but rather reminds of a ghostly haunted bygone. They are marketed as catechin bombs and emphasize a beneficial health effect. Those who are interested in it, should look for the word カテキン meaning catechin on the packaging of such powder teas.

PRESSED TEA

Tea pressed into discs, bricks, mushrooms or other shapes may be the cheapest stuff or contain the highest quality. Originally, tea was ground into powder and pressed for easier transport on horse or mule backs, sometimes stuffed unground into bamboo canes or woven baskets. Later the most common form of tea, the bing, also known as cake, was developed.

Pressed tea is almost only popular in China, especially as heicha, the dark tea. More about it and its shapes will follow later on.

SOURCING OPTIONS

Nowadays the procurement of tea can be as simple as it can be complicated. Lucky are those who have found "their" tea, have obtained it year after year from a trusted source and are completely satisfied with it. The rest of us carry the burden and the joy of constantly searching for new teas and new sources of supply, true to the motto "The journey is the reward".

SUPERMARKETS

I suppose one can get decent tea in a supermarket. After all, it is usually large multinational corporations that provide products which should be carefully composed and tested. Cannot go wrong with that, can we? Well, without any sarcasm one might say "Whom the tea tastes, let them bear it." All well, one gets the always identical taste from the well-known brands, predominantly in tea bags and carefully blended, that is, mixed from different batches of tea, which reliably tastes bland. Certainly drinkable, but not necessarily desirable.

I personally consider the huge quantities of teas in the trade which are mixed with artificial, natural or nature-identical flavors to be sad. On the other hand, if the majority of consumers want to drink it and are not prepared to pay a little more for real flavor, then the market is simply arranging the supply. In my opinion, a search for top-quality teas in classic food retailing is in vain, but you will not find a Château Pétrus there either.

While with black tea one often at least has the choice between Darjeeling, Assam or sometimes even Ceylon, in many cases there is only exactly one green tea on offer. Whether it comes from South East Asia, from the Indian subcontinent or from Africa does not matter, as it only tastes "green" anyway. To once again use my favorite analogy, wine: it is like choosing between red from France, Spain or Italy or white from who-knows-where.

LARGE TEA RETAILERS AND YOUR LOCAL SMALL TEA BUSINESS

Perhaps you know the most prominent top dogs in your local tea market. Established for decades and also served in many restaurants, they offer a comprehensive range of teas and other infusions that are considered tea.

Some even offer a franchise model and supply numerous independent entrepreneurs with their goods, others operate their own stores and yet others operate merely online.

In contrast to these big players, there are smaller classic tea shops throughout the country, which often still possess an individual charm and carry the supposedly more select assortment.

Almost all of them have one thing in common: in addition to tea, they offer coffee, confectionery, pastries and sometimes even wine.

What I appreciate about "the big ones" is their extensive range of products at mostly moderate prices. Whether their teas always justify their prices may be questionable, but due to the large quantities purchased, these traders at least have the chance to buy and offer at reasonable prices. As a consumer, however, one should not forget that it is usually not the aim of merchants to sell cheaply. And so even the most trivial plantation teas may be verbally praised as rare treasures and underlaid with pretty pictures of happy tea farmers and romanticizing tales.

If one were to classify the supermarket teas as preschool level in regards to teaducation[62], I would see these big traders as middle to high school. They offer teas from all over the world and have well-established suppliers or even their own plantations or trusted wholesalers since decades. You should be able to expect at least a decent to higher quality product without pesticide residues, but you will hardly find exotic specialties, qualitative surprises or the best tea among all teas. And how could you? After all, the business model of the "big ones" is mainly designed for mass consumption, so it is not worthwhile to search for, import, test for residues, put online and distribute small quantities to far too many branches.

Some smaller shops, on the other hand, are (some more and some less) successful persuaders who know their products and give intensive advice, sometimes also in a desperate defensive fight against "the big ones" and "the Internet", i.e. online trade. Some smaller tea shops, out of sheer economic necessity, also offer the boring standard teas or flavored monstrosities, which they either buy from large chains mentioned above or purchase directly from wholesalers. The more ambitious of these "little ones" are often also networking with other smaller retailers and complementing each other's respective portfolios. While one may be an expert on Japan, the other may have greater expertise in the field of Pu'er or have better sources of supply there.

Some large retailers can afford their own buyers for each country or region. Smaller traders, on the other hand, usually travel to a particular tea country only once a year, if at all. They then spend a considerable part of their annual holiday visiting as many regions, plantations or tea farmers as possible and, in a short period of time, filter out the teas to be included into their product portfolio for their customers at home. Blessed are the consumers whose taste preferences are similar to those of their trusted tea merchant. Once you have found this merchant, you should keep him in business with regular purchases in order to have his palate available for pre-selecting for your own enjoyment for as long as possible.

I am rather skeptical when small shops offer many hundreds of different teas at the same time. How they guarantee the freshest[63] possible tea is a mystery to me, unless the turnover in these shops is tremendous. However, I rarely see long queues in front of overcrowded tea shops, so I stick to my skepticism.

If one has found a nice little shop with friendly staff and a reasonable repertoire, I think it is advisable to ask where the exact expertise of the house lies. This way it should quickly become clear whether the often owner-managed establishments have a main focus and where it is to be found. And this leads us to the specialTEA shops.

SPECIALTY TEA SHOP

We just had a look at the regular tea shops. Let's now turn to the specialists, with some of them only running their business online. We will get to that shortly. First of all, we are generally interested in any specialization. As mentioned above, the communication with the sellers often provides further help if at first you cannot tell what the shop's focus is. If the Internet address or the inscription on the shop window already advertises Chinese tea, then one should rather expect no or only little know-how in the field of Japan or India. In a Japanese tea specialty shop, on the other hand, I would not hunt for old Pu'er in the first place.

It is especially pleasant when shop owners themselves hail from the region whose products are the target of your sourcing. For example, I would rather buy my Taiwanese oolong from a person who regularly visits their home country and can speak to the producers in their native language than if the source is just any wholesaler, distributor or importer. Of course provided that said Taiwanese is not only a good merchant, but also someone with a fine palate and the ability to respond to the preferences of their clientele.

European tea dealer during quality control on site and harvesting for his personal supply

Selected treasures can of course also be discovered by non-asian traders who either live or did live in the country of a tea's origin, who know the language at least a bit and have a talent for tasting the finer nuances. These traders often cover a wider range of regions because they do not always (only) research and buy in their home region.

No matter whether Asian or European, I am always happy to talk to dealers in person, by phone or online and ask them what they are passionate about. Then the conversation does not revolve around whether one should rather buy the Dong Ding or the Tie Guan Yin, for example, but rather whether they also offer such treasures aged, i.e. whether they offer specific vintages and which ones they personally prefer - and why. Such treasures and rarities are often not to be found online or on the shelf. But for loyal customers or at least interested hunters, some dealers are willing to open their private treasure chests. Personally, I am often amazed that the much rarer and older teas are not necessarily many times more expensive than the better known younger ones. However, the price is not the decisive factor here, but the exceptional taste.

I have the highest respect and admiration for those specialty tea shops that really and truly offer only top quality products. When I use the term top-quality products, I do not necessarily refer to the most expensive teas, but to honest teas, teas of which their producers can be proud. Unfortunately, one has to search for these shops with a magnifying glass, as it is very difficult to achieve a sufficient turnover with a decent margin, if a dealer does not primarily cater for the taste of the masses.

TEAHOUSES

The line between specialized tea shops and tea houses is often blurred. Even the term teahouse is neither a protected nor an easily defined term.

If an establishment is named English Teahouse, for example, it may be a humble shop with bar tables or a stylish Victorian ambience with comfortable chairs, armchairs and sofas. There you can expect the higher quality "English" teas, paired with scones, clotted cream and strawberry jam - or the refreshing cucumber sandwiches. Certainly a great thing, and even the spoiled specialty tea fan should be able to feel at home here every now and then. And nobody is being forced to put milk into his Assam.

The Turkish/Moroccan/Arabic/Afghan teahouse can certainly offer a nice ambience and on top of that the delicious culinary specialities of the Levant, complemented by quiet niches to play some tavla. Unfortunately, however, the tea selection is usually very digital: tea or no tea. Almost always it is a product called Chai (Arabic-Turkish black tea, rarely from Turkey or Georgia, mostly from Sri Lanka) or Thé à la Menthe (North African, a mixture of Chinese gunpowder with the aromatic Nana mint). In these teahouses the company is often more interesting than the tea.

I also consider it worth mentioning the option offered by some upscale Indian restaurants. In addition to chai (black tea with spices, milk and sugar), which is often even available gratuitously, select Indian or even Ceylonese teas are on the list of beverages of the top houses. If the menu does not only indicate the region, but also the village, the mountain or even the plantation, you can hope that the caterer is making an effort to provide quality. Or, pessimistically speaking, that he is a marketing expert...

Personally, I consider a teahouse to be a gastronomic establishment that appeals to me, which clearly focuses on drinking tea and where food is a secondary consideration. In an "English" oriented house I expect a pot of ready-to-drink tea or preferably the tea leaves and separate hot water for individual preparation. Some tea houses brew tea (multiple steepings) at the bar and then refill their guests cups again and again.

In my opinion, the ideal teahouses offer their guests a complete equipment for the Gong Fu Cha method at each table. Those are quite hard to find outside of Asia, but in big cities chances are improving. Often called Chinese or Japanese teahouses, these are restaurants that I consider top of the tea chain. They not only provide an ideal atmosphere for cultivated enjoyment, but also offer snacks or small meals - but the tea always takes centre stage.

ONLINE

Two hearts are beating in my chest when it comes to shopping online on the Internet. I am fully aware that online shopping poses more and more challenges for the stationary trade, i.e. the common local store. However, since one cannot ignore this disruptive development, some traditional retailers with retail stores are also successfully facing the challenges of the new technology and using the new sales channel of the Internet. Provided that they are clever and market their products in a targeted manner, they can attract new groups of buyers and offer a wider range of products.

Some retailers are exclusively selling online, and without this modern technology they may never have existed. As they are sometimes proven experts for specific regions or they have special expertise in the field of tea ceramics, they enrich the market quite considerably.

Of course, the Internet is also home to the top dogs, who are already known nationwide.

However, for me personally it is quite exhausting to visit the online shops of most dealers. Many times I have to virtually put aside all the fruits, rooibos, herbs, mate and flavored "teas" before I have unhindered access to the more interesting offers. After that, distribution formats such as infusion bags, diamond bags or tea pyramids have to be filtered out.

Although I like sniffing, testing and buying at local retailers, I also enjoy online shopping a lot. Many of the often owner-operated small and medium-sized shops provide telephone advice and one should not hesitate to pick up the phone if in doubt or when interested. Many times I was able to avoid potential misunderstandings in advance or to discuss special requests in a quick and easy way.

DOMESTIC OR INTERNATIONAL SOURCING?

As a European, when buying online in other EU countries, consumers enjoy the same rights everywhere and there is no customs barrier. A halfway useful command of English considerably increases the choice of shops where you can indulge your addiction, as many European vendors offer an English language option on their websites.

Many retailers are located in China, Japan, Singapore and other East Asian countries and offer a great variety of teas that are not available elsewhere. Even though this may sound tempting, I strongly advise beginners in the top tea segment to visit the local (online) shops first, in order to be able to venture out into the wider world later. My few complaints up until now have always been solved reasonably, even with Japanese or Chinese suppliers, but if worst comes to worst, Asia might feel far away.

If you have gained more experience, you will sometimes find larger tea farmers who only sell their own, as I call it "friends&family tea" or shops that specifically market several small tea producers or farms. These differ noticeably from the somewhat more anonymous large suppliers who offer tea from many regions and factories. With a little research, you can quickly find out what makes each shop tick and stock up exactly where you feel most comfortable as a buyer. Vendors with a large and diversified portfolio may not always know their goods as well as the smaller specialists, but with the latter you may sometimes have difficulty reaching the minimum order quantity.

I consider producers who market directly to be especially noteworthy. Here one can distinguish between individual suppliers who only offer their own products on their website or cooperatives who jointly set up small web presences. Personally, I prefer these providers whenever possible, because they are very close to the product, thus it massively reduces the risk of buying inferior or counterfeit products.

Which leads us to large websites. As an example for all, I would like to mention Taobao or eBay. Such portals provide practically everyone with the opportunity to sell their products, and not all products necessarily have to be of poor quality. However, one should be aware that sales are made quite anonymously and a dishonest seller rarely runs the risk of being held liable. Vendors with many thousands of ratings may seem more secure, but everyone has to decide that for themselves. Just for fun, I made some test purchases of teas via such portals and I was usually quite lucky. By luck I mean that I personally did not receive any fakes and did not have to record any losses in delivery, but the quality was sometimes very questionable. But why should quality be sold off? The rule is once again: "You get what you pay for."

Unlike Taobao, the Tmall platform, which is also Chinese, is limited to the sale of professional providers to end customers, which is nowadays called business-to-consumer or B2C. If you are looking for teas from more well-known producers (Dayi, Xiaguan, etc.), you can find them there at reasonable prices. Since most of the suppliers on Tmall only ship within China, you have to use so-called "Agent Services", which commission your own shopping cart for a premium and then ship it abroad.

If you have your tea shipped directly from Asia, there are further advantages and disadvantages. Gourmets can have the first Darjeeling of a year delivered from India, and the freshest possible Matcha from Japan. Other green teas should also not be kept in transit for too long, but rather be stored in a cool place as quickly as possible. Therefore, one has to calculate quite high shipping fees, because those who are looking for the freshest tea do not want to wait six or eight weeks until the mule has traveled the Silk Road, so they choose airmail, which can easily be twice as expensive.

And then there is also customs. Because of the rather marginal duties in many countries, most teas are more or less duty free in many countries anyway, but from a certain amount upwards import sales tax might apply. Although these rates are mostly manageable and fair, the occasional trips to the customs office to release a package are way more unpleasant. This happens when the foreign trader forgets to correctly attach[64] the customs declaration on the outside of the parcel, or someone in the logistics chain loses the declaration, or it is simply your turn in the lottery of random checks by customs, or...

In the past, I have very rarely been asked to visit customs in person, but lately it has happened more and more frequently. Furthermore, because of different tax rates for tea and non-food, I order either tea or accessories, but never combine the two. This way I can at least make sure that the duty-free tea is not being mixed with other goods and that it does not cause irritation with the customs officers on how to apply the correct duty rate per category. Otherwise it has happened that the friendly postman was standing at my door needing to collect the full VAT on everything. Of course one may refuse to pay this and rather go to the customs office in person, asking for a corrected tax calculation. This is not a big issue, but one needs to take this effort and possible additional costs into account if they decide to shop outside of their country of residence (or outside of the EU in my case).

These are just my personal thoughts from an EU-centric point of view. Your results may vary...

TEA MASTERS

As in any other industry, there are apprentices, advanced students and true masters in the tea world. In many countries, one becomes a master craftsman after completing an apprenticeship, gaining a lot of experience, and undergoing further training and one or more subsequent examinations, in which one has to demonstrate a high level of knowledge and also the ability to properly train others or ensure adequate knowledge transfer. In some Japanese industries an apprenticeship can last for 10 or even 20 years.

It is certainly safe to assume that a master craftsman's title was presumably somehow earned in most cases, even if the title holders have not passed examinations in front of a Chamber of Industry or Commerce as it is usual in many countries nowadays. Given the high quality of many teas, I cannot help but notice that most people in this business do know what they are doing. Some experience and mastery should have accumulated after two thousand years or more. And indeed, there are some real authorities to whom we as tea enthusiasts owe a great debt of gratitude. Often these are older gentlemen or ladies whose natural humbleness prohibits them from calling themselves masters, even if it may be justified. Sometimes tea marketing, by its very nature, turns this into something less humble. I find it more appealing when proven experts and teachers prefer to call themselves eternal learners. There is certainly nothing wrong with modesty and humility in the infinite tea universe.

In principle, there is nothing to be said against tea traders advertising their products as works of Master X or Grandmaster Y. Self-proclaimed masters add the finishing touches to the colorful bouquet and are all well and good, but for a good reason did the Chinese authorities announce in 2016 that the title Tea Master is no longer considered a state-recognized profession. There is no officially regulated, standardized training and certification in China and therefore no officially regulated standards for this title.

The Tea Taster, on the other hand, is apparently still recognized as a profession and is subject to requirements similar to those of teacher training.

There are a lot of tea schools in China (or India and Sri Lanka), mostly run by the big tea factories, but there are no officially regulated standards, the schools and factories create their own. There is nothing to be said against that, after all this contributes to a better understanding of their products and ideally also an increasing quality.

While some traders make a lot of fuss about their tea masters products, others let their products speak for themselves, sometimes sourced from the same masters, but without making a lot of noise. Mastery is good, and experienced producers are important, but if recruiting famous people for marketing only leads to more expensive tea, then that is not helpful. Bad tea from heavily advertised tea masters has not yet come to my attention, but often, together with other tea connoisseurs, I have not been able to detect significant differences in taste when we blindly compared them to teas of similar grades. I have nothing against tea masters (I only despise the self-proclaimed) as long as people do not freeze in awe. In the end, it is still one's own taste that counts.

FRIENDS

Of all possible tea sources, however, I still prefer my tea friends with whom I can drink together and who generously share their own treasures with the group. Be it for a serving that is infused and sampled together, or the tasting samples that you have to take home, because after hours of collaborative tasting, you simply cannot manage to steep even one more round.

Allow me to make a recommendation for drinking together with friends. A tea friend had brought this to my attention because he is highly allergic to perfume and artificial fragrances. Before a tea session it is particularly advisable to avoid perfume, lipstick, fragrant deodorants etc. Not only in order not to irritate the other drinkers, but also to be able to develop a neutral perception of one's own scent and taste.

In order for tea acquaintances to become (and stay) tea friends, I would not want to miss out on mentioning the topic of smoking. For smokers, especially those who smoke in their own homes, it may be hard to hear, but teas take on bad smells in smoking households and tea gifts from smokers (or their contributions to tea gatherings) hardly contribute to the enthusiasm of the other participants. As a tea and chocolate addict, I have no intention of rising above other addicts (nicotine addicts, in this case), but since this book is dedicated to drinking better tea, this should not go unnoticed. It is not easy to fight an addiction and get rid of it, but the enjoyment of tea can be greatly increased immediately if you stop smoking, at least some time before drinking. In any case, smokers who are perhaps joining a tea party for the first time should wear fresh clothes and also avoid my smoking breaks.

THE FAIR PRICE OF TEA

The price of a tea is generally regulated like the price of all other goods which are sold in a free market economy and without cartel activities.

The price of the same tea can be several times higher in the rest of the world than in the countries of origin. This is easy to understand, because western traders bear the cost of capital, transport, customs, certification, storage and much more, but they also want to earn a margin. Those who envy the traders or want to feel the thrill of importing directly can except some savings, but also a bit more stress.

QUALITY CRITERIA[65]

Unfortunately, many dealers only provide little detail about the teas they offer. However, if these are given, it is advisable to study and evaluate them attentively:

- Does the tea derive from wild plants or are the bushes grown from seeds, or were only cuttings planted?
- Was it picked and sorted by hand or mechanically?
- Were essential processing steps done manually?
- Did the withering take place outdoors, or was hot air used?
- Has the material been dried in pans or baskets over fire, or in an electric oven?
- Did people roll the material elaborately by hand?
- Has it been fixed in a wok (pan) by hand, or in the drum of an electric oven (similar to a clothes dryer)?

It is true that manually processed teas do not necessarily have to taste better than machine-processed ones. However, if many steps are done by hand, it gives a master tea maker more control and it is increasingly done with high-quality raw material and in prestigious tea gardens. Thus, the reference to handcraft in the description is at least an indication of better quality, provided the information given was correct.

COMPETITION TEA

Annual competitions are conducted in leading tea-growing countries and regions to select the best tea of a particular variety or growing region. The reputation of these competitions means that the prize-winning teas are subject to exponential jumps in price which are hard to grasp with reason and can only be explained by the consumer's greed for prestige.

Today one may buy one gram of top-quality tea for about one Euro. The so-called competition teas on the other hand can easily cost five or ten Euros and even more per gram.

Are these now the best teas in the world? Perhaps they are. And perhaps you will have the opportunity to visit one of these competitions or tea auctions while on holiday in Asia? If so, you will have the best opportunity to taste the tea directly on site and, if necessary, purchase it.

If you do not have any other hobbies or a well-filled piggy bank, you can of course buy competition finalist or even winning teas, but then you should be able to drink these teas directly on site, prepared with the same water and by the same people who prepared them at the competition, for that exact experience. Otherwise, the experience at home with your local water might be a very different one. Personally, I prefer to buy tea based on how good it tastes at home and with my local water.

Especially for the most sought-after, rare, old Pu'er, ten Euros per one gram is by no means the end of the story. For vintage bings usually weighing 357 grams, six-digit (dollar) amounts are routinely called at auctions. And these teas do not even have to have won competitions. Speculators make sure that the harvest of the most expensive and prestigious locations is sold long before it is brought in. The raw tea from a special garden or single tree may then cost up to 20,000 Euros per kilogram.

However, all tea lovers who do not want to be driven wild can be consoled. Competitive tea does not necessarily have to offer the ultimate taste experience. On the contrary, some competitions select tea that tastes typical and well-balanced and is virtually a reference for this type of tea. Very often, I even like teas of a slightly lower quality or price range much better, precisely because they are not perfect, but often special nuances. Of course, this does not refer to any off-flavors or poorly crafted teas.

SOME THOUGHTS ON PRICING

But let's return from the cloudy heights of the auction or competition teas back to the real tea world. For those who are used to spending 2€/100g in a supermarket or elsewhere, it might seem quite exorbitant to get only one gram of tea for these same two Euros. This is not unusual and can be illustrated by the example of Matcha.

The cheapest Matcha, which is only suitable for cooking or baking, costs about ten to 20€ per 100g in retail shops. Drinkable qualities start at 50€, premium at 150€ and top offerings end around 300€ to 400€ per 100g.

However, these teas are usually only available in small portions of 20 to 40g, so one rarely faces three-digit prices.

Things look different with heicha, which in its pressed form usually weighs 357g and in its finest version, the Lao Ban Zhang Sheng Pu'er bing, has a four-digit price tag. 1,500€ for a young bing is not unusual here.

As you can see, even outside of Asia, four to five Euros can easily be charged for one gram of tea. I buy the majority of my teas in the range between 20€ and 70€ per 100g, above 0.50€ per gram one can already find high quality products, and even below that. Teas under 30€/100g I usually receive from friends or acquaintances visiting from China or by placing an order directly in Asia. Retailers abroad have to calculate differently, of course.

So let's just calculate what tea enjoyment really needs to cost.

For the preparation of Matcha I need two to three grams per person. The gram costs between one and two Euros. On average, a Matcha of excellent quality costs me four Euros. This allows for 80 to 120ml of foamy beverage.

As you will read later in the chapter on preparing tea, high-quality teas can usually be infused several times. This obviously does not apply to Matcha.

So for other teas, let us calculate with about one gram of tea per 20ml (0.7 fl oz), which is a good rule of thumb, so I use ten grams of tea for a 200ml (6.7 fl oz) pot. At an average of 0.50€/g the tea costs me five Euros. Quite a lot of money for 200ml, one may think. But depending on the type of tea, I can steep the tea leaves from three to 20 times and this way I get 600ml (20 fl oz) to almost four liters or one gallon of tea, enough to make it through the day. In other words, what some people pay for a glass of simple, open wine in a restaurant or a fancy frappu-cappu to go keeps me hydrated all day long. Even some mineral waters cost more; if I get four liters of beverage from ten grams of old Shu-Pu'er, it is only 1,25€ per liter.

But even students and regular earners, for whom five Euros per day for tea are still out of budget, do not have to do without good tea. Good teas are even available for less than 0,10€/g (especially red teas and simple heicha), and thanks to the Gong Fu brewing method, the palatal pleasure to be extracted from them is much higher than when using the western steeping method.

FAKE TEA

But be warned about fakes, i.e. forgeries. Teas that are too cheap to be true should be handled with caution or ideally not at all.

If greed and ignorance come together on the buying side, fraudsters have an easy game. The documentary film *Sour Grapes* from 2016, which is well worth seeing, tells a story from the world of wine in which rich collectors have been cheated out of millions.

But millions need not be the issue. Anyone who is offered a Lao Ban Zhang for less than 1,000€ from dubious sources should be alert, and even a famous 20 or more years old Sheng for less than 100€ per bing is hardly kosher. Not only high-ranking Chinese teas are being counterfeited, also the Sri Lanka Tea Board, for example, is leading a well-documented fight against product piracy - despite the rather modest prices of the original products.

It does not always have to be direct fraud, often it is also extremely creative or careless marketing, which can be misleading. If dealers offer Pu'er from Thailand, Myanmar or Laos, which often happens, it doesn't have to be a bad tea, but it is certainly not a Pu'er. At most, it can be a tea that has been produced from similar plants and with the same methods as the eponym from Yunnan.

One should also not put the tea farmers in general under suspicion of fraud. Often it is factories or traveling sales agents who buy raw tea directly from less renowned tea farmers' estates and then press and market it under their own label. Unfortunately, tea cannot be tagged with a precise label like, for example, an egg. Also, areas of Laos and Myanmar are bordering China, and the chance of infiltration of second-class material from still emerging regions is quite high. This is again well illustrated by the example of Lao Ban Zhang[66]. The market offers about four times as much Lao Ban Zhang as the small region actually produces. This speaks for itself. The occasional one or two sacks of tea may easily be "accidentally" re-declared, who would notice?

But there is reason for hope. Those who know the real thing will notice it. And good, serious, experienced traders do a lot to recognize such fakes and offer their customers affordable goods at fair (but not cheap) prices.

This is why I allow my trusted suppliers their well-earned margin, not looking for questionable bargains elsewhere. Price comparisons are of course always advisable, but I do not compromise on quality. I prefer to buy tea from small farms or from less renowned areas, because hardly anyone will want to counterfeit these teas. Moreover, these teas often cost a little less and often offer a similar high quality as the more well-known regions.

STORING TEA

Storing tea is a chapter in itself. But it will be quite short, because the most important rules can be summarized quite well and are mostly self-explanatory.

As a general rule we can state that tea should always be stored in a cool, dry and dark place, and usually airtight. Otherwise, tea will quickly lose its flavor due to contact with oxygen, moisture, heat or light, and will also readily absorb foreign odors.

So there are some basic, optimal storage conditions for tea, which almost always apply:

- Dark
- Dry
- Airtight
- Rather cool
- Free from unpleasant odors

Darkness in this case means the absence of UV light, which means that translucent glass is excluded. Well-closing containers made of porcelain, glazed ceramics or tins are recommended. Heicha, as an exception, may benefit from containers made of open-pored clay with a lid that is not necessarily airtight. For Japanese green teas and especially Matcha, finely lacquered tins and bamboo are also used, which are called natsume 棗 (for thin Matcha or Usucha) or chaire 茶入 (for thick Matcha or Koicha).

I need to confess that I willingly and intentionally violate the principles of optimal storage. I am aware that this does not make the teas any better, but some Pu'er bings are so beautiful to look at that I display them in a showcase. At least they are halfway protected from direct sunlight, but I could certainly store them better. However, I would not buy tea that is displayed for weeks in a shop window, I would rather donate the money directly to charity.

Air humidity should not pose a major problem, as long as one does not store one's teas in the bathroom or close to possible ironing areas or indoor pools.

Tea should also always be stored away from any other odors, such as kitchen fumes or cigarette smoke[67], because it absorbs such foreign odors all too easily. Storage in the kitchen or cellar should therefore be avoided.

Airtight storage does not only mean protecting the tea from unpleasant odors, but also from too much oxygen. If I may again compare it to wine, there are devices for keeping away or extracting air (oxygen) from opened wine bottles, so that they can keep their aroma as long as possible. Some Matcha producers also seal their products under a protective atmosphere right from the start.

The following table provides an overview of noteworthy additions to or deviations from the above mentioned basic conditions.

Storage recommendations

Type of tea	Storage	Remark
White	Dry	Can improve even more with proper storage, provided good raw material is used.
Yellow	Dry	Better shelf life than green tea, but will not improve with longer storage.
Green	Cooled	Should almost always be drunk as fresh as possible, especially Japanese teas which are not roasted but steamed. Those sometimes lose aroma faster than one can drink them. Heavily roasted/baked green teas are less susceptible to this, but one should still not overdo in terms of storage time.
Steamed green	Cooled	
Matcha (Japanese green in powder form)	Cooled	
Oolong	Dry	Aged oolong may also be lightly re-roasted at home every two or three years to remove excess moisture and give the taste a boost.
Red (black)	Dry	Good shelf life, but no improvement due to aging to be expected.
Dark (post-fermented)	Dry (airtight or ventilated) or humid (then in any case well ventilated)	Heicha and especially Sheng Pu'er will continue to mature for many years or even decades. Provided that the base material is well selected, the taste often changes and improves considerably. In contrast to all other teas, some aeration may be helpful and desirable, provided that the influence of foreign odors can be avoided.

I put small bags of silica gel or the iron-filled oxygen absorbers into the containers in which my aged oolongs are stored. This helps to better keep my treasures from deteriorating.

High quality green teas should be stored neatly chilled, preferably in the refrigerator. This is especially vital for Matcha, which otherwise degrades or even spoils quickly, recognizable by its brownish color at the very latest.

This can easily be verified by storing one half of a freshly bought green tea in the refrigerator and the other half at room temperature. After a few months you are able to make a comparison. The aroma and taste will have clearly diminished in the portion that was not refrigerated. In addition, the bright green color of Matcha quickly darkens, particularly badly stored Matcha may even turn grayish.

Tea stored in a refrigerator should be allowed to acclimatize to room temperature for 15 to 20 minutes before opening its container. Otherwise the tea might become moist due to condensation when opened and thus spoil faster.

If necessary, it is advisable to store a small portion in a separate container for short-term use, so that you do not have to keep warming sensitive tea to room temperature several times a day just because you want to prepare a fresh brew.

Similar to the delicate storage of cigars in a humidor[68], some collectors even build or tinker with a so-called pumidor[69]. This can be a discarded and converted camping cooler, or even a room within a room with an elaborate air conditioning system. So far I did not have to go to such extremes in order to keep my collection pleasantly drinkable, but in extremely arid or wet climate zones, one may feel differently.

Small tea urns

By the way, wine refrigerators that are no longer needed can easily be repurposed for storing high-quality green tea or Matcha.

STORAGE PERIODS

The deliberate aging[70] of **white** tea is currently quite en vogue, if one wants to talk about trends in the world of tea. Thank Buddha, tea trends are rather rare, but sometimes they can be huge, for example the bubble tea hype, but this seems to be more or less over now. Good candidates for aging are naturally sun-dried white teas, no matter whether they are large or small leaf varieties. Beautiful examples in my own collection are Bai Mudan and Shou Mei, each about ten years old, and some bings of Lao Bai Cha.

The former gain body and even tingle a little on the tongue, while the Lao Bai Cha are more reminiscent of mild Pu'er. Artificially and quickly dried whites do not age to their advantage, but do not spoil as quickly as greens.

Yellow teas also last better than green teas. Although not as oxidized as white teas, they have already lost some of their sensitivity through fermentation or composting. An age of two to three years is no problem for them.

Since **green** tea is the most natural tea because it has not oxidized, it changes most rapidly after production. The quality goes down fast, and fastest in the case of (mostly Japanese) steamed green teas. As a rule of thumb, these should not be stored for more than half a year after purchase and open packages should be used up quickly. Air is toxic for their taste.

The situation is somewhat less dramatic with roasted green teas, there are even specimens that are extremely durable[71] without losing much taste, but these are rare exceptions. Those teas should not get much older than a year, especially as they are generally not brought home immediately after harvest.

Anxi **oolong**s produced the modern way and also Taiwanese oolongs produced rather green are best drunk fresh, red oolongs like Wuyi Yancha, on the other hand, win massively by leaving them untouched for at least one year[72], also to allow the effect of an often strong charcoal roast to set in. Here I can only advise to experiment and to find out the best storage times for your own taste. A distinction can also be made between spring and autumn picking. A green spring oolong should be drunk as fresh as possible, an autumn oolong, which is also green, may be allowed to ripen a little if desired.

Oolongs that are processed especially for aging are a completely different matter. They do not taste as fresh and flowery, but heavier and yet light, with notes of plums and dark berries, sometimes even cocoa. They are almost always red oolongs, heavily roasted and often lovingly re-roasted every two or three years to keep them dry and aromatic. The oldest treasures in my storage are almost half a century old and will keep their aroma for many years to come, making them ideal for collectors. However, one should not expect any significant quality increase in aroma from these so-called aged oolongs, the quantities in which they are stored at home are simply not sufficient for that. I also do not recommend to simply leave any oolongs lying around. What is not sold as aged oolong right from the start is unlikely to develop the desired aromas just by forgetting the tea somewhere in the back of the cupboard. My oldest oolongs date back to the seventies and in comparison I can say that every decade of age brings new and extraordinary nuances. For me, "old" starts at about 20 years, but some shops also market seven years old teas as "aged". Of course, those teas cannot be compared to specimens that were allowed to mature for several decades.

Carefully produced **red** tea made from high quality leaf material has a much longer shelf life than most green teas, but it does not get any better than when fresh. It is important to store it dry in an air- and light-proof container, so it can keep its quality for up to several years, and thanks to its almost complete oxidation, the taste will not change much. As an exception, somewhat weaker oxidized first flushes are to be mentioned, e.g. from India. Only rarely can one find black teas that have been deliberately aged (and not only forgotten in the warehouse).

Dark tea (better known as **heicha** or its most prominent representative, the Pu'er) is often sold with the claim that it gets better with age, but this is not quite that simple.

True to the motto "garbage in - garbage out", the rule of thumb is that nothing can be expected from inferior material, not tomorrow and not in a hundred years. Buying cheap Pu'er today and then enjoying the finest drinks in a decade or two does not work, just as a large bottle of Lambrusco does not magically mutate into Château Pétrus just by being stored for a long time.

When talking about the shelf life of **Pu'er**, I almost always mean the **Sheng** (also called raw Pu'er). This is close to green tea in terms of production technology and is therefore capable of changing considerably. A Sheng that is only a few days old can be bitter, ultra-strong and almost undrinkable, then after a few months it may already be very enjoyable, and after ten years it can become fully matured and balanced. However, the taste does not change or improve in a linear fashion, usually these teas enter a so-called in-between phase, being between two and five years of age. Within this time frame the taste often decreases significantly and can be quite disappointing.

After enjoying a young sheng for a year or two, one may sometimes not recognize it anymore. The consolation is the great certainty that after a small break of one or two years, one may rediscover a usually better, but certainly different tea, deep down in one's collection. But this is only true if one has already acquired a good quality. If it was produced quickly and cheaply and with too much heat, you may wait for a long time, but not much change or even improvement will occur anymore. If a Sheng has reached an optimal aroma, you can put it into resealable plastic bags and thus deliberately suppress further ripening.

The in-between time may vary depending on the location and humidity of the storage site. Retailers like to add labels like Dry-Storage (Gancang 干仓) or Wet-Storage (Shicang 湿仓) to their products, i.e. dry or moist storage. This means that the respective warehouses may be physically located in different climate zones. Sometimes Chinese tea is even stored in Malaysia because of the tropical humidity. The advantage of this wet storage is faster ripening and also an earlier and shorter in-between phase. The microorganisms do a faster job than when stored in low humidity. Whether they also do a better job, everyone may judge for themselves, but dry-storage heicha is usually more expensive. The disadvantage of wet-storage is the danger of mould and mildew, so I recommend to be very careful when buying.

The oldest Pu'er vintages that I have tasted so far are from the 60s, so they are a good half century old and worth every single cent. Sheng up to the age of ten to 15 years is called young, up to an age of 30 years it is called aged or old Pu'er and beyond that it is called vintage.

Shu Pu'er ("ripe" or "cooked" Pu'er) has already been artificially aged by its special production process and does not gain or lose as much taste as a Sheng during storage, but also offers an extremely long shelf life.

Pu'er teas and other heicha can be stored together quite well and may have a positive influence on each other's taste. However, you will want to make sure to store Sheng and Shu Pu'er separately, as they possess very different aroma characteristics which should not interact.

PREPARING TEA

Having familiarized yourself with the tea varieties, you will easily master purchasing and storing, which now takes us straight to the most difficile challenge, namely preparing the tea. After all, what use is the right tea, fresh, of high quality and bought at a reasonable price, if we do not get the most out of it? And sometimes it is not even supposed to be the very best taste, but a certain nuance is to be achieved or a tea party with friends is supposed to be especially pleasant.

Of course, we can simply put tea into any vessel, add more or less water, and then let it steep for a certain time. Most of the time you can certainly drink the resulting liquid, and sometimes it just has to be quick and straightforward. Fine with me, we will consider that, too. But the steeping or brewing process is not all that may be considered in order to get as much pleasure, taste, relaxation or Qi 气 as possible out of the leaves.

Despite the extremely low minimum requirements of tea preparation, there are some topics that we want to take a closer look at now. Let us turn our attention to the tableware and also look at the second essential ingredient, water. Then we will discuss the brewing process and its variations and finally we will do some tasting.

DISHES AND OTHER ACCESSORIES

Many Non-Asians are used to preparing tea in and drinking it out of china (porcelain, not the country) or glazed earthenware pots and cups, and some also prefer glass teaware. First of all, there is nothing wrong with this, as these vessels do not influence the taste. Most of the time they are even dishwasher-safe and therefore easy to clean, but often they are also very big, too large for certain methods of steeping.

It is not by chance that the so-called tasting sets of tea buyers are always made of porcelain. So if the crockery does not influence the taste, they can taste the tea relatively genuine (of course, other factors such as water quality or temperature may still produce different results). However, an unaltered taste may not be the most ideal taste. A good example of this are once again the professional tea tasters, who always brew each tea with boiling water and always let all varieties steep for an equal length of time. Here, it is not the hunt for best taste is at the forefront, but the desire for optimal comparability. Neutral vessels and the same water temperature at all times are certainly beneficial to that purpose.

Glass pots and jars are also popular, and often there is no need to buy anything special, one may simply repurpose a large glass cooling jar for steeping. In glass pots you can watch (green) teas unfold, sink to the bottom and rise up again. Also art- or flower teas are displayed to their best advantage. A major disadvantage of glass (for brewing purposes) is its poor thermal conductivity, it cools down too quickly - which makes it a perfect choice for cooling.

Yunomi and gaiwan

THE BREWING VESSEL

Porcelain vessels are not always the first choice among tea lovers. Sometimes one simply wants to brew the tea of one's heart in the pot of one's trust, which is believed to have properties that promote brewing success. Especially open-pored clay pots of various origins are appreciated here. Some are said to smooth down young, edgy Pu'er teas whereas a pot made of iron-bearing clay is considered particularly suitable for increasing the desired amount of minerals in certain teas.

And maybe soon you find yourself deeply engaged in acquiring a small collection, often starting with one pot each for green and black tea, quickly followed by another pot for oolongs, only to discover that it is better not to brew strongly oxidized or even charcoal-roasted oolongs in the same pot in which you want to prepare a delicately floral green oolong next time. With Pu'er and other dark teas, a separation into Sheng, Shu and maybe even Fu is also a good idea, and you may want to keep white teas separate as well. Who wants to drink a delicate white tea steeped in a pot in which either red or even darker tea has been prepared many times? It would be better to forget about the white one and just pour hot water directly into the well-used pot, the resulting infusion may well be powerful enough to completely cover a delicate white tea's aroma.

Hence there is a growing tendency towards specialized pots, which are not absolutely necessary, but each of them offers its own advantages. Especially strong or smoky teas leave their residues quite remarkably in an open-pored clay and should really be dedicated their own brewing vessel. But fear not, the above only applies to open-pore clay pots.

You often get the advice that teapots should only be rinsed with plenty of clean water to preserve their patina, but this is only true for open-pored materials. For porcelain or glass, a cleaning agent can safely be used.

Although teapots made of iron[73] or cast iron are sometimes used for brewing in their countries of origin, in fact they were originally designed as kettles for heating water. Cast iron teapots, which are often found in the markets and in which the sieve is much too small, are often enameled on the inside and are therefore not even suitable for their original purpose, namely to add some iron ions to the water but without enriching the taste of the water. Some teas do benefit from this, so that even marginal rust is often accepted.

Those who fancy such cast iron models can of course use them to serve tea in them, after all the tea stays warm in there for quite some time. But their weight makes them hard to handle, thus I cannot advise acquiring such a teapot.

Often teapots are accompanied by a tea pot warmer, but I have a problem with them. Most teas taste especially good when prepared fresh, but keeping them warm does not improve any tea. Still, if you brew tea according to western methods (more on that later), you usually have to or want to keep larger quantities of tea warm, unless you drink in company.

So let us get back to the fancy pots which are popular among fans and tea addicts, because they are suitable for brewing tea in the Gong Fu style (again, more on that later). Sense and purpose of these rather small and unglazed clay pots is the positive influence of the minerals in the clay on the taste of the tea. Small here means that my personal clay pots cannot hold more than 50 to 250ml of water, and even less once tea is added.

Although there are smaller and larger ones around, I am well equipped for brewing tea for one to six people with these sizes, and tea rounds rarely get bigger.

One might ask how much tea is allotted to each drinker in a four-person round, if the smallest pot only contains 30 to 40ml of tea? This is not a real issue, you can choose the tea cups to be as small as you like (in all seriousness they can be as small as a thimble), and in case of doubt you can brew two or three times in a row and collect the tea in the fairness cup before serving it into the individual drinking vessels. There is no time-related problem here either. Particularly high-quality oolongs, which are often brewed in tiny pots, are initially only steeped for seven or ten seconds per brewing cycle.

Chinese and Japanese pots for approximately 100ml[74]

KYUSU

In Japan, the teapot with the characteristic handle is called Kyusu 急須. The most popular ones hail from the city of Tokoname and are characterized by their fine, often thin structure and the famous iron-rich and often anthracite-colored clay.

Especially for the purpose of preparing Japanese green tea, Kyusu usually feature integrated sieves with large surfaces and very fine pores, which are located directly in front of the spout. I also prepare Chinese green teas in Kyusus. The built-in sieve with its large number of rather small holes is more suitable for green tea leaf grades. Yixing teapots are mainly used for oolong and heicha.

Black Kyusu pot from Tokoname

More suitable as cooling vessels are the Yuzamashi 湯冷まし, which are similar in style to the Kyusu, but they do not have a lid or strainer. They are useful if you want to observe the brewing phase and the soaking of the leaves, but you can also use them as a cooling vessel. In this case, however, an additional sieve might be useful.

CHA HU

Chinese teapots are called Cha Hu 茶壶, but are widely known as Yixing[75] 宜兴. Those originate from the city of the same name, a large part of the production comes from there. Depending on their origin, clay and color, Chinese teapots may also be called Jianshui (a popular purple clay originating from around this city), Chaozhou (with the characteristic red color) or they come from many other cities and regions and look plain, elaborately decorated or even rustic (from Qinzhou).

Three Chinese teapots in Xishi style

When sourcing teapots, it is advisable to buy from a shop where you can judge the quality. Is it single clay, i.e. one single type of clay, or do you have to deal with dual or even triple clay? Apart from the fact that the latter often looks particularly pretty, can the taste-enhancing properties of clay from several different mines perhaps have a special effect? What is the size of the sieve? Can the desired tea be poured perfectly into the intended pitcher? Or will it clog up quickly because the holes are too large? Does it have too few holes, so that pouring takes too long and the desired infusion time is severely exceeded?

As a rule of thumb, Japanese green teas require a larger sieve than others. The consistency of the leaves after the brewing process can best be described as mushy, even with high-quality teas, and would quickly clog smaller sieves. When cleaning after use, a soft brush is helpful to remove leaf residues with little effort under plain water.

There are also some basic rules when purchasing a teapot. First of all, the top of the spout, the fill opening and the handle of an Yixing (and many other pots) should be on the same level, because this is the ideal way to handle them and pouring is easy without spilling too much. Also take a close look at the lids. It is nice if they have a small hole, which prevents a negative pressure in the pot. It can easily be covered by putting the thumb or a finger of the other hand on it. This way, it is easy to stop the flow of tea until you have moved the pot over the next drinking vessel, because you may not always have a fairness cup available.

The lid should be thoroughly checked for accuracy of fit. Inferior pots are often characterized by the fact that the lid does not fit exactly, but has too much tolerance. Thus, sometimes when pouring tea quickly, hot tea might spill out, which is something you do not want. This would also prohibit to apply the popular pouring technique where you place the pot vertically in a suitably sized pitcher and allow it to empty unsupervised. You just need to be able to rely on a tight-fitting lid.

Typical size of the sieve in a Chinese teapot

Typical size of the sieve in a Japanese Kyusu

Generally speaking, there are three qualities of teapots. The simplest are the ones made of cheap clay and pressed quickly into moulds, which are sold to tourists or in Asian retail stores around the world. The clay is often cheap mud and not really open-pored, the lid rattles, and optionally strange characters or decorations are meant to cover up the low quality or to evoke authenticity. The next quality level are the moulded pots with some manual finishing, whose clay quality at least promises some positive effects, and at the top end of the scale are the masterpieces, which call for corresponding prices both because of the material and the entirely handmade quality.

I also order pots online (search for terms like Yixing or Kyusu tea pot), but mostly these are variations of what I already own and where I put my trust in the competence and quality of the dealers.

The prices for clay[76] teapots range from 20 to 2,000 or more Euros. What you can buy in Europe for 20€ is sold for about a tenth in China and is quite questionable in terms of quality. Acceptable quality start at about 80€ and range up to 400€. For this you may get partially handcrafted pieces, which may have been designed and drafted by masters, but are finished by means of moulded parts and assistants. Only from about 500€ upwards you may expect masterpieces, which might have been formed entirely freehand and with first-class craftsmanship or which might show small irregularities, which are practically not found in the middle price range, because despite their good quality, they are more likely to be made on an assembly line. The masterpieces are almost unlimited in price, especially if they are antique pieces that collectors are chasing after.

Personally, the middle class models are sufficient for my needs, because it is not important to me to have a very unusual look or a maker's stamp. but A good quality clay and decent craftsmanship should result in a pot which can be handled easily and rounds the tea off nicely. Therefore, I am happy to shell out 150 Euro or more for a pot that should serve me well for many years, as long as I handle it with care. This means rinsing it after use exclusively with fresh water, dry it with a cloth on the outside and then let it dry with the lid off.

If a Japanese teapot does not have a handle, it is called shiboridashi 搾り出し or ho(u)hin 宝瓶. The hohin is closer to the pot, because although it does not have a handle, it does have the typical sieve of a Kyusu. The shiboridashi, on the other hand, is more similar to a gaiwan with a pouring lip.

So what is the difference? The gaiwan is a Chinese teacup (similar to a very small rice bowl[77], supplemented by a saucer and a lid), while the shiboridashi has a practical pouring lip. However, both cups often require a separate strainer in the case of Japanese tea, unless you want to have a lot of small fragments in the cup.

Simple test to make sure that spout, filling opening and handle are at the same level by turning it over

A shiboridashi (right) with matching pitcher or fairness cup (left)

With particularly high-quality whole leaf teas, such as Gyokuro, the experienced brewer[78] does not need a sieve, because in this case the large leaves remain almost completely in the brewing vessel, and the small particles which end up in the drinking vessel do not irritate at all.

If you are still at the beginning of your tea journey, you should not feel urged to buy many expensive pots or other brewing utensils. As long as it can be easily cleaned, one single pot (made of china or glass) is sufficient, but those who want to refine their preparation skills may consider acquiring a piece of quality clay and see how it goes. Good advice is indispensable for beginners, preferably in a local specialist shop, as it is hard to judge the feel of a pot online.

Countless books have been written about the selection of teapots and the ideal clay, but most of them have never been translated from Chinese. Every tea lover and pottery collector wants and has to make their own personal experiences, only tendencies can be formulated in general terms and are based on personal observations and the exchange with far more experienced pottery experts.

The Zisha[79] clay teapots from Yixing are said to increase the perceived thickness of the infusion and make it softer and rounder, thus significantly improving the mouthfeel and reducing bitterness. Jianshui pots have a much lesser effect here, and the most neutral ones are those from Chaozhou and Tokoname. Both Yixing and Chaozhou release noticeable minerals into the tea, so that they can even level out a low-mineral water to a certain extent. Yixing is generally appreciated for Pu'er tea, although some drinkers find it too dampening. Chaozhou and Tokoname provide more purity, in general they are more suitable for green teas, where they can gently emphasize the very fine nuances.

In conclusion, for personal use I prefer:

- porous[80] Yixing for Pu'er and dark (red) Yancha and older oolongs
- Chaozhou[81] for Dancongs and fresh, green oolongs
- Tokoname for Japanese and some Chinese greens
- Jianshui or Duanni Yixing for red tea

With white tea I have not yet decided, I like to alternate between glass, Duanni clay pottery and also pottery made by some Eastern European craftspeople. I am not yet completely at ease with the infusion in silver pots or a silver-plated gaiwan[82], as the silver ions generally influence the tea more than I prefer. My personal conclusion is that I have not yet found the ideal tea to go with the silverware, but isn't it nice to still have something to quest for? Maybe the journey is my reward here.

Gao Shi Piao made of Zhuni clay

Apart from these suggestions, which I follow loosely, I buy teapots primarily on suspicion. I check the type of clay, the tight fit of the lid, the good water flow when pouring, but then it is still a wonder bag which tea works best in the new pot at home.

In case the subject of teapots is still rather confusing to you and you would first like to get to know and try out the basics of tea, do not put yourself under any unnecessary pressure: glass or china is always suitable, only then you cannot expect any additional effects from the material used. First and foremost, the quality of the tea and the water is essential. Everything else is a bonus. Not the tea finds the pot, but the pot finds the tea...

WESTERN TEAPOT

As far as I can see, the teapots usually used outside of Asia are made of porcelain or earthenware, some of them even of glass or metal, and hold 400ml to 1.5 liters of tea. The major advantage of porcelain and glass is that they are suitable for everyday use and dishwasher safe. The common statement that all teapots should only ever be rinsed with water and that the dark stains inside are a sign of quality belongs into the land of fairy tales and legends.

If you always use the same teapot with the same tea, you will certainly not have to clean it thoroughly after every use, but if you switch between black and green tea, for example, do not be afraid to clean it thoroughly with detergent and a brush.

Either bags are hung in the pot or loose tea is poured in spoonfuls and then usually boiling water is added. After a few minutes, the bags are then removed or the infusion is emptied through a sieve into a second pot, from which the tea is served. Larger pots are then placed on a teapot warmer and often kept warm for hours using a tea light. Whether this improves the taste of the tea is more than doubtful. Teapot warmers, tea lights and such are mostly unheard of in Asia. There has to be a reason for that.

Due to my limited enthusiasm for brewing tea in large pots in the western style, almost all further statements refer to the Gongfu Cha method.

COOLING AND SERVING VESSELS

Several times I already mentioned cooling and serving jars or the fairness cup. The latter is the literal translation of the Chinese term Gong Dao Bei 公道杯 or Gong Dao Hu 公道壶, in the English-speaking world we know it as pitcher. But the common term in China and also in trade is Cha Hai 茶海. Cooling jars have a different purpose, but they can still be one and the same utensil. Cooling is required when boiling water from the kettle has to be quickly taken down to a temperature most beneficial to the leaf material. After brewing the tea, pour it back into the cooling jar it magically becomes a serving jar.

Depending on the material of the cooling jar, the water temperature can be suddenly reduced by 5° to 20°C. Once you know your dishes and have tested the process with a thermometer, you will soon know from memory which vessel provides which level of cooling. For example, I have a very thin-walled glass jug that cools boiling water down to just over 80° in a matter of seconds, at least if I fill in exactly 200ml of water. Ceramic vessels cannot keep up with this.

Sometimes I also misuse a cooling vessel for brewing a nice Chinese green tea, because I do not have a glass teapot for the reasons already mentioned.

So what about the term fairness? Well, pouring a teapot into a single cup is simple. However, if you want to fill several cups directly from the pot, a standard pour (one after the other) will result in the last cup containing an infusion that has steeped considerably longer than the first one. After all, emptying a pot can take up to 15 seconds. To avoid this unequal distribution, in some tea ceremonies[83] these pots circle over the cups, but this is not very accurate and also leads to spilling the liquid treasure. Exactly for this purpose the fairness cup is used, because only from this cup the tea is poured out to all participants and everybody gets the same strength of infusion.

Finally, the aroma or smelling cup should be mentioned. Some connoisseurs in the East and the West enjoy special tall and narrow cups, which are also called appreciation cups in English and Wen Xiang Bei 闻香杯 in Chinese.

This aroma cup is used exclusively for olfactory evaluation, and the valuable tea is transferred back to the serving vessel or the actual cup after the nasal test. Of course, one may also drink well from of tall and narrow vessels, but then it takes much longer until a pleasant drinking temperature has been achieved. In my community we usually do without the smelling cup, but sniff the inside of the lid of the pot or gaiwan after the first steeping, but there is a clear difference to the smell of the finished tea (the lids often smell much more intensive).

TEA CUPS AND BOWLS

Although tea is not only brewed in gaiwans, but can also be drunk out of them[84], other cups are usually used for drinking. Of course, everyone may choose to their liking, but many connoisseurs prefer to drink in authentic Asian style.

In principle, for the materials used, the same applies as for the teapots. Glass or porcelain can be used in many ways, whereas open-pored clay cups darken quickly and a patina builds up. For this reason it may be advisable to use a separate drinking vessel for each type of tea. In addition, you will soon find out which type of cup you enjoy the respective tea from best. By type I do not only mean the material, but also the wall thickness and the size and general shape.

Teas brewed in a pot of only 50ml are unlikely to be drunk from a 250ml cup or bowl. Of course, a tea cup does not have to be filled to the brim. Matcha, for example, is prepared and drunk in quite large bowls (called Chawan 茶碗 in Japan[85] and China), but only filled up to about 20%. The rest of the space is needed for creating the foam with the bamboo broom. In China, tea bowls are also called Cha Bei 茶杯, which simply translates as tea cup and means smaller vessels. In Japan the drinking vessels are mainly known as Yunomi 湯のみ. They are smaller than a Chawan (and more cup-shaped) and therefore meant for normal tea. Very tiny versions are called Guinomi, which is also the name of the iconic and petite sake cups.

Tiny drinking bowl handmade in Europe, inspired by the Japanese Wabi-Sabi style 侘寂

I do not intend to differentiate any further here, so what more crockery, cutlery and other accessories do you need? Nothing really, but a few small items shall be mentioned, although many them may easily be substituted with available kitchen utensils, but if you are looking for something stylish or exotic, you will certainly be able to find some suitable and well proven specialty items.

TEA CUTLERY AND OTHER TOOLS

Depending on the preparation method or the type of tea, you may want or need to buy utensils such as strainers and teaspoons.

The Chinese call a tea presentation container or plate Cha He 茶盒 (open box). It is often used on more formal occasions to allow guests to appreciate the dry leaves in style. The Cha He often serves as a practical filling aid, with which the valuable leaves can be easily moved into the sometimes narrow openings of the teapots without spilling any of them.

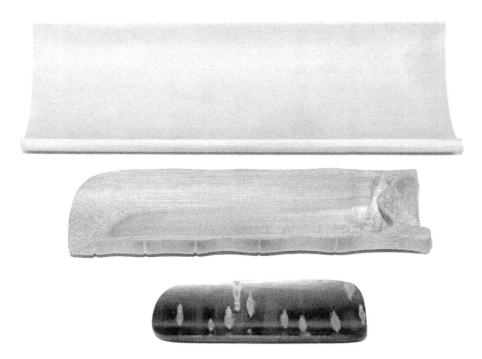

Two simple Cha He made of bamboo and one high-quality version made of Japanese cherry tree bark in direct comparison (from top to bottom)

Tea can glide easily from this tray onto the Cha He or directly into the brewing pot

For pressed tea (mostly heicha) you will probably need a Cha Zhen[86] 茶针 (tea needle or awl). Of course you could also use a knife or a letter opener as an alternative, but in this case you might want to have some band-aids ready just in case. The bing or brick is then skillfully poked with the needle in a practical tray with an opening at one corner to break or lever out portion-sized pieces.

Tea needle with built-in brush

Whichever tool you choose, always use it in a way that does not endanger your other hand (which holds the tea) or your body!

A scale with tenths of a gram division and a stop or countdown clock are further useful utensils. Experienced brewers often only estimate the amount of tea following their nose, they count the seconds in their head, and in case of teamergency, one almost always has a watch or a smartphone at hand these days.

However, I advise against buying unnecessary things just because they are on sale. Some retailers sell or even give away measuring spoons of non-standard size and then offer their preparation recommendations in their in-house unit of measure, rather than in grams. Shame on them.

The idea of a measuring spoon may seem to make sense, but spoons are not a good unit of measurement for almost all teas, unless the tea is in the form of powder. In that case it is usually a Japanese Matcha and should be portioned with a special spoon, the Chashaku 茶杓. Preparing Matcha also means you will need a Chasen[87] 茶筅 (tea whisk).

Tongs or tweezers are also popular, made of wood or bamboo, sometimes also of steel. With their help some tea lumps or balls can be handled or during tea ceremony the drinking vessels of the guests can be moved and rinsed now and then without having to touch them with the fingers. In private, however, I consider these to be negligible.

Bamboo chasen and chashaku right before use

WATER COLLECTION TANKS

Tea can be prepared very simple or a little more sophisticated. Most of the times, it is a rather soggy matter. And if one does not steep in a kitchen but cozily at the table, excess water needs to be collected.

In Chinese teahouses, entire tables or table tops made of stone or wood are equipped with drainage holes, from where small hoses drain off excess water. Top retailers also offer such devices for home use, starting at 250€ with the sky being the limit for built-to-order stoneware. But you can also buy them much cheaper and still authentic. Mostly made of bamboo, simple to elaborate boxes are being offered, which cost between 20€ and 150€, depending on size and quality. They are called tea boats, boards or tablets, in Chinese Cha Chuan 茶船

or Chapan 茶盘. In the Japanese tea ceremony these are less common, as one tries not to let the water spill over and is often content with an absorbent cloth.

Simple tea boat in full use

KETTLES AND WATER HEATERS

The next section is dedicated solely to water, but of course heating it is also part of the preparation. As the final utensil we will now have a look at how to heat the water for tea.

One might wonder why one has to think about the boiling of water at all. Well, according to some culinary legends, there are supposedly such talented people who even manage to burn water; but most of the time, boiling water is still the easiest exercise in the (tea) kitchen. The trick, however, is at least to have the water conveniently available at the right temperature at all times.

Kettles have already been mentioned, and even today they may still be practical, especially if you have an open fire or a constantly burning stove.

Especially in tea ceremonies and in Japan, hot water kettles are still in use today, which are permanently kept hot over electric or charcoal fires. Usually, however, simple water heaters are being used in Asia. Kettles with temperature pre-selection are popular with those who frequently brew different teas with varying temperature requirements.

In today's modern kitchen, us Westerners also use electric kettles, and that is all right. These can be simple low-cost models or even high-tech appliances that can be controlled using a dedicated app.

As with teapots, I think the truth lies right in the middle. I use several different models (at home, in the office, when traveling), also because I simply have not found the boiler of all trades yet. I usually use a heater made of glass with built-in water filter, as well as models made of plastic or metal, with and without inserts for filtration systems. The water filter is incredibly practical, as it allows me to use my dearest Munich tap water directly, avoiding any separate filtration steps or appliances. I could not make space for them anyway, as the woman of my heart has to have her huge fully automated coffee machine dominating in the kitchen. Anyway, at least I am allowed to spread out as much as I like elsewhere - and also there is nothing wrong with good coffee either.

Glass has the advantage that it does not release any contaminants into the water. There are also models made of BPA-free plastic, and I use one of these with built-in temperature control in the office. There, I usually do not handle thermometers, cooling or serving jugs, as I prefer to reserve some space on the desk for secondary utensils such as computers etc., and also often brew in the so-called grandpa style, i.e. directly in the cup. Since my water heater with electronic temperature control does not have a built-in water filter, I only use soft mineral water in it. Unfiltered tap water is not recommendable in many regions of the world, as it is often much too hard or even chlorinated.

I also use a stationary hot water dispenser with filter insert, which provides different temperatures at the push of a button, so every tea friend can find something for his or her needs and preferences. This additional device may seem a bit exaggerated, but only those of you who do not own a second car may cast the first stone...

For longer trips I prefer to use a durable plastic water heater with a filter insert, because glass seems to be too fragile for traveling. Some other tea lovers also use electronically controlled heaters made of stainless steel, but I have never been able to find one with a filter insert. That does not bother these snobs anyway, because they only prepare their teas with the mineral water they trust or draw their supplies directly from fresh mountain springs. Which brings us to the subject of water.

THE RIGHT WATER

The taste of tea is significantly affected by the water used. Water which is too hard hinders the development of aroma and tends to make the tea bitter and limy. In turn, water that is too soft contains too little minerals and makes tea taste bland.

I am neither a chemist, nor am I a maritime creature, thus no expert on water. Therefore I can and want to judge water by taste only. However, I limit myself to what is absolutely necessary and do not delve into details on which many books can be (and have been) written. I am neither interested in implying that my knowledge of chemistry is greater than it is (quite limited), nor in giving splendid water recommendations. That is why I avoid technical terms as far as possible.

Most of us will likely use one of three basic types of water for tea preparation:

- tap water
- filtered tap water
- spring or mineral/bottled water

TAP WATER

In areas where local suppliers do not chlorinate tap water or do so only to a limited extent, pure tap water may taste quite well and an increasing number of people share the laudable opinion that it is called drinking water precisely because one can and should in fact drink it. The luxury of drinking bottled water is increasingly being abandoned by more and more of my acquaintances, at least in their own homes. This is more sustainable than any sophisticated reusable logistics, but unfortunately the majority of tap water ruins a good tea faster than you can pull the bag out of the cup again. I can almost never get the full aroma out of the leaves using pure tap water, no matter in which region. In my experience, pure tap water is almost always unsuitable for tea, but this may simply be the case because so far I did not live in an area with water soft enough.

Fresh, soft, oxygen- and mineral-rich water allows for full-bodied tea enjoyment. Soft (measured in degrees of hardness) it should be, but never distilled. This would make it ultra-soft, but it would also eliminate all the minerals that add flavor to water. Tap water does contain minerals too, and if you are one of those lucky people whose waterworks deliver soft water to the tap, you only have to worry about the mineral content, which might either be detrimental or beneficial to the enjoyment.

FILTERED TAP WATER

Wherever waterworks supply moderately hard water, you may use activated carbon filters or sticks or blocks of charred wood (bamboo, oak, etc.) to minimize the degree of hardness and also reduce other undesirable particles.

Again, filtered tap water here does not mean distilled or denatured water produced by reverse osmosis. These variants are the other extreme, because they lack virtually all the minerals that influence the taste. Therefore rainwater or melted snow is not a real alternative. When catering companies or restaurants use reverse osmosis devices, they re-mineralize the purified water as they see fit.

Calcium and magnesium have the most significant effect on the taste of the water. Unfortunately, the calcium content in tap water is often too high.

This is where commercially available activated carbon filters may help. They all lower pH and water hardness, thus filtering out some calcium and magnesium; some other pollutants may also be reduced this way. However, if you have to live with very hard tap water as in my Munich home, you will usually not be able to achieve the desired maximum hardness for tea, even after filtering.

You may try for yourself and prepare the same fine tea once with unfiltered and then again with filtered or bottled water. I am certain you will taste the difference.

While water merely passes straight through activated charcoal filters, the charcoal sticks mentioned above remain in the water jug for a few hours and can be reused for several months. By boiling them up they may be recycled several times until they can finally be used as natural fertilizer in the flowerbed.

Activated carbon filters, which usually come in a practical plastic container, probably have a less positive eco-balance. With ultra-hard tap water, even these filters are of limited effect. In my experience they hardly manage to reduce the hardness sufficiently. In some regions, bottled water is simply indispensable for tea.

If tap water is acceptably soft, but contains a lot of chlorine, you can let it boil open for a few minutes and often the unpleasant taste will disappear - the downside being a lot of oxygen vanishing from the water, which is also not ideal.

THE MINERAL WATER YOU TRUST

As a teetotaler I am well aware of the differences in taste of many bottled waters and I have my personal top ten list, too, but that does not matter here, because how delicious a pure water actually tastes has little to do with the taste of the tea steeped in it.

No matter how deep you want to go down the abysses of water, do yourself a favor: taste your favorite tea blindly and in direct comparison with (preferably) filtered tap water and the spring or non-sparkling mineral water you trust. If you do not taste any differences, then you either live in a mountainous region with perfect tap water or perhaps have less sensitive taste buds.

I do not intend to advertise any mineral waters, especially as they may not be available in your part of the world. The fact that I know the two mineral waters Volvic and Black Forest is for two simple reasons. Volvic is always carried into my house by a tea friend in handy eight-liter container (unfortunately not returnable) and Black Forest is conveniently delivered to my doorsteps by the friendly delivery staff of the local retail giant. The latter at least comes in returnable bottles and optionally in glass bottles. I am painfully aware of the general idiocy[88] of moving water over thousands of kilometers, however, some of my guests also firmly reject filtered local tap water, which I can totally understand with some very delicate teas.

WATER COMPARISON

Choosing a suitable mineral water is actually quite simple. Start with a few (at least two) still waters, which are readily and affordably available at your place of residence. Make sure that one contains rather low and the other significantly higher levels of calcium and magnesium. This will ensure that the teas steeped with these waters differ considerably in taste.

Now taste your chosen teas blindly, i.e. someone else prepares several infusions with the same amount of water, with exactly the same amount of tea and the same brewing time, allowing for comparison of the bottled waters and ideally also the filtered tap water. Then compare the taste on your own or together with friends. The water that best accentuates your tea may now become your favorite one.

However, if you intend to widen your search for more suitable mineral water, there is a great tool on the Internet. Gerolsteiner's mineral calculator provides the data of a large number of different waters for convenient comparison.

Gerolsteiner's water is not particularly suitable for making tea. The company is rightfully proud of the rather high mineral content in its water, but for the preparation of tea this is too much of a good thing. Nevertheless, I am happy to recommend the mineral calculator on their website for the purposes of tea friends who need to get an idea of the options without having to travel all over the world and purchase random samples for comparison.

You simply enter the names of the waters to be compared and in no time at all you will get a neatly arranged overview that answers all the important questions. There is even an app available for the quick check in the aisle of a supermarket. You may look up the Internet address in the section References, at the very end of this book.

	Gerolsteiner Sprudel/Medium	Plose Naturale	Spring water ❶ Highland Spring	Volvic	Spring water ❶ Crystal Geyser Natural Alpine Spring Water
	Comparative quantity = 1 litre	Percentage = Proportion of recommended Daily requirements				
Calcium	348mg | 44%	2mg | 0%	40mg | 5%	12mg | 2%	27mg | 3%
Magnesium	108mg | 29%	1mg | 0%	10mg | 3%	8mg | 2%	6mg | 2%
Bicarbonate	1.816mg | -	14mg | -	150mg | -	71mg | -	0mg | -
Potassium	11mg | 1%	0mg | -	0mg | -	6mg | 0%	2mg | 0%
Sodium	118mg | 8%	1mg | 0%	5mg | 0%	12mg | 1%	13mg | 1%
Chloride	40mg | 5%	0mg | -	6mg | 1%	14mg | 2%	6mg | 1%
Sulphate	38mg | -	3mg | -	5mg | -	8mg | -	36mg | -
Totalmineralization	2.479mg	21mg	216mg	131mg	90mg

The online mineral calculator in action

CONCLUSION

Instead of searching for the optimal water for tea, I tend to look for the tea that tastes good using my local filtered tap water. However, the more premium tea I buy, store and collect, the more often I have to surrender to mineral water. In my experience, almost any tea can win with an appropriate mineral water, or to put it in other words, almost any high-quality tea loses detail and finesse when using most tap waters. But the teas I drink most often, namely heicha and aged oolongs, lose comparatively little, so I stubbornly brew them with tap water. Even strong black tea (namely Assamica) is quite forgiving, as it is not very subtle by nature (thinking of English Breakfast or East Frisian blends in particular). A friend of mine who is in the tea trade drinks all his teas of any kind with his local tap water, which makes much sense, because this way he knows what the resulting brew will taste like for his customers - at least if they are supplied by the same waterworks.

I usually keep three or more different still mineral waters at home for use with certain teas that demand a higher quality than tap water. While many teas taste at least a bit better to me with Volvic than with filtered tap water, I prefer some other teas with Black Forest (Hansjakobquelle), especially young, green oolongs from Anxi. I also like the latter quite well in order to emphasize the umami of Japanese shaded teas. But again, there are so many waters around and your personal results will certainly vary, so I do by no means intend to recommend any waters here.

THE BREWING PROCESS

"Brewing tea with boiling water and letting it steep for 3 minutes makes a stimulating tea. If the infusion time is extended to 5 minutes, the tea is soothing."

Adhering to the above statement, this subchapter could already be finished. For this is still the scope of numerous instructions in print or online media and often even on the packages of simple supermarket products. But it is not that simple after all. We will take a closer look at this in the next section.

It is true that a large part of the stimulating caffeine is already released in the first one or two minutes and the tannins that dissolve later compensate that a bit. If you follow the above rule, however, you will in most cases only get one thing: an unpleasantly bitter[89] tea.

Have you read the section on tea bags in the chapter Sourcing tea? Well, then you will not be surprised that they do not play any role here. With low quality tea bags, it makes little difference anyway how long they are exposing their dusty ontaents to the water.

As a tea dealing friend of mine would put it, "We are not drinking for fun here!" Or, alternatively, "We are serious about tea." Now, that does not sound like much fun, but it is meant at least partly in irony. The hidden hint is that you should at least have some idea of what you are doing in order to maximize the taste experience.

We all know the preparation recommendations on the tea boxes that we have so joyfully acquired. No matter what the importer or retailer recommends in terms of preparation, somehow it never seems to be the ideal way.

In general, you are being told the

- amount of tea
- water quantity and temperature
- brewing time

and sometimes other suggestions are also offered, e.g. whether a tea is more suitable for consumption in the morning (typically strong caffeine breakfast blends such as English/Scottish/Irish Breakfast or the infamous East Frisian blend) or for consumption in the evening (e.g. low-caffeine Japanese Bancha).

With higher quality teas, it is often suggested that they should be infused several times. In principle, this information is very important, because many consumers simply do not know that and therefore often waste high quality leaves by disposing of them directly after the first and only infusion. On the other hand it is a banality for anyone who knows a little bit about good teas, because practically every tea can be infused several times, of course with the exception of foamed powders, like Matcha. Japanese green teas usually tolerate two to three infusions, oolongs six to twelve and Pu'er even eight to over 20 repeated infusions.

The quantities of tea and water and the different infusion times are the basis of brewing methods whose common[90] names are similar to the following

- Western style
- Gongfu Cha style[91]
- Grandfather or grandpa style
- Cold brew

We will now take a closer look at these four basic concepts.

WESTERN STYLE

What is it about the so-called western way of brewing tea? Quite simply, it means how it is mostly done in the non-asian world, where the classic brewing method is very different from the Eastern, or Asian, method.

To quote[92] a large supplier of bags and loose leaf teas:

> *"Black tea should steep for 3 to 5 minutes. Up to 3 minutes it has a stimulating effect, over 5 minutes it no longer has a stimulating effect, and then it usually becomes bitter.*
>
> *For green and white tea, the water should cool down for about 3 minutes after boiling, so that the delicate, flowery nuances of the tea are preserved and do not get burnt. The brewing time should not exceed 3 to 4 minutes."*

How should such a statement be evaluated? After all, it is partly correct, tea should steep (one can and must argue about the length) and yes, caffeine is being released quite early and only later the tannins, which have a bitter effect and are an antagonist of caffeine. After all, it is not claimed here that tea has a calming effect after a brewing time of about 5 minutes. Boiling hot water for white and green tea has a suboptimal effect, I can agree with that, and I also agree with a brewing time of less than 3 minutes.[93] We should also tolerantly ignore the term "get burnt", which is quite an exaggeration.

But why am I so upset about here? Simply because one can do much better. Many of my tea friends and I have brewed for years using this method because we did not know any better and unfortunately the tea never turned out as great as we got to know it by now.

Of course, the quoted supplier and many others offer mass-produced products whose consumers are not interested much in further details and often the tea would not even be worth more efforts. If you make consumers believe that with just a couple of grams of tea and some liters of water they are capable of creating a drink that has any taste at all, then you just have to recommend a rather lengthy infusion time. Unfortunately, this will not make the resulting infusion very amicable.

In order to defend the suppliers' honor, it should not go unmentioned that for instance consumer associations recommend to always pour boiling water over the product and let it steep for at least 5 minutes in order to "obtain a safe foodstuff".

On the other hand I do not want to entirely disapprove of the western style. Red Chinese tea is the tea that reached Europe first. Later, those early teas mostly came from India. The qualities these days were certainly far from today's standard, and the preparation (water, temperature, etc.) was probably less thought about than nowadays. Red teas have always been infused with boiling hot water and (outside Asia) left to infuse for several minutes and the leaves were discarded after just one brew. Indian black tea in particular, which (and this is not meant to be mean) is often not as subtle as red Chinese tea, can easily tolerate this type of preparation. But a comparison with the preparation in Gong Fu style could well reveal new aspects of the tea.

Just compare a "normal" Darjeeling (black tea) with a white Darjeeling, ideally (but not necessarily) from the same vintage and plantation. The white variety will seem much more delicate, lighter, more sophisticated and the aroma is more of a breeze compared to the power of the strongly oxidized black variety.

I prefer an alternative way of preparing a white or green Darjeeling for better taste results. So, western tea preparation means more or less:

- a small amount of tea
- lots of water
- long steeping time
- single infusion

The tea is thrown away after just one steeping, as it is usually exhausted by then. You may notice that my enthusiasm for this style is quite limited, so let's look at a, in my experience, much more suitable alternative.

GONGFU[94] STYLE

Did you ever see instructions on how to prepare Chinese teas on packaging? I am referring here to Chinese teas produced in China for national consumption, not the produce intended for export. Seldom or not at all one finds recommendations there.

This is not necessary, because even if many Chinese also have little in-depth knowledge of tea, because many drink the same (locally grown and available) tea day in, day out, one can certainly assume a fundamentally broader tea knowledge. The number of connoisseurs, lovers and collectors of tea is also much higher in China than in other countries, and they dedicate themselves much more to the subject of tea and its many facets. In return, we may know more about coffee, wine, bread or cheese.

If you manage to brew a halfway aromatic tea in western style with, let's say, 1g of tea and an infusion time of 2 minutes (the amount of water depends on your taste), now try six times the amount of tea with the same amount of water, i.e. 6g, and one sixth of the infusion time, i.e. 20 seconds, in a small pot or in a gaiwan. Did you notice the difference? Then we are on the right track.

Critical consumers could now argue that the cost of tea is higher with this brewing method, but this can easily be refuted. One does not pay six times more, because they can infuse the tea more often and may even receive more tea in the end.

Compared to the western method the Gongfu method essentially means (bluntly ignoring all ceremonial details):

- a larger quantity of tea leaves
- less water
- shorter infusion time
- multiple infusions

The water temperature does not change compared to the western method. You can also take breaks between the individual infusions.

In this case it is important to empty the pot of the liquid (the leaves stay in) and leave it without a lid. Avoid leaving the leaves even partly immersed in water, otherwise the tea at the bottom of the pot will continue to infuse, which you do not want. The lid is kept off for the heat being able to escape quickly and thus the leaves cool down fast and no steam robs the tea of any aromas.

It is encouraging to see that an increasing number of tea dealers, in addition to the western method, also mention the Gongfu style and offer respective preparation recommendations.

Preparation

IN THE TEAPOT	GONGFU CHA METHOD
⚖ Quantity: 6g / 500ml	⚖ Quantity: 3g / 100ml
🍵 Water temperature: 100°C	🍵 Water temperature: 100°C
🕒 Infusion time: 4 min	🕒 4 infusions: 30, 60, 60, 90 sec
	For best results in gongfu cha, brew in the traditional gaiwan.

Different brewing methods being specified in an online shop

The statement given in the above screenshot is already a nice approach, even if I do not quite agree with it. With the Gongfu method, the retailer recommends 20% water quantity and 50% tea quantity. I would personally recommend more leaves, but I know this dealer and his fine sense of taste and understand that he always brews his teas more lightly than I do. So he stands behind his recommendation, and his customers appreciate his advice. As a guideline for beginners, such a statement is definitely desirable until one is absolutely sure about ones own taste. One may always deviate later, according to ones preferences. I particularly enjoy the fact that the recommended number of infusions and the ideal time per infusion are given, as these vary quite often depending on the type of tea.

Another retailer suggests 3 to 4 tablespoons per liter for the same tea. Is that more or less than 6g per 500ml then? Unfortunately, spoons are not really standardized in size, and the 2 to 2.5 minutes brewing time recommended there is not very beneficial, because this (otherwise quite renowned) retailer was advising for this tea to be brewed in the Gongfu style, only in that case the brewing time would have been way too long and nobody prepares half a liter at once in Gongfu style. Hm, that is confusing.

Approximate rule of thumb for converting from western to Gongfu brewing method:

1. double the amount of tea
2. half the brewing time and even less

Before taking a closer look at individual teas and their recommended quantity, temperature and brewing time, we will start with a brief overview. The following table contains some very basic suggestions for the preparation of the different tea types according to the Gongfu method. You should only use them as a quick reference or for initial orientation. The quantities are intended for beginners and very light infusions. Personally I also like to use up to double the amounts of tea, but this might be a bit too much for some subtle palates.

Approximate guide values for Gongfu preparation: dosage, temperature and infusion time

Type of tea	g/100ml	°C	# of steepings	Duration in seconds
White tea	2.5 to 4	80 to 90	6+	30 to 60
Yellow tea	2 to 3	75 to 85	2 to 3	45 to 120
Green tea	1.5 to 2	60 to 80	3 to 5	30 to 90
Steamed green tea	1.5 to 2	40 to 70	3	45, 30, 60
Matcha	1.5 to 2.5	70	1	-
Oolong	3 to 5	95+	5 to 8	First infusion 5 to 30 seconds, depending on degree of roasting, increase slightly
Red (black) tea	2 to 2.5	95+	2 to 5	60, 45, 60, 90
Dark tea	2.5 to 3	100	8+	**Sheng**: 30, 20, 30, 40, 50, 60, … **Shu**: 7, 14, 21, 28…

The above table alone can already lead to heated discussions at the tea table, as everyone has their own preferences and their own experiences.

For your convenience, I have included a few more tables which might come in handy when dealing with preparation suggestions from international sources, starting with weighing the main ingredient, the tea leaves.

Weight conversion

g	oz	Pound imperial	Pound metric
1	0.04	0.002	0.002
28.3	1	0.063	0.057
100	3.5	0.22	0.2
453.6	16	1	0.91
500	17.6	1.1	1

Considering myself to be lucky being born and raised in a metric world, I rarely had to bother with unit conversions, except when traveling. How I miss converting units, especially when it comes to fluids... ;-)

Volume conversion (liquid)

ml	fl oz UK	fl oz US	Cup US	Cup metric
100	3.5	3.4	0.42	0.4
28	1	0.96	0.12	0.11
30	1.04	1	0.13	0.12
237	8.3	8	1	0.95
250	8.8	8.4	1.05	1

Finishing with the most confusing scale of all. Must be simply too boring to live with a freezing point of zero degrees and a boiling point (at sea level) of 100. So, I give you Fahrenheit conversion as well and Kelvin as a free bonus. Enjoy.

Temperature conversion

°C	°F	K
40	104	313
50	122	323
60	140	333
70	158	343
75	167	348
80	176	353
85	185	358
90	194	363
95	203	368
100	212	373

One of my tea friends has his very own simplistic view on the ideal amount of tea vs. water, which surprisingly often turns out to be correct. He recommends to always use **1g of tea** (no matter what type) on **20ml** (0.7 fl oz) **of water** and we do manage quite well with this **rule of thumb**.

Experienced drinkers, and those who think they are, often do not weigh their tea at all. The desired amount is poured freehandedly into the brewing vessel and flooded with water until the leaves are at least completely covered. The brewing time is determined on the basis of intuition and experience, and many aficionados know their teas so well that the result is very satisfactory.

GRANDPA[95] STYLE

This brewing method may sound more interesting than it really is. It is probably one of the most original methods of preparation, because it is also the most simple, apart from the cold infusion, which is more of a modern fashion.

Tea is put into a rather large cup or glass, you let it steep and start drinking it as soon as you are no longer in danger of scalding your tongue. Meanwhile the tea is infusing (without interruption) and this process certainly does not improve the taste. But you can refill your (quite large) cup many times.

Almost any tea can be prepared this way, but especially dark oolongs, red teas and heicha are very sensitive to prolonged infusion times, and grandpa style is not recommended. With whites and greens it is not that bad, though.

Now let us take a closer look at the particular details for each tea type, but before we do so, I would like to give you a few hints on how to awaken the tea, also known as washing.

THE WASH

When brewing oolongs and heicha, I always do a washing or rinsing cycle first, and even two cycles with Shu Pu'er. This is for two reasons. Firstly, most teas benefit from this, especially pressed heicha and heavily rolled oolongs, which can develop and loosen up a bit; secondly, one far too often sees that tea in China, especially during the drying phase directly after plucking, is left unprotected on mats, factory floors or even in front of the halls and is thus exposed to various impurities. This is not supposed to be panic-mongering here, I have never found unappetizing residues in tea (yet) and tea has never turned my stomach or that of my fellow drinkers, but if the tea actually benefits from it, an additional hygiene step is not the worst thing to apply.

If you have a personal connection with your tea producer and know that you could eat off their floor, or if you have a very insensitive stomach, you could also do without a wash for oolongs[96], but never for Pu'er and especially not for Shu Pu'er. Residues of the microflora involved in fermentation should always be rinsed, especially in the case of Shu, to which a cocktail of starting cultures is usually added during production. This cocktail or process is called wodui[97] 渥堆 or wet pile. Also the unpleasant aftertaste that results from it is called wodui, and it is the reason why Shu Pu'er should actually be rinsed twice. There is not much lost in content and taste, since a decent Shu will be steeped for 8 to 20 times anyway. So two short washings do not really matter, do they? Since heicha and aged oolongs are often several decades old, a gentle dust removal is also a good idea, it can only improve the taste.

"Washing" may sound a bit more exciting than it actually is. You briefly infuse the leaves with the hottest possible water and then immediately pour it out. That is it. A few tea lovers also rinse white or red teas for hygienic reasons, but I refrain from that.

The washing procedure offers another positive side effect, because you save the warming of the pot, which is adjusted to the upcoming task by means of hot water. This ensures that the teapot does not cool down too quickly after the boiling water has been added and the desired temperature is maintained.

For purists and masters of ceremony I would like to point out that in our private rounds we sometimes lazily warm up the drinking cups with the rinsing water. The rinsing water is then poured out shortly before the first drinkable infusion is being served. In an elaborate tea ceremony, one would certainly prefer to warm up the drinking cups with clear water.

WHITE TEA

White tea usually works quite well with a water temperature above 80°C. Personally I like to take at least 4g of tea per 100ml of water. A short wash and then, depending on the type of tea (many buds, loose or pressed, young or old), I usually let it steep for 20 to 30 seconds and repeat this up to eight times, depending on the quality. Other white tea fans swear by 5g or up to 7g of tea and then brew for a shorter time, for example 10 seconds, 15, 20, 30, 45, 60, etc. Since this method requires a little more care (in terms of timing), I practice it in the relaxed tea sessions with my co-addicts. For a quick preparation during work I usually use the former method. On a working day I am sometimes too impatient for the finer nuances and immediately want my Boom! in the cup.

You can easily recognize the pattern: more tea allows for shorter brewing times. The latter method brings out the aromas bit by bit, the taste can develop noticeably from one infusion to the next. If it is light, almost clear and rather floral at first, the later infusions may become slightly darker and gain more body.

YELLOW TEA

Yellow tea is brewed slightly hotter and a little longer than white tea. Due to its after-treatment during production, it is also considerably more robust than green tea and tolerates, or better requires, correspondingly more heat to release its full aroma. I use a little less tea than I would with white, raise the temperature to a maximum of 90°C, and then let it brew noticeably longer. Only if the infusion proves too coarse, too strong, I reduce the temperature to a little below 80°C and extend the infusion time to up to 90 seconds.

GREEN TEA

Not all green teas are the same, many are similar, but there are huge differences in taste nuances. I happen to know people who do not like green tea at all but do not refuse an occasional Matcha, while others have only ever known one type of green tea and have then been positively surprised by alternatives.

As a rough differentiation, I separate green tea into Chinese, Japanese and Matcha. The latter is authentic Japanese, but deserves a unique approach and individual consideration.

CHINESE GREEN TEA

Most of the Chinese green teas perform quite well at 80°C, extremely fine and small-leaved representatives sometimes benefit from 70°C or even less. When trying out, remember to extend the infusion time accordingly, because lower temperatures dissolve the leaves contents more slowly. In general, Chinese green teas can be brewed without any problems, and they only requires a glass jar and not even a sieve. One or the other tiny tea leaf may (if you do not mind) simply be swallowed together with the brew.

JAPANESE (STEAMED) GREEN TEA

In contrast to Chinese tea, Japanese tea requires a bit more care during the brewing process; although Japanese green tea can be classified quite clearly, the different types have their own typical requirements regarding temperature and brewing time.

It is important to keep in mind that Japanese teas are never subjected to a washing cycle. It is probably due to the steaming process that it is already "fully awake" at the first brewing cycle, although the first infusion is slightly prolonged. In addition, almost all Japanese teas are exhausted after three infusions, just another reason not to waste a cycle to washing.

Sencha, more or less the standard tea, should never be brewed above 70°C[98], the second and third infusion should be done even cooler (60°C and less), I suggest infusion times of 45, 30, 60 seconds. In general, the rule of thumb is almost always that the best is out after two minutes, so the maximum overall infusion time should never exceed three minutes with Japanese green tea. In addition, the first infusion is typically quite long, the second infusion much shorter (because the remaining water and the heat from the first infusion continue to have an effect) and the third and often last infusion needs to be much longer. Of course there are exceptions like Bancha, more about it later.

For **Kabusecha** or very high quality Sencha you should already keep the first infusion well below 60°C, for the second and possibly third pass you may slightly increase the temperature. Infusion times of 60, 30, 60 seconds are a good starting point. Kabusecha ranges between Sencha and Gyokuro in terms of production and taste, and in fact its taste may deviate in both directions. If the temperature is raised up to 80°C, a bitterness that is appreciated by some drinkers may be obtained, of course by reducing the infusion time by up to 50%.

To me, **Gyokuro** is probably the most challenging topic, or at least the one that can be argued about most. Each person has a different taste, but in general, the higher the temperature and the longer the brewing time, the more bitter the taste of the tea. You can also generalize about the amount of tea: the higher the quality of the tea, the more tea you may use (especially with Gyokuro). However, to achieve the best balance with most Gyokuro, you should never go higher than 50°C for the first infusion, some even go as low as 40°C in extreme cases. At 60°C and above, too many tannins (bitter compounds) are extracted which overpower the other flavors. However, this is just a personal opinion, everyone has to find out his or her preferred infusion settings. In any case, at higher temperatures, as with other Japanese green teas, the infusion times should be reduced accordingly.

Top-quality Gyokuro may tolerate up to five or six infusions, but personally I often find the fourth infusion already slightly bland. Three infusions are enough to bring out the very different aromas. One infusion is full of umami, the next one is heavily grassy, and then the third one offers a delicate flowery taste. With three infusions, very high quality leaves and very low temperatures you may allow the first infusion to steep for up to 90 seconds and then continue with 45 and 60 afterwards. Lower or average qualities do not improve with long infusion times, so in worst cases 60, 10, 20 might be a better start, and whoever wants to give it a try may finish with a final infusion of up to one or two minutes. This one may be slightly disappointing, but at least you have wrung out everything then. No matter which temperature you started at, an increase in temperature of five degrees Celsius per infusion has proven to be favorable.

With all the previously mentioned tea types, but especially with Gyokuro, one may also increase the amount of tea considerably, up to doubling it, given an excellent quality; this results in a special flavor kick, similar to a ristretto compared against an espresso, the tea then turns almost sirup-like. One then uses about 1g per 10ml (sic!) of water.

Bancha, Hojicha, Kukicha and **Genmaicha** can all be prepared quite similarly, they all tolerate at least 90°C and are therefore among the most robust Japanese teas. A brewing time of about 30 seconds is a good starting point, only the number of infusions varies a lot. Genmaicha usually loses its magic for me after the third steeping, Hojicha lasts a bit longer and (especially aged) Bancha sometimes lasts for up to six rounds.

Bancha and Hojicha can also be brewed quite well western style, even if this do not make them taste any better. Every now and then I prepare a few liters of them (or a simple Indian Assam) in a very large pot, cool them down and store them in the refrigerator to drink during cycling or hiking trips. If tea gets warm on the road in summer, that's fine. Warm water on the other hand is less tasty, if you ask me.

MATCHA

Even though some people seem to shy away from preparing Matcha themselves, it is actually a very simple. Beginners may be confused with the terms Usucha 薄茶 (thin tea) and Koicha

濃茶 (thick or concentrated tea), and in fact both are used in the Japanese tea ceremony. However, the differences are quite simple: for Usucha, one takes about two to four grams of powder with approximately 80ml of water (at 70 to 80°C), and for Koicha only about half of the water is used - or twice the tea. Furthermore, the Koicha is not whipped as frothy as the Usucha.

With their premium qualities, dealers specialized in Matcha sometimes indicate for which preparation variant a Matcha is best suited, but generally the best qualities are used for Koicha, because the enormous concentration prohibits the use of mediocre material.

Let us now look at the preparation method for Matcha, which can be structured into a few and easy steps. This is how I do it myself:

1. Place a small sieve in the Chawan.
2. Put the desired amount of tea into the sieve using the Chashaku (bamboo spoon). With a little experience you can even avoid weighing the amount, you simply count how many spoons you use.
3. Add a little bit of water to the Chawan and thoroughly stir the powder to a creamy paste by using the Chasen (bamboo whisk)[99].
4. Add the rest of the water and mix well with the Chasen.
5. Whip quickly and vigorously from the wrist.[100] The hand hardly moves at all, trembles rather in high frequency from one side of the Chawan to the other, at maximum the amplitudes reach one inch. After about 20 seconds[101], a tender, delicious foam hood should already have formed.

From powder to foam

OOLONG

Oolongs are very easy to brew, at 95°C+ and with steepings lasting 7, 10, 15, 20, 25, 30 seconds etc. Personally, I often start with 20 or 30 seconds if the oolong is quite green and mild, or if I have very little material available, but most connoisseurs prefer it as I described at first, and especially if you fill your gaiwan or tiny clay pot full to the brim with tea, then five to seven seconds is the maximum for the first steeping cycle. By the way, this does not mean that you start pouring tea after these seven seconds, it means that you start pouring right after you have filled the pot with water. Put the lid on, take the pot in your hand and pour off immediately, a few seconds are always needed to release all the water. If you do not have a good pot with a nice flow rate at hand, be advised to rather use a gaiwan, here the pouring speed can be easily controlled by adjusting the gap between the lid and the bowl to your liking.

RED (BLACK) TEA

Red tea works best with boiling or almost boiling water, at least 90°C. Small leaf teas should be handled more carefully, Assamica, on the other hand, tolerates boiling water well without becoming very bitter. I vary its infusion times according to its origin.

Chinese red teas are brewed almost like oolongs, but I let them steep about 50 percent longer, i.e. 10, 15, 20, 30 seconds. In my opinion, red tea loses most of its strength after a maximum of three or four brewing cycles. Oolong usually lasts longer.

For teas from the Indian subcontinent I prefer 60, 45, 60, 90. I can hardly explain this preference, but as I keep pointing out, everyone brews and drinks for themselves, and no one has to justify themselves to others.

POSTFERMENTED (DARK) TEA

The nice thing about dark tea or heicha is the fact that you do not need to worry about the water temperature. Boiling water at 100°C, a preheated pot or gaiwan, and this is it.

The only thing to keep in mind is that without exception you always have to do a wash, with older teas and Shu Pu'er you should even rinse twice. Older tea wants to be awakened strongly and the dust of time, or various microbes, should not be drunk; with Shu and other artificially aged heicha it is also important to avoid the taste of wodui, i.e. the production-induced inoculation residues or, in other words, the starter cultures.

As an orientation for your own experiments I suggest two different infusion intervals to try for a start. Young and tender Sheng: 30, 20, 30, 40, 50 ,60 seconds and so on, very powerful and older Sheng, as well as Shu: 7, 14, 21, 28 , 35...

For Fu Cha and other heicha, the truth lies somewhere in between, but one thing is for certain: if the taste becomes unpleasantly bitter, then the infusion time was definitely too long.

COLD BREW VS. COOLED TEA

I have already talked about cool tea further ahead, i.e. normally brewed tea, which then waits in the refrigerator for one or two days to be consumed. Cool tea, that is, tea left in the open and cooled down to room temperature, is a double-edged sword. On one hand it can still taste quite delicious, but on the other hand tea tends to lose its taste very quickly when exposed to air and may become stale or even bitter. Aroma is quite a volatile thing. White and green teas are most likely to be cooled and drunk later, but especially with Sheng Pu'er I have not made many positive experiences.

The term cold brew refers to tea that is not made with hot water, but rather with water at room temperature or even below. This infusion is then left to steep for at least an hour and at most a day, ideally in the refrigerator.

I have prepared almost every kind of tea as cold brew, with mixed results. Many teas brewed with hot water and then chilled can provide a lot of pleasure, but I consider almost only green Japanese teas to be perfectly suited for the cold brew method. I suspect that its special suitability for cold infusions is due to the fact that the tea was steamed during production, whereas tea from other origins gets treated with dry air.

The Japanese call the traditional method of infusing tea with hot water Nurudashi ぬるだし. Mizudashi, on the other hand, uses cold water and Korimizudashi even uses ice-cold water.

MIZUDASHI 水出し

Tea is mainly brewed with warm to boiling water and also drunk warm. However, nothing could be easier than brewing tea leaves with cold water.

The Japanese term Mizudashi 水出し, literally water extract, is quite common among connoisseurs. Some Sencha or Gyokuro are marketed especially for this purpose[102] and result in a particularly lively and refreshing drink, for example Mizudashi Gyokuro. In general, Japanese or steamed green teas seem to be the most suitable for cold infusion, they release the desired ingredients more easily than other green teas.

Cold infusions may be produced in two different ways. If you have a lot of time, pour water over the desired amount of tea leaves and leave them in the refrigerator overnight before pouring the tea off and enjoying it chilled. Alternatively, the tea does not steep in the refrigerator but is placed in the blazing sun for several hours and then strained off before being chilled in the refrigerator. This second variant lets other, stronger aromas and ingredients dissolv, because the water is warmed by the sun and offers a clearly distinguishable taste.

The drink obtained through the Mizudashi method can be found everywhere in Japan as Reicha 冷茶 (cold tea), just like hot infused tea. In order to prepare Reicha by yourself, you do not need anything but tea (I recommend one to two grams of tea leaves per 100ml of water), water and a vessel. It tastes much more delicate than hot brewed tea, the typical umami tastes rather sweetish when infused with cold water, and a refreshing light acidity is usually present - at least if shaded tea is the basis. With Bancha, of course, there is not a lot of umami to be felt.

Personally, I prefer Reicha made of Gyokuro, even if the raw material is a bit more expensive than the modest Sencha. But if only the latter is at hand, I like to add a spoonful of Matcha powder to achieve more body; this is also helpful when making a second infusion with the same leaves, which tends to come out a tad weak. The addition of Matcha to other teas is called Matcha Iri 抹茶入 in the trade and is also done e.g. with Genmeicha, which I like quite a lot.

KORIMIZUDASHI 氷水出し

Also worth mentioning is the even cooler[103] method where no infusion is made at all, but rather a dripping takes place. It is called Koridashi or Shinobi Cha for short. This technique is ideal for high-quality Japanese green teas. Instead of hot water you simply put ice cubes[104] on the tea leaves in the kyusu and after some time you get an umami bomb, which drips almost viscously from the beak of the pot when pouring.

This way the cold infusion idea is taken to the extreme, due to the fact that the liquid never reaches room temperature (provided that you intervene as soon as the last ice has melted).

Whether you should simply use icy water instead of dealing with the ice cubes, I leave it up to your urge to experiment or play. Even if the umami can be amazing, I find the ice infusion a bit of a gimmick, tea offers so much more when hot.

GURIN TI グリーンティー

On the lower end of the cold tea spectrum, Gurin Ti is a rather sad lowlight. Japan has adopted the English word green tea into its own language and as usual harmonized the pronunciation. Since it is a foreign word, there is no Kanji and therefore it needs to be written in Katakana.

These teas, which are mostly available in bottles, are made of ground Sencha or Bancha. Still better than pure water, but these creations certainly do not cause much rapture.

ISO 3103

Unsurprisingly, there is also an industry norm to extract the contents of tea leaves. ISO 3103 is an international standard describing the most standardized approach to infuse tea, particularly bizarre or (depending on ones point of view) boring. The purpose of this method is by no means to maximize taste. Its sole aim is to extract all soluble ingredients from the leaves.

The method precisely describes the size of the cup, the amount of tea to be used per 100ml of water (2g) and the water temperature (>95°C). A shocking fact for every connoisseur is the fixed infusion time of six (sic!) minutes. There are even instructions given on how to optionally supplement the concoction with milk.

So who would come up with such an idea to prepare a tea like this? The most tasteless adulterators? Au contraire! This is how tea tasters, buyers and blenders prepare the tea about which they will later make purchasing decisions or which they are considering as an ingredient of a house blend. No surprise this tea is not swallowed but rather spat out like at professional wine tastings. This method has nothing to do with enjoyment, it serves a completely different (professional) purpose. This is how one ensures that the tea has truthfully revealed everything, a factor which is very important for quality assessment. One does rather not drink such infusions.

TRAVELLING WITH TEA

Many times, tea enthusiasts are not at home or at work, but rather traveling, staying in a hotel or other people's homes. Their own extensive tea selection, their usual utensils and preferred waters are not available to them. Coffee drinkers are to be envied as they get at least halfway drinkable produce almost everywhere, while we often only get a tea bag thrown in our direction.

While Europe has certainly copied many nice ideas from the US, the world certainly has no need for the tea-to-go fashion (formerly known as coffee-to-go). Nowadays, if you aim to appear young, fit and hyper-dynamic, you obviously have to take in food or at least drinks in passing. Well, dehydration does not occur very often in an urban environment, and the ubiquitous cardboard or plastic cups glued to many pedestrians hands do neither improve the taste of drinks nor the environment.

I make an exception when it comes to endurance exercises. On excursions lasting several hours or when on bike tours, I sometimes use a water backpack equipped with a hose and mouthpiece. I tend to fill it with a simple oolong or black tea instead of water. This is not only because I prefer tea over pure water.

I use rather simple, inexpensive or already slightly older tea for two reasons then. When exercising, I do not focus on the drinking experience, but rather on preventing dehydration. Furthermore, high-quality tea in a plastic tube appears to me like casting pearls before swine. To prepare tea for this purpose, I use a little more water and let it steep a bit longer than usual. The result is a light and refreshing drink that is always at hand. Or in the mouth.

As I like tea hot, lukewarm, cold or even chilled, this method offers me yet another advantage. While I do not like to drink water which is too warm, it does not matter much to me if tea warms up in the sun or cools down in winter or when the wind blows.

While in Japan I was quite happy with the ubiquitous vending machines offering green tea at almost every corner, or at least every (subway) station. Certainly that tea is not of the highest quality, but compared to the rest of the world one can be grateful that it is available at all. In other places, vending machines mostly sell sugary soft drinks or artificially flavored so-called iced teas, and even the water is often only cheap table water, not spring water. Tea without added sugar does not seem to be very popular outside of Asia.

It is known that especially in Italy, a good espresso for one Euro or little more can be enjoyed while standing at the bar. This takes little time and usually costs only half as much as sitting down to enjoy the coffee. But somehow the Italian baristas seem to have forgotten this traditional price difference during their long journey north, across the Alps. At least in my home town Munich, you have to pay around three Euros, even when standing at the bar. But I digress, thinking about Italy always makes me daydream.

Now back to tea. The challenge is to achieve an acceptable quality while traveling. What do we need for this? Nothing much different from the familiar surroundings:

- (Hot) water
- Brewing vessel (+ optional sieve)
- Tea

In order to avoid unnecessary efforts while on the road, we intend to limit ourselves where appropriate. What should be considered regarding the travel equipment?

WATER

Tap water is available almost everywhere in drinking water quality. In addition, tea water will be boiled anyway, so it is even safer than fresh from the tap. When booking a room I usually check if a water heater is provided within the room. Provided that it is low in lime, the water in the hotel can even be used unfiltered, and personally I do not carry a water filter around when traveling. In some world regions I still prefer bottled mineral water, which I bring into the hotel. Not so much because of thriftiness but rather because most of the mini bars do not contain enough water in order to brew sufficient amounts.

BREWING VESSEL

If a water heater is available in the room, cups are also supplied. So you may want to consider which of your teas is best suited for brewing grandpa style - or you bring your own brewing vessel. Taking a high-quality fragile clay pot along can be quite risky.

Provided that there are cups in the room, a gaiwan, hohin or shiboridashi might be a good choice. If you own the latter, it probably is the preferred choice, because their spouts make it easier to pour the water into the cup drip-free. If you travel with a tea boat, a gaiwan will do as well.

A number of dealers also offer shiboridashi in handy sets with drinking bowls, which can be stacked in one another and thus are particularly suitable for traveling. However, since shiboridashi usually do not have a built-in strainer, a hohin may be more practical.

SIEVE

Sometimes I carry a tea sieve or strainer with me, but I rarely need it. A few small particles at the bottom of the cup do not really bother me, especially as high quality teas tend to give off very little broken tea or dust. I mainly use the filter when preparing tea for fellow drinkers. Even if I personally do not bother, I try to keep their cups free from particles out of simple courtesy.

TEA

Most of the time I have two Shengs and one or two oolongs with me, but I also like to carry a Huang Pian or Batabatacha, the latter two especially because they are so uncomplicated and ideally suited for grandpa style. I can also prepare all of them in a gaiwan and drink out of another one or a porcelain cup. If possible I bring my small tea boat along, so even the rather humid preparation using the gaiwan is no obstacle. The market offers an enormous selection of small travel sets, typically consisting of a handleless pot, cup and maybe a small tea boat, often in a fitting box or bag, in which one may also store some other utensils (sieve, Pu'er knife, spoon, tongs etc.). Just a little bag of tea on top, and you are ready to go on the road.

If you are not traveling to a hotel or a holiday apartment, but instead visiting friends or family, you may choose different combinations of your tea baggage.

For those who wish to travel with rather light luggage, perhaps just some tea will suffice. In this case, one is only dependent on a good soul or a host who provides soft and boiling water plus a brewing vessel. Very small quantities are especially practical (I like take samples on the road with me). You can find portions weighing just a few grams, conveniently wrapped in mini pouches, mostly of the oolong type. If necessary, these can also be prepared grandpa style, but most of the times, one can find a simple pot just everywhere.

Another very exotic treat is the essences of (mostly Shu) Pu'er, weighing one gram or even less. They are made from boiled down tea which in the end visually reminds of small malt candies. Shu lovers may turn away shuddering, but as an instant infusion this is at least an emergency solution for me, quite similar to a freeze-dried coffee.

CONCLUSION

As could be expected, the preparation "away from home" is always a compromise. The above considerations are only meant to be food for thought, you will certainly find your own ways that suits you best.

My personal travel kit for tea and accessories

THE PERFECT TEA

There is no such thing as the perfect tea, like there is no perfect person. However, each person may define for themselves what the perfect tea may be for them at a certain moment and in a certain situation. For one individual this can always be the same morning wake-up drink and for another the spontaneous "to-go" with extra knick-knacks. Many people have an affinity for "their" tea, which means a growing region, a blend or a brand. Then they speak of their Darjeeling, their East Frisian blend or mention the name of a (bagged) tea from an international food company. Others appreciate afternoon tea or a more ritualized Asian ceremony.

My perfect tea is not always the same either, it has changed over the years . I select increasingly higher quality and sometimes also rather unpretentious teas, but certainly more and more consciously.

However, finding, storing, preparing and consuming the favored tea in the highest possible quality is an issue that can never be fully dealt with. The fun is in endless discussions among tea friends. Anyhow, first of all we should always work on adjusting the following main reasons for faulty brewings:

- The water was too hot
- The infusion time was too long
- The tea was too old or stored improperly
- The tea has been produced poorly

The wrong leaves to water ratio can also lead to dissatisfaction, but you cannot please everyone anyway, and even a tea which is subjectively too strong or too faint can still be of high quality and taste appealingly.

Thus, for the perfect tea, only a little attentiveness is needed, and of course it is possible to further increase the wonderful experience, be it in the context of a tasting session or in combining tea with matching dishes, the following two chapters will address this.

TEA TASTING

The majority of us tea lovers are not professionals, traders, nor paid tea testers from the major importers and no certified or self-proclaimed tea sommeliers either. Therefore we can drink what and how we want it and we can say and write what we want about tea. The only thing that is important is our own sense of taste, however well or poorly trained it may be.

Therefore, no one has to be afraid of the process of tea tasting. However, respect is due to the tea and the efforts of the producers, and there are different approaches to pay tribute to them.

The simplest tasting is the conscious infusion and consumption in solitude. One single tea is all it takes, but the appeal certainly lies in the comparison of teas, and also in the company of other tea fans.

If you are planning a tasting, which may lead to a combined order if you liked the tea, it is a good idea to agree in advance with the other participants whether you intend to taste horizontally or vertically. As it is also the case in wine tastings, horizontal means to compare teas from different producers of the same region and year. Typically, this is done by tea traders until they find the specific teas of a region and variant they want to order. For groups of tea lovers or individuals who concentrate on a small number of teas and are looking for the best qualities or at least the best value for money, this is also a decent approach. One obtains samples of the current year from various suppliers and the tasting begins.

Personally, I prefer vertical tasting, i.e. comparing the teas of a particular farmer or a particular type, trying different vintages. Of course, most green teas are eliminated here, because the fun usually stops at a maximum age of one or two years. But for instance the comparison between early and late harvests of different vintages of an oolong often shows that a domestic storage of 6 to 12 months after the harvest is usually beneficial to the taste.

If you buy the same Sheng Pu'er of a certain tea garden or factory year over year, you can appreciate the pleasure of being able to continuously monitor and compare the different vintages and assess their development over the years.

Regardless of whether they want to taste just one tea, or let a larger quantity run horizontally or vertically through their throats, many tea lovers prefer to take notes more or less regularly. How far one wants to go, how many notes one takes and which details one collects, everyone has to decide for themselves. Some enthusiasts write blogs and even create graphics that visually represent the spectrum of flavors.

The aroma of a tea makes up most of the taste experience, provided the water is right, the temperature, etc. Five different impressions can at least be evaluated:

- the smell of the dry leaves
- the scent of the washed/moist leaves
- the fragrance of the finished infusion
- the taste when drinking
- the aftertaste[105]

Unfortunately, or interestingly, whichever way you look at it, these impressions do not always match, nor do they have to. What counts in the end, is what reaches the palate.

It would be nice if one could judge a tea already in the shop, by its look and smell. However, one can (almost) never judge a tea only by its smell or dry appearance, and most of the time, retailers have little motivation to allow for an unplanned, extensive tasting. Therefore I like tea houses, where you can buy every tea in single portions for immediate tasting conducted by yourself. Some top products hardly smell at all when dry, but develop a firework of taste in the pot or at the very latest in the mouth. Others smell great when dry, but fail on first contact with water. It would be tragic if some teas were rejected or sorted out according to the smell of the dry leaves. Some may smell almost disgusting when dry, but taste delicious after infusion. As a typical example, I can think of some Lapsang Souchong or other smoked teas. When dry, they may smell unpleasantly reminiscent of fried pork bacon, barbecue sauce or charred whisky casks, but the finished product in the cup may show very little or nothing of that, but rather offers a fine and only slightly smoky experience. Provided you have acquired the right quality, of course. Also the smell of some dry Shu Pu'er remind of dead fish or worse (I am thinking of certain Menghai V93, for example) and then develop pleasant aromas for palate and nose when steeped.

Nevertheless the smell of the dry material is still an important quality indicator. Especially if you already know a tea quite well it will be easy for you to recognize even small losses of quality with your nose. Assuming, of course, that the tea in question has a significant odor when dry.

While reading this book, you may already have noticed my frequent comparisons to wine, and will continue to do so. Naturally, this is also the case when it comes to aromas. Wine connoisseurs and lovers have been using the aroma wheel developed by Ann C. Noble for a long time now, and various tea lovers have developed variations of it for our purposes. The following table lists the most well-known aromas that can be smelled and/or tasted in natural tea. Due to the emphasis on "natural", you will certainly not find taste abominations such as artificial strawberry cream or other fascinating achievements of modern laboratories nor genuine bergamot oil (an ingredient to the infamous Earl Grey). No added flavors, be they natural or artificial, shall irritate us now.

If the table[106] on the following pages seems to be a bit exhaustive, it should be said that these are only the most common aromas that one encounters again and again in tea. While you will probably never notice all of them, others are more common[107], depending on your personal tea preference. If you prefer Dancongs, you will usually taste fruit and flowers whilst woody notes are unlikely to occur, you are much more likely to encounter these in Shu Pu'er or Kukicha. Other taste experts such as Charles MacLean[108] also focus on additional attributes for the perception of taste and mouthfeel. These are: sweet, sour, salty, bitter, warming, cooling, sparkling, viscous, obtrusive - certainly an approach that can be combined well with the specific aromas in order to communicate one's own taste sensations to others.

One thing that is practically never mentioned among the aromas is the different types of bitterness. Of course, tea brewed too hot and which does not tolerate such a heat can show an unpleasant bitterness. I call this bitterness the one where the hairs on your forearms stand up like goose bumps. This is a bitterness no one needs and it should be avoided at any cost. However, there is also a desired bitterness which can be astringent or bittersweet or medical, like letting an aspirin slowly melt on the tongue.

Like bitterness, mildness can also vary, with adjectives such as sweet, smooth, luscious or strong, and some teas may even want to have their level of maturation put into words, with attributes such as old/stored, fresh/young, damp/musty/muddy or dry. A certain kind of enjoyable bitterness I would describe reminiscent to "the white under a grapefruit's peel", which is certainly not a professional description, but an accurate one.[109] A particularly strong bitterness in Pu'er teas is found in Bulang and some other very young green shengs, which could be described as medicinal, really a bit like sucking an aspirin pill. In China, some drinkers judge a tea by the Qi 气 or energy it gives them and tolerate a mediocre taste if only the tea high it provides is satisfying.

A tea high can be experienced from time to time, and this certainly does not come from the caffeine but other active substances contained in the leaves, but without top taste this alone would be lacking.

Dominating flavors in tea

Main flavor	Sub flavor	Aroma
Plants/Herbs	Grassy	Asparagus
		Bamboo
		Bean sprouts
		Bell peppers
		(Freshly cut) grass
		Green beans
		Hay
		Kale
		Peas
		Pumpkin
		Spinach, chard
	Herbs	Basil
		Camphor
		Eucalyptus
		Fennel
		Lavender
		Mint
		Parsley
		Rosemary
		Sage
		Thyme

Floral (fragrant)	**Summer meadow**	Chrysanthemum
		Jasmine
		Orange blossom
		Osmanthus
		Pomelo blossom
		Violets
	Garden flower	Daisies
		Gardenia
		Orchid
		Peony
		Rose
Nutty/Milky		Almonds
		Chestnut
		Creamy
		Fresh butter
		(Roasted) nuts
Sweet		Beeswax
		Cane sugar, molasses
		Caramel, toffee
		Honey
		Malt
		(Maple) syrup
		Vanilla

Fiery/Animalistic		Leather
		Roasted, toasted
		Smoke
		Stable
		Tar
		Tobacco
		Wet fur, wild animal
Spicy		Cardamom
		Cinnamon
		Clove
		Cocoa
		Ginger
		Liquorice
		Nutmeg
		Pepper
		Star anise
		Vanilla
	Tropical	Banana
		Fig
		Longan, Lychee, Rambutan etc.
		Mango
		Melon
		Pineapple

Fresh, dry or candied fruit	Stone fruit and grape	Apple
		Apricot
		Cherry
		Grape
		Muscatel
		Olive
		Peach
		Pear
		Plum
	Citrus	Bergamot
		Lemon
		Lime
		Orange
		Pomelo
		Tangerine
	Berry	Blackcurrant
		Blackberry
		Blueberry
		Raspberry
		Strawberry
Marine		Fishy
		Oysters/Shellfish/Shrimps
		Sea salt
		Seaweed

Category	Subcategory	Descriptor
Mineral		Brass
		Chalk
		Damp stone
		Flint
		Granite
		Petrichor
		Volcanic
Earthy	Forest	Compost, humus
		Forest soil
		Moist leaves
		Moss
		Musty (mostly off-flavour)
	Wood	Cedar
		Eucalyptus
		Mahogany
		Oak
		Pine
		Sawdust
		Wet wood

Speaking of taste: in the second part of this book I will describe many teas in detail. In the field of taste I usually do not distinguish between the smell (the "nose") of the liquid and the actual taste in the mouth. Smell and taste are always personal impressions and sometimes differ significantly from person to person. Therefore, I prefer to give all impressions, which may differ at least in nuances even with the same tea from different suppliers. They are my personal impressions, no more and no less.

Personally I do not keep extensive tasting notes anymore, I simply categorize the taste in my online database into five levels, giving up to three stars as follows:

Minus	-	The world doesn't need this tea. I would not even want it if it was free.
Plus	+	Decent quality, but I would not buy it again.
Stars	*	Good quality, I would buy it again or recommend it, but it is not one of my favorites.
	**	Great tea, if I can get it cheaply, I will gladly buy it over and over again.
	***	Top, I always want to have it at home and I am willing to pay a premium for it.

This classification is all I need to have a relevant memory aid even after years. Additionally, I keep all other important details such as name, origin, cultivar, harvest, leaf grade, degree of roasting, date of purchase, dealer and price, because otherwise a collection can easily become unmanageable.

Finally, I think it is worth mentioning that depending on the outside temperature and humidity, a tea[110] can taste clearly different than what one might be used to. Even though I always taste teas with the same water and usually at home, I am sometimes disappointed, particularly in very warm and rather humid weather. Thus, in order to really do justice to a tea in terms of evaluation, one should try it several times - ideally not after having tasted ten other teas beforehand. At some point our taste buds will just start acting up and perceive considerably less impressions.

FOOD PAIRING

The term food pairing is so ubiquitous in the current eating and drinking culture that I cannot think of anything better than to name this small chapter accordingly.

Why only a short chapter? Without question one may write many books on this subject, the possible combinations are shear endless. But as we only intend to deal with the basics here, we will concentrate on just a few principles, namely what, when and why one should eat with tea. Or, to put it the other way round, which tea goes with which food.

My first and most important principle is "never eat when tasting". This means that in the case of a targeted tea tasting, i.e. an evaluation of its exact details and facets, any food will be irritating. No matter what you eat, and no matter how mild or neutral it may be, the food still distorts the taste impression for some time afterwards. Smelling is not affected as much, but the taste buds on the tongue recover quite slowly from strong flavors. So if the tea is in the centre of attention, I would refrain from any distraction. When tasting wine, one uses light, unroasted white bread to neutralize the palate. Still, water is ideal there too, because chewing bread always creates a feeling of sweetness in the mouth (the starch from the flour converts into sugar through the saliva). While the strong wine, thanks to acidity and alcohol, can easily drown out this sweetness, with delicate teas it is easy to falsify their assessment.

I know what I am talking about, as I have often found myself during cheerful tea rounds noticing a particularly strong almond aroma in a Xingren Xiang or a strong hint of banana in a Tie Guan Yin, which my fellow drinkers could not follow. It is indeed true that high-quality Xingren Xiang possesses more than just a slight almond aroma and sometimes I also perceive a hint of banana in TGY. But when I then realized that I had thoughtlessly nibbled an almond or a slice of dried banana from the confectionery bowl, it suddenly became clear to me why one should eat nothing, nichts, nada, naught at a real tea tasting. At least if you want to classify teas or make objective notes for your own records.

A professional has to behave as described above, but us normal teaheads may keep it casual, however it suits us. One or two hours before a tea party with friends, I eat a light meal to have a basis, especially because our parties can sometimes drag on. Otherwise a little hunger might quickly appear. For snacks, unroasted and unsalted nuts, almonds or cashews have proven to be ideal, but not walnuts, whose slight bitterness can be quite distracting.

But our topic here is food pairing and not reasoning about "what do I eat before drinking tea". By food pairing I mean the targeted combination of a suitable tea with a certain food. As I drink almost only tea from morning to evening, this is rather an unconscious decision for me. Targeted planning is more likely to occur when visiting restaurants or eating with family and friends, where the focus is on the food and not on tea.

I used to like combining cheese and wine up until I became a teetotaler. Now it is tea instead of wine, but my love for cheese remains. Similar principles still apply, however: acidity goes well with fat (think of the popular cocktail skewers made of diced Gouda, garnished with grapes), salty is a good contrast to sweet, sweet mitigates bitterness well, etc.

Since time immemorial, Chinese people have always paid attention to a balance between the "five tastes"[111] of sweet, sour, hot, bitter and salty in all their dishes, and used to add prunes, salt, mint and other spices to tea; it is not without reason that they also called it tea soup.

As a rule of thumb, the heartier, greasier or hotter the food, the stronger the tea should be. For example, I combine white tea with very mild, young and tender cheese. It would not be recommendable with a spicy Thai curry.

It is also worth mentioning the combination of hot or at least warm tea with colder cheese. Cheese connoisseurs know that cheese tastes much more aromatic at room temperature than fresh from the cooler, and it often increases in aroma when heated. It is not for nothing that cheese is often sprinkled on pizza or pressed between burger halves. Cheese that will melt in the mouth is also considered enjoyable by most people and a warm tea helps melting it, plus it often helps to squeeze even more flavors out of the cheese. However, cheese can also compensate for too much bitterness in tea due to its fat and delicate melting, and bring out nutty, floral or fruity flavors.

The table on the next page shows combinations that I, and often our guests, appreciate and I can recommend with a clear conscience.

The umami, the ocean breeze and the mild herbaceousness of Sencha correspond excellently with the sometimes slightly pointed or pungent note of goat cheese, the tea also benefits from the cheese's salts.

The milder sheep's milk cheese tolerates the light, unroasted oolongs and benefits from their floral notes. If you want to emphasize the milkiness of the sheep's milk cheese, choose a Jin Xuan rather than a more floral cultivar. If you desire more strength from the tea, you may choose a good Yancha or a Mi Xiang, whose honey aroma goes nicely with sheep's cheese. Darker or aged oolongs with their rather fruity (e.g. plum) notes are also recommended with medium to strong semi-hard or grated cheese.

Sushi is not listed in this table. Sencha, Bancha, Gyokuro, it doesn't matter, as long as it is Japanese. After all, Japan has spent many centuries to optimize the tea coming from China according to its dominant diet, there is no second opinion. But there can always be two opinions as to whether tea should complement or contrast the food.

Not as a pairing, but as a substitute, I would like to mention two more Japanese infusions. Instead of an alcoholic aperitif, a fresh, tangy, slightly sour Cold Brew Sencha or Gyokuro is an excellent fit, and for or instead of dessert or espresso I recommend the thick Koicha version of a Matcha.

If it shall only be a little piece chocolate to finish off a meal, I recommend powerful Shu Pu'er or other vintage heicha, which ideally offer a peaty aroma, like some single malts, which also go perfectly with dark chocolate.

Suggestions for combining food with tea

Food	Tea suggestion
Appenzeller, Cheddar, Emmental and other full-bodied semi-hard cheeses	Aged, strongly oxidized or heavily roasted oolong; robust Chinese green tea
Barbecue, grilled meat or vegetables	Iced black tea or Japanese cold brew green tea
Blue cheese (Gorgonzola, Roquefort, Stilton, etc.), Muffone	Intense Ceylon tea
Brie, Romadur, Taleggio, Tilsiter	Darjeeling black or green, Hojicha
Buffalo mozzarella or ricotta (perhaps with a drop of honey)	White tea, e.g. Shou Mei
Cakes and sweet pastries	Shu Pu'er or Assam with cream cake, Black Darjeeling with sponge or marble cake
Chicken	Japanese green tea with strong umami
Curry (Indian, Thai, etc.) and other spicy dishes	Sheng Pu'er, Ceylon tea, robust Chinese green tea
Dark chocolate	Shu Pu'er, aged oolong
Fish	Hearty Darjeeling (with tender white fish), Huang Zhi Xiang or other floral oolong
Goat cheese	Sencha, chilled Pouchong
Ham sandwich	Smoky Lapsang Souchong
Lamb	Moroccan mint tea
Raclette or cheese fondue	Assam with especially spicy cheese, otherwise Dian Hong
Risotto al Funghi	Sencha
Sheep's cheese	Oolong

HEALTH

Oh, really? Health? You want to drink tea to live more healthy? I am sure there is nothing wrong with that. A healthy life depends not only on genetics and social environment, but on a healthy diet, too. And, besides clean water, tea is certainly one of the healthiest beverages.

But health claims of salvation like "green tea fights free radicals, cancer and whatnot" or "Pu'er tea makes you slim" just freak me out. To fight radicals from the right or left I favor the police and the constitutional protection, where available. For weight loss I think that avoiding refined sugars and saturated fats will contribute much more than massive consumption of Pu'er. But in a journalistic environment people roll out one circus after another in the superfood area every year. Chia seeds or kale smoothies may quickly become boring, but when it comes to tea, many readers will notice and click on the periodically recycled pseudo-scientific article about tea's benefits.

ORGANIC AND PESTICIDE FREE TEA

Personally, I drink tea simply because I like it. I do not expect it to make me healthier or a better person. I am perfectly happy if a tea is not unhealthy.

As an insecure consumer, one may of course orientate oneself towards sales-promoting attributes such as "organic" or "pesticide-free" and put a few extra coins into the bag of the savior or tea merchant, but to what extent one acquires more health by that is open to question.

I do not intend to discredit the subject of organic farming at all or trivialize the problem of pesticide use in agriculture. I often and gladly buy organic food and avoid palm oil, but I do not believe that these products always are particularly healthy or low in residues. This is likely and desirable, but my motivation is a different one. With the voluntary additional payment for organic products I want to reward the efforts of farmers in general who decide against the current fast and cheap mass production of increasingly irrelevant food and who do not take the easy way. I am sure that I am also being cheated sometimes, but I am also certain that too much thriftiness in food procurement certainly does not promote better health nor better taste.

It is by no means possible for the average consumer to trace the validity of organic certifications from farmer to table. But then how shall one trace organic certificates from foreign farms, especially when their goods are loose and weighed individually? Of course, reliable farmers, buyers, middlemen and importers have documentation of the processes, but is it always complete? And who can guarantee that the amount of organic teas has not been doubled "by mistake" in the warehouse"? What really does end up in the tea bag?

In conclusion I do not care too much whether tea is certified organic or pesticide-free, or not. If it tastes good and is organic, all the better. It could be true. But that is only my personal point of view. If you decide to only buy tea with labels certifying organic or pesticide-free produce, you will find a wide range of teas, for which the supplier should be able to provide a certificate. And indeed, some suppliers also make this considerable effort. We are hopefully promoting a movement into the right direction by paying a bit extra for organic, even if we are occasionally being cheated by rogue suppliers.

By the way: organic does not mean pesticide-free, but only that less pesticide use is permitted in tea cultivation. The most important thing for the drinker is that no residues can be detected in the tea. At the same time, nature also cares about the damage that pesticides do, but that is another story.

ACTIVE SUBSTANCES IN TEA

Tea contains a variety of beneficial ingredients. The most important group are the tannins (bitter substances) which are part of the polyphenols. The most valuable tannins in terms of nutrition are the catechins, with a share of about 50%.

Another important group of ingredients are the alkaloids. Besides the well-known caffeine (theine), theophylline and theobromine are also found in tea in smaller traces. All alkaloids have a stimulating effect.

Saponins belong to the secondary plant substances that the plant uses to protect itself against fungal attack, for example. There is a great variety of saponins whose multiple functions, despite intensive research, are still not completely understood. However, like the tanning agents, they are often advertised with health promises and are supposed to prevent infections of any kind.

Tea contains a variety of vitamins as well. Besides a high content of vitamin C, vitamins of the B-group are particularly abundant. Vitamin B2 (riboflavin), like vitamin B3 (nicatin), is involved in metabolic processes. Vitamin B7, which is also contained in tea, is said to support cell growth and promote good hair growth, which I personally cannot confirm in any way.

Many of the leaf constituents mentioned influence the taste and vary depending on the time of harvest. The first harvest may contain three times more L-theanine and other amino acids compared to the leaves of later harvests. In comparison to other plants, the tea leaf contains a great number of water-soluble compounds, so its composition also explains the great differences in taste between the different harvests and regions of origin, which particularly influence the proportion of the tasty minerals.

GABA

A special amino acid, the gamma-amino acid or γ-aminobutyric acid (GABA for short), is said to possess so many health-promoting attributes that resourceful producers have developed a method of artificially raising its content in tea. In Japan in particular, a special cultivar is farmed whose crop is treated with nitrogen in the tea factory for about half a day, making the proportion of the desired amino acid up to ten times higher than regular versions of this tea. Apart from green tea, this material is also used to produce oolong, which is often found in the trade as Gabalong (GABA + oolong). It is said to have a fresh and sweetish taste. Well, great, many other teas offer that as well, I usually perceive GABAs as rather dull, similar to removing the higher notes from music. No GABA tea has ever really convinced me, but I also never really searched for it; I must have tasted a mere 25 different samples of it. In general, I would describe GABA as inconspicuous. If only for their taste, I would not buy them again. In Japan you can search for Gabaron ギャバロン茶, and those outside Japan just google for GABA. In China you can find Gabalong as Jia Ye Long Cha 佳叶龙茶 (good leaf dragon tea).

CAFFEINE

By nature, tea contains the alkaloid caffeine, which has a stimulating effect. In the past, the caffeine in tea was called theine. In contrast to coffee, the caffeine in tea is present in a bound form, so that it develops its stimulating effect more slowly than when drinking coffee. It is therefore commonly said that tea stimulates, but does not arouse. The caffeine content of tea fluctuates, as it is a natural product. The dry leaves contain 1 to 5 percent caffeine, on average about 3 percent. When using 5g of tea, infused with 500ml of water (at temperatures between 70°C and 95°C) and infused for several minutes, a cup of tea (according to studies) contains a maximum of 60mg of caffeine. Adults of normal weight can easily tolerate 200 to 400mg of caffeine per day, so I do not see any danger for healthy people, but your doctor or pharmacist may have a different opinion and has the final say in the matter.

It should also be noted that the amount of caffeine tolerated differs from person to person, and some get fidgety, nervous, tachycardic, get headaches or experience sleeping problems. I have always had the privilege of being very immune to caffeine. I was able to tolerate 20 espressi per a day at times and also survived long-lasting tea sessions with up to 30 different teas; at the most, my dreams were quite hectic during the following night. But I also know a number of people who are more sensitive or who are in poor health. Excessive self-experiments are certainly contraindicated and in our tea rounds these people simply skip a round or only drink every second infusion. It might help to eat before and during the session, but if you feel uncomfortable, you should listen to your body and switch to plain water.

Sensitive people or those with insomnia often ask for particularly low-caffeine teas. There are hardly any decaffeinated teas on the market, although decaffeinated coffee is widely available. While it is well known which teas tend to give off more or less caffeine, the differences between cultivars, terroirs and production methods are so enormous that it is not possible to make any serious statements, only tendencies can be communicated with a clear conscience.[112] With many exceptions, both upwards and downwards, it can be said in simple terms that tea gives off less caffeine than coffee, with white tea giving off the least, followed by green tea, oolong and topped by the strong black tea.

Even with these tendencies it is a tricky subject. Often people claim that white tea has less caffeine. However, I have read comparative studies that have shown only about 15mg in a Silver Needle tea, but 40mg in white Bai Mudan. No surprise, because not that much caffeine has been able to develop in the still closed buds of the silver needle. The rather delicate and almost translucent Green Tai Ping Hou Kui even showed 50mg, while Sencha was clearly below 20mg, but there were again deviations upwards when special cultivars were used. Black (red) tea is often found in the upper range, but there are also some cultivars that are clearly lower in caffeine. The only way to know for sure is to try it for oneself. In general, one seems to be on the safe side with Bancha, which is unanimously determined as extremely low in caffeine in all publications known to me. Pu'er has personally amazed me a little in this regard, as it is often in the low-middle range - but where does the popular tea high come from, the excitement you feel especially after enjoying Pu'er? That must be due to the other alkaloids.

Tea drinkers who worry about their night's rest because of the caffeine may apply a very simple relief method which takes advantage of the fact that caffeine has a half-life of about six hours in humans. So if you want to get going in the morning, you will feel the effect of the tea after a few minutes, but in the early afternoon the body has already broken down half of the caffeine. But should one then stop enjoying tea? Things are much easier.

Instead of brewing several teas one after the other, i.e. using new leaves after the umpteenth infusion, you can start brewing the daily supply directly in the morning, in two or three separate pots, and then continue using all the pots throughout the day. So you drink the first infusion from pot #1, then the first from pot #2, etc., then you continue with the second infusion from pot #1, the second from pot #2, etc.

This is to ensure that the highly caffeinated early infusions are being drunk in the morning. That way, follow-up infusions to be enjoyed later that day will automatically contain much less caffeine. The quality does not suffer much, but it is important not to close the lid of the jug so that the leaves will not continue steeping in a moist warmth, but rather spend the time up to the later infusions rather drily.

DIET

The subject of tea and weight loss is always a popular one. Studies suggest that the catechins, especially the esteemed epigallocatechin gallate (EGCG) of tea, can absorb fat in the intestines. Furthermore, EGCG is believed to accelerate lipid metabolism. Unfortunately, many studies have been carried out on mice and other small rodents and are therefore rather less relevant for humans. In addition, the doses for the mice were often so high that humans would have to drink an awful lot of tea to achieve comparable results.

I can simply state that I have always been a heavyweight fighter, and massive tea consumption did not change that.

But enough about this unpleasant topic, in the second part of this book we turn to the observation of selected teas. I do not hide my preference for China and Japan, but other regions also offer delicious qualities, so read on…

CHINA 中国 AND TAIWAN 台湾

This chapter covers both China[113] and Taiwan[114]. This is simply for pragmatic reasons. Traditionally only grown on the mainland, teas are now also produced and marketed in Taiwan under similar names. Moreover, the cultivation methods and terms are so strikingly similar that an unnecessary split makes little sense.

The international legal status of Taiwan is controversial. Placing Taiwanese teas in the context of China is not intended as a political statement in one direction or the other. The political views and positions of the two countries do not matter to me here, I only want to drink good tea. I do by no means share the Chinese view that Taiwan is just a rebellious province; still I do not want to deny China the right to consider Taiwan as part of its state. De jure, China has its opinion; de facto, Taiwan acts like a sovereign state. Everything else will hopefully be settled pragmatically and peacefully among the people themselves.

Tea growing areas in mainland China are located in the southern, more water-rich provinces. As the cradle of tea, China produces all kinds of tea imaginable, benefiting from the ginormous size of the country, the different climatic zones and the great diversity of terroirs.

Taiwan has excellent conditions for growing tea, but compared to China, the quantity produced is relatively small. Taiwan is especially known for its great oolongs, sometimes still referred to as Formosa tea.

HARVEST TIME

Before purchase, like in Japan or on the Indian subcontinent, interested parties pay attention to the harvest time. This is sometimes even part of the tea's name and mostly emphasized in the retailers' tea description.

These harvest times are named according to the Chinese calendar, in principle there are 24 periods of 15 days each in the lunar calendar, each starting on the first and middle day of a month. The most important period begins on April 5th[115] with Qing Ming 清明 (spring festival and commemoration of the dead), followed by Gu Yu 谷雨 (rainy season) on April 20th, Li Xia 立夏 (beginning of summer) on May 6th and so on. Apart from Qing Ming you do not have to remember much, the other Chinese periods hardly play a role in the day-to-day (tea) business, wherever it makes sense the traders indicate the harvest period according to the Gregorian calendar, sometimes even to the day. Differences in picking dates are particularly noticeable with green tea, and Qing Ming is above all a clearly visible price hurdle.

The tea called Pre Rain (before the rain) or also Pre Qing Ming or Ming Qian 明谦 is therefore harvested very early in the year and one may expect to get the highest quality here, albeit at the highest prices. Often very light and delicately sweet, this tea yields everything the plant could extract from the soil during the winter months. This goes primarily into the buds, the plant intends to push all the energy into the young leaves. Moreover, the rainy season after the spring festival makes many connoisseurs doubt the quality of the tea harvested afterwards, and often not without cause. Harvesting in the rain is prohibited, and excessive humidity also delays drying after harvesting, which results in negative effects on the quality. This is just one reason why so-called rain tea is often offered quite cheap. However, tea from other regions is also traded under this term, but it is harvested in summer or autumn during the monsoon season.

PICKING METHOD AND LEAF QUALITY

While the harvest season still receives quite a lot of attention in China, at least in western marketing, the picking method and leaf quality is less obviously taken into consideration. In the case of white tea, the plucking method is already implicitly mentioned in the name, but otherwise the well-known Indian product attributes such as BOP and such are omitted, at least for the consumer.

Categorization of the top picking methods in China

Pinyin	中文	English	Note
Ya	芽	Bud	Available in the retail market as Ya Cha or Cha Ya
Yi Ya Yi Ye *or* Yi Xin Yi Ye	一芽一叶 *or* 一心一叶	Bud and a leaf	Mostly the finest leaf quality, typical for the earliest harvests
Yi Ya Liang Ye *or* Yi Ya Er Ye	一芽两叶 *or* 一芽二叶	Bud and two leaves, somewhat stronger and less subtle than the Yi Ya Yi Ye	Comparable to the typical Indian picking term "Two leaves and a bud"
Yi Ya San Ye	一芽三叶	Bud and three leaves	
Yi Ya Si Ye	一芽四叶	Bud and four leaves	Even very high quality tea (especially oolong) may have been plucked in that way, this type of picking does not necessarily reduce the quality of some Chinese teas.

The table above lists the best known picking styles for those who are interested, but this classification is rarely found in retail procurement, although it is still more common than the Indian one.

This is all the more surprising as on the one hand in China the appearance of dry tea is much more important in the assessment than elsewhere. On the other hand, all that counts in the end is the taste, and if blends of different leaf grades and even breakage produce good results, so much the better. Some specialities are even deliberately made from shredded leaves, but as a rule of thumb the youngest whole leaves are always considered the highest quality.

THE BEST TEAS FROM CHINA

If you search the Internet for the best Chinese teas, you will often find lists of the supposedly best known, or most popular, or best, or most famous teas, originally called Ten Famous Teas or Shi Da Ming Cha 十大名茶. These lists often tend to contain slightly different teas but fortunately some of these can be found in almost every list which is at least an indicator for a certain relevance.

Almost all the teas in those lists will be covered in the following, but I do not intend to flag them explicitly.

With more than 10,000 different teas in China alone, however, no list can ever claim to be truly complete. The teas described in the following sections were therefore in some cases selected arbitrarily. Of course, the world-famous and popular big names, i.e. the "must haves" or at least "must knows" are included, but I also list some of my personal favorites. They usually became favorites because in my opinion they represent something very special. There is no claim to completeness of the whole compilation, as this would be impossible.[116]

WHITE TEA (BAI CHA) 白茶

Although white tea plays a much smaller role in the market than almost all other teas except the yellow one, its reputation is consistently good and always worth a look (or brew). However, the range of varieties is much smaller than that of green or black teas. Fujian, Zhejiang, Yunnan, these are the three renowned provinces of China whose white teas stand out above all others. Little known are some white teas from Guangxi, but still worth mentioning.

Fujian is at the top of the league and teas from the following districts are particularly popular

- Fuding
- Jian Yang
- Songxi
- Zhenghe

White teas may be divided into two basic subtypes:

- Bai Ya Cha 白芽茶
- Bai Ye Cha 白叶茶

The best known white tea, Yinzhen or Silver Needles, is made exclusively from buds, making it a Bai Ya Cha. Ya 芽 means bud in this context. Ye 叶 on the other hand means leaf, and thus Bai Ye Cha white teas are made from whole leaves with no or only a minimum amount of buds. The name Gong Mei almost sounds a bit ironic, because tribute tea made of third class material seems strange. However, one should not conclude on quality and taste by leaf grades. A perfect Shou Mei is certainly better than a Yinzhen made without love.

Picking grades of Chinese white tea

English	Pinyin	中国	Note
Silver Needle	Bai Hao Yinzhen	白毫银针	Buds only
White Peony	Bai Mudan	白牡丹	Top one or two leaves with an addition of 10 to 50% buds (blend)
Tribute Eyebrow	Gong Mei	贡眉	Third leaf quality grade, including second and third leaf
Longevity Eyebrow	Shou Mei	寿眉	Fourth grade, more than three leaves per branch, sometimes with breakage

You may also not always want to taste the delicate and dominating sweetness of the bud, sometimes it may or should consciously be the more robust, simpler material. Personally, I always have at least three of these types in stock, but rarely a Gong Mei, because it is less common to find in stores.

White tea from Yunnan is much cheaper than the one from Fujian, probably because the large leave varieties mainly used. Yunnan produces much more red and dark tea. And so white teas in Yunnan are often produced from cultivars that are mainly known for the production of the darker tea types; for example the Yue Guang Bai is made of Da Ye Zhong.

BAI HAO YINZHEN 白毫银针

Silver Needle, Yinfeng, Silver Needle White Fur	
Origin	Fuding, Ningde, Fujian Zhenghe, Nanping, Fujian
Color	Silvery white
Cultivar	Da Bai or Da Hao
Taste	Very sweet, mild, delicate
Harvest time	Mid March to mid April, only on dry days
Suggested preparation	75°C, 10 to 30 seconds depending on quality, approx. 5 infusions

This tea has been known for almost 140 years and can be found in every top ten Chinese tea list. It is produced exclusively with unopened leaf buds surrounded by white or silvery fluff. Although it is similar in taste to some green teas, the sweetness resulting from the flowers is almost unique.

White Silver Needle

Yinzhen can be plucked two ways. Either one picks only the young buds and ignores the leaves, or one plucks much more of the respective branch and then sorts or separates the leaves after harvest. The latter method is more common, as it saves time during picking. Although it takes more time to sort the material afterwards, it can be done with much more precision than in the hot outdoor conditions. The visible difference between the two growing regions Fuding and Zhenghe is due to the stronger oxidation in Fuding. This makes the buds look a little darker and the aroma is slightly stronger. The difference in taste is not necessarily due to the growing regions, but rather to individual differences in quality. Top qualities often release a lot of aroma within seconds, others require a much longer infusion time. Varying the water temperature can also help improve quality a little.

BAI MUDAN 白牡丹

White Peony, White Monkey	
Origin	Fujian, today's top qualities coming from Taimu Shan
Color	Greenish, partly darker and more reddish leaves
Cultivar	Da Bai or Da Hao
Taste	Sweet, Rose blossom, Chrysanthemum
Harvest time	Mid March to mid April, lower qualities also later
Suggested preparation	90°C + for 30, 45, 60 seconds

Typical Bai Mudan with clearly visible buds

The white peony is also commonly transcribed as Pai Mu Tan, which is the same tea. Probably Bai Mudan is so popular among the white teas because it perfectly balances between buds and high-quality young leaves. This way the tea gains body and still does not lack refinement. Bai Mudan is harvested at the same time as Yinzhen and beyond, because later in the year the buds are not as tender as at the beginning, there is a significant reduction in quality in later harvests.

GONG MEI 贡眉

Tribute Eyebrow	
Origin	Fujian
Color	Greenish, partly darker and reddish leaves
Cultivar	Da Bai, Da Hao, also Xiao Cai Cha
Taste	Dark wood, chocolate, delicate acidity
Harvest time	All year round
Suggested preparation	90°C + for 30, 45, 60 seconds

Gong Mei is not found for sale as often as Shou Mei. While Shou Mei, as the officially fourth ranked white tea, is offered openly and proudly, Gong Mei is probably rather offered disguised as Bai Mudan to uninformed customers. Gong Mei is often produced in autumn, when the buds are growing somewhat larger than in summer. A Bai Mudan that looks unattractive or tastes too strong or hard could therefore actually be a Gong Mei sold at a higher price.

GUSHU CHA YA 古树茶芽

Old Tree Bud Tea	
Origin	Yunnan
Color	Light yellow like fresh hay
Cultivar	Ku Cha
Taste	Very sweet, very present floral aroma, with notes of anise
Harvest time	February, shortly after the snow melted
Suggested preparation	90°C, length and number of infusions as desired

So far, in this section on white tea we have talked about buds, but these are rather half-finished leaves, which are still quite small and completely rolled up. The fact that a large part of the closed bud has not yet seen UV light results in the particularly fine taste.

The buds of Gushu Cha Ya are harvested even earlier than Yinzhen and Bai Mudan. It is a white tea made from old Yunnan trees, often categorized as wild. Gushu means old tree and in this case also large leaf tea, because in Yunnan the raw material is mainly Assamica trees and bushes, not Sinensis shrubs.

The harvest is usually wilted exclusively in the sun and then dried. Due to the extremely early harvest time and the Assamica variety, the tea looks different from a Yinzhen. Assamica produces larger leaves and buds. This tea speciality is sometimes also simply sold under the name Wild Buds.

Gushu Cha Ya

LAO BAI CHA 老白茶

Old White Tea	
Origin	Fuding, Ningde, Fujian
Color	Like white tea, depending on leaf quality
Taste	Similar to white tea, but stronger, more mature, with the authority of age and less freshness and acidity
Suggested preparation	95°C at 20, 30, 40, ... seconds

Pressed Lao Bai Cha

Many teas of different varieties, regions and cultivars are referred to as Lao Bai Cha. One thing they all have in common is that they are white teas which have been aged deliberately long and well, and ideally they have developed much more in quality than their dewy-fresh relatives. If one refers to an especially old tea, it may also be classified as Lao Shou Mei or the like.

The trade does not always advertise this tea as Lao Bai Cha, sometimes only the regular name of the tea is mentioned, supplemented by a year. Merchants who have kept close contact with their sources for many years sometimes offer the opportunity to purchase white tea in different stages of aging, produced by the same farmer. Such a comparison is always a special experience to me.

Lao Bai Cha is usually marketed in the form of a bing or brick, made from Gong Mei or Shou Mei leaf grades. That is why suppliers whose Lao Bai Cha is made of Bai Mudan, which is much more aromatic (and more expensive to produce), will point this out at the point of sale.

Unfortunately, Lao Bai Cha has become a trendy tea and according to the law of supply and demand the market is being satisfied, however questionable. The leading producer, the Fuding Bai Cha factory with its own gardens in the Taimu Shan National Park charges several Euro per gram for top-notch aged Yinzhen these days.

Very cheap Lao Bai Cha can hardly be top quality. Sometimes older stocks of lower leaf grades seem to have been blended and pressed. To simply moisten old leaves and sell them in pressed shape does not result in the product the collector is looking for. Taking fresh or only a few years old white tea, pressing it into shape and then letting it age for many years, maybe even allowing for some post-fermentation, is the only way to guarantee top results.

The format offered does not always have to be the bing or brick. Lao Bai Cha of various quality levels is also offered in the form of Dragonballs. As with dark tea, a quality enhancing effect of a slight post-fermentation is more likely to be expected in larger bings than in small balls. The maturing of an old tea takes place slowly from the outside to the inside, it may take several years until the microorganisms have arrived at the centre and accomplished their transformation work. With as little material as in a Dragonball even after a very long aging process there is not much to be expected compared to a somewhat younger one, especially since the ball dries much faster after pressing than a Bing. The desirable microorganisms, however, need some moisture, especially at the beginning of the process, to motivate them to do their good deeds.

SHOU MEI 贡眉

Longevity Eyebrow	
Origin	Fujian
Color	Greenish, partly darker and reddish leaves
Cultivar	Da Bai, Da Hao, also Xiao Cai Cha
Taste	hay, white wine, slightly sweet, balanced
Harvest time	All year round
Suggested preparation	90°C+ at 30, 45, 45, 60 seconds

Shou Mei

Among the four classic white teas, Shou Mei is on the lowest level, due to the less attractive leaf material. Nevertheless, it deserves as many compliments as its siblings on the podium. It only depends on which taste one prefers. Shou Mei, especially in the aged variety (at least 5 or rather 7 years old), does not have to hide behind its relatives.

YA BAO CHA 芽苞

Bud tea	
Origin	Dehong and Lincang, Yunnan
Color	Light green (occasionally with purple tips)
Cultivar	Assamica Dehongensis or special hybrids
Taste	A touch of rose, marginal pine or vanilla
Suggested preparation	90°C, length and number of infusions as desired

Ya Bao[117] Cha is picked very early in the year, because all that is desired is the buds. Like green tea, it should be drunk fresh, but rewards longer storage in a pressed form. Ya Bao Cha is also produced as Mao Cha to enrich Pu'er blends and add floral sweetness.

The category Purple Tea does not officially exist. Nevertheless, various teas that have been produced according to the methods of white or dark tea are sometimes listed separately as purple tea in literature and trade, due to the fact that their buds or leaves are partly and seldom predominantly purple. Even though I may appear to be rather unimpressed by the color purple[118] in the very short section on this topic later on, the Ya Bao is one of my favorites in the purple segment and it does not have to hide among the regular whites either.

YUE GUANG BAI 月光白

Moonlight White, Moonlight Belle	
Origin	Jinggu, Yunnan
Color	Almost black on one side and greenish-white on the other
Cultivar	Da Ye Zhong
Taste	Greener in taste than normal white tea, sometimes also delicately bitter
Suggested preparation	90°C+ at 45, 60, 75, 90, 120 seconds

Loose leaf Yue Guang Bai

There are legends surrounding the Yue Guang Bai, which still claim that it is a) only picked by moonlight and/or b) only dried under moonlight. If there should be esoteric tea farmers, option a) might make at least some sense, option b) however sounds completely senseless, because what advantage should it provide to not let it dry in daylight, which in my experience gives more heat than even the brightest moon? It seems to be fact that this tea often dries in the shade and not under the blazing sun. Thus, it oxidizes more strongly and a bit longer than common white tea, thus coming a little closer to the taste of red tea. Its lyrical name is most likely due to the fact that the white buds between the dark leaves look like the bright sickle of a crescent moon during a dark night - or due to the color differences between the upper and the lower sides of its leaves.

Recently unwrapped bing of Yue Guang Bai

Yue Guang Bai is commonly made of the same large-leaf material that is used to make Pu'er. Similar to Pu'er and some red teas, Camellia Taliensis is used instead of Camellia Sinensis, the former being considered a higher quality or at least a rarer variety. From the same material (Da Ye Zhong) producers also process the red tea Dian Hong.

Leaf quality may range from something reminiscent to Silver Needle down to Bai Mudan or even Shou Mei. You can easily recognize the differences by comparing top quality loose leaf YGB with the leave grades pressed into the bing. Both taste really nice but offer a different aroma.

Try brewing Yue Guang Bai in larger quantities and put it in the fridge for a few hours, it tastes especially refreshing and strong. Due to the long shade drying it offers significantly more body than other white teas. Sometimes this tea can also be found under the name Yue Guang Mei Ren 月光美人 or Moonlight Beauty.

YELLOW TEA (HUANG CHA) 黄茶

The overview of the better-known white teas already was quite compact, but when it comes to yellow teas, things get even simpler.

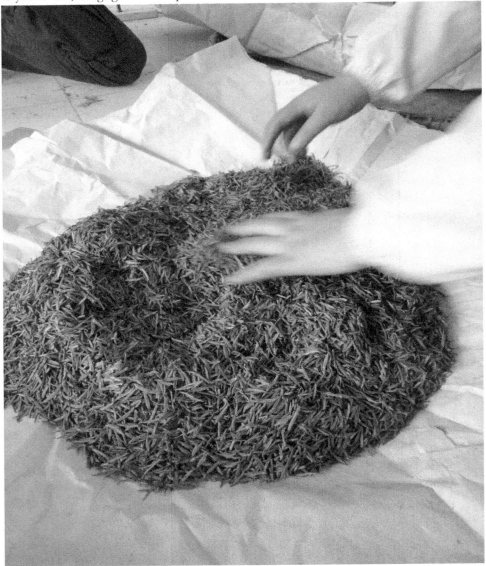

Yellow tea production

Even in China there is only a comparatively small supply, and on the international market there is far less. Nevertheless, some teas that we will now look at are particularly excellent.

For those who like green tea but cannot tolerate it very well, yellow tea may be a somewhat milder alternative. The production process makes it gentler and more digestible than its green siblings.

We distinguish three main variants:

- Huang Ya Cha (Yellow bud tea)
- Huang Da Cha (Yellow large leaf tea)
- Huang Xiao Cha (Yellow small leaf tea)

However, you will hardly find them under these names in the market, they will rather be offered as Junshan Yinzhen or Meng Ding Huang Ya (both bud teas) and Huoshan Huang Ya (made of small or large leaves).

The latter, however, should not be confused with Huang Jin Ya 黄金芽, a tea which is named after its cultivar of the same name.

Huang Jin Ya - not a yellow but a green tea

Although it looks bright yellow and its name means golden buds, it is a green tea cultivar that was practically cultivated as an albino and is usually harvested in the Yi Ya Yi Ye picking method, i.e. bud and first leaf.

JUNSHAN YINZHEN 君山银针

Jun Mountain Silver Needle	
Origin	Junshan Island, Dong Ding Lake, Hunan
Color	Yellowish
Cultivar	Yinzhen #1, Bi Xiang Zao, Tao Yuan Da Ye, Fu Yun
Taste	Slightly sweet, fresh hay, notes of tender corn
Harvest time	**Start:** Early or mid March **End:** Before the Spring Festival / Pre-Rain / Qing Ming
Suggested preparation	75°C at 45, 60, 75, 90, 120 seconds

Junshan Yinzhen is sometimes confused with Bai Hao Yinzhen. This is understandable as both are made exclusively from buds. Both are usually counted among the ten famous teas of China. Apart from the similar shape and name, they have little in common. The Junshan is basically (at first) a green tea (although it does not taste green or grassy at all), which gets its extraordinary aroma from its two short composting (fermentation) periods during production, which then makes him a member of the yellow tea category. It also receives a special kick through the final drying over charcoal.

Genuine Junshan Yinzhen is harvested "before the rain" (in English Pre Rain or also called Pre Qing Ming). This means "before the spring festival", usually before the 4th or 5th of April. Later harvests with less fine leaves are processed into green teas like Junshan Mao Jian or Junshan Lu Cha.

Whether the Junshan Yinzhen is counted among the top teas because of its rarity (the growing area is tiny by Chinese standards), its history (tribute tea to the emperor in the Qing dynasty) or its taste - I leave it up to you to decide.

Genuine Junshan Yinzhen of the best qualities (which are mostly state-marketed and officially not exported at all) can be very expensive, you may rather want to consider buying other teas for your budget - but often the question does not even arise. If Junshan Yinzhen is offered for considerably less than 1€/g, it will most likely be a fake, I like to compare this with a Wiener schnitzel (veal cutlet) versus Viennese style schnitzel (made from pork). The latter may also taste appealing, but is not made of veal. As a precautionary measure, fair traders specify the origin of their product, e.g. from nearby Pingjiang or Taoyuan.

Other yellow "needle teas" originate from Yunnan and are called Yellow Needles from Yunnan or similar in the trade. Due to the use of a Yunnan cultivar, I find their taste a bit coarser and not quite comparable to Junshan Yinzhen.

HUANG YA 黃芽

Yellow Sprout	
Origin	**Huoshan Huang Ya:** Huoshan, Lu'an, Anhui **Mengding Huang Cha:** Mingshan, Ya'an, Sichuan
Color	Yellowish
Cultivar	Yinzhen #1, Bi Xiang Zao, Tao Yuan Da Ye, Fu Yun
Taste	Slightly sweet, fresh hay, notes of tender corn
Harvest time	**Start:** Early or mid March **End:** Before the Spring Festival / Pre-Rain / Qing Ming
Suggested preparation	75°C at 60, 90, 120 seconds

Huang Ya

Although both variants are called Huang Ya, the yellows from Huoshan and Mingshan differ significantly. The latter typically consists of buds only (rarely one also picks the first or the two youngest leaves) and tastes fresh, but also offers sweet notes of bamboo leaf and sugar cane.

The Huoshan Huang Ya tastes more aromatic, fuller and slightly reminiscent of roasted bell peppers. The leaf material is often less fine than that of the Mengding. The name Huang Ya is rather a euphemism. Huoshan Huang Ya is also produced less "yellow" than the Mengding and is therefore closer in taste to green tea, although less tannic and therefore sweeter.

Unfortunately, there have been a lot of reports lately that sly producers from Huoshan massively shorten and even completely omit the complex yellowing process and actually market green Huoshan as more expensive yellow tea. Caution is advised here.

Sometimes you may also find Huang Ya from Zhejiang, but I have not tasted it yet and cannot say anything about it. Let us instead look at another of those rare representatives of the yellow tea species, the Kekecha.

KEKECHA 可可茶

Cocoa Tea	
Origin	Guangdong
Color	Dark green
Cultivar	Kekecha
Taste	Slightly nutty, a little peach or papaya, very mild
Suggested preparation	80°C with several, longer infusions

Kekecha

Kekecha is quite rare even among the yellow teas, but it has been appearing more frequently in the shops lately. It should not be confused with the Japanese Kukicha, the names may sound similar but the teas are completely different.

Its name means cocoa tea, even if the tea does not taste like cocoa or chocolate. It got its name because, in comparison to other teas, it contains a particularly large amount of theobromine, as is the case with cocoa. On the other hand, it generally contains much less caffeine than most other teas and is therefore said to be particularly suitable for sensitive individuals or an evening cup of tea.

I do not find Kekecha particularly stunning, but if I can buy or drink a well-produced batch, it is a nice alternative. Because of its very light character you will want to let it steep a little longer, the way you would not do it with other teas.

GREEN TEA (LÜ CHA) 绿茶

Almost all Chinese green teas are dried or roasted in a pan or wok and thus differ fundamentally from most Japanese green teas. They are characterized by a great number of varieties, but if you are looking for the grassy, vegetal and sometimes savory, you better stick to Japanese green teas.

Chinese green tea is also usually more robust and lasts longer than the steamed Japanese, but it still should not be stored for too long.[119] Freshness gets lost quite quickly and means a loss of aroma, both in fragrance and the infusion.

ANJI BAICHA 安吉白茶

Anji White Tea, Anji White Virgin	
Origin	Anji, Zhejiang
Color	Very light green
Cultivar	Bai Ye Yi Hao (White leaf number one)
Taste	Delicately sweet, with a hint of citrus and vanilla
Harvest time	Spring, preferably before April 5
Suggested preparation	80°C at 30, 45, 60 seconds

Anji Baicha[120] and the next in line Bai Long Jing are Chinese green teas. However, one often finds them in the wrong place in trade under the category white tea. This is certainly due to the name, which describes the whitish appearance of the fresh, still unpicked leaf.

Anji Baicha contains many polysaccharides and has a correspondingly delicate and sweetish finish. Personally, I like it brewed at 80°C, with an infusion time of 30 to 50 seconds depending on the mood and amount of leaves. A second or third infusion may also be done for up to 1 minute.

Young leaves (above) and ready to brew Anji Bai Cha (below)

BAI LONG JING 白龙井

White Dragon Well	
Origin	Zhejiang
Cultivar	Bai Ye Yi Hao

Despite its name, the Bai Long Jing is by no means a real Long Jing and it is also not a white tea. As with Anji Bai Cha and some other green teas, the word Bai 白 in the name can easily lead astray. It is made from the cultivar Bai Ye Yi Hao like the Anji Bai Cha, but produced like a Long Jing. Compared to other green teas, it is said to contain twice as many amino acids.

BI LUO CHUN 碧螺春

Green Snail Spring	
Origin	Wuxian Taihu, Suzhou City, Jiangsu
Color	Silvery, emerald green
Cultivar	Spring
Suggested preparation	75°C at 60, 60, 90 seconds

Bi Luo Chun or Pi Lo Chun appears in almost every list of the ten famous teas of China. It is a green tea which is preferably grown on the mountain Dong Ding 洞庭 near Tai Hu (or Tai Lake). Tai Hu is located in the Chinese province of Jiangsu. Translated literally Bi Luo Chun means "green spring snail". The name derives from the appearance of the processed tea leaves, which remind of curled snails. Bi Luo Chun is popular for its elegant appearance and flowery-fruity taste.

The "black" Bi Luo Chun from Yunnan is a Dian Hong and has little in common with the popular green tea except the shaping of the leaves and sometimes the cultivar Yunkang. Some sources also classify (green) Bi Luo Chun as particularly high-quality Mao Jian, which can be easily understood due to its appearance and taste.

Bi Luo Chun

Dian Hong offered as black or golden Bi Luo Chun

GUZHU ZI SUN 顾渚紫笋

Purple Bamboo Shoots from Guzhu	
Origin	Changxing, Huzhou, Zhejiang
Color	Dark green to slightly greyish brown
Cultivar	Gu Zhu Qun Ti
Taste	Hay, grain, barely earthy, hint of roasting
Suggested preparation	80°C at 60, 60, 90 seconds (Loose leaf) or 100°C (Cha Bing)

Guzhu Zi Sun is not a purple tea, just as Anji Bai Cha is not a white tea. It got its name from the appearance of the unopened buds, which resemble budding purple bamboo.

At the time of the Tang Dynasty (618-907 CE) tea was still unknown in the western world and loose leaf tea was not yet widespread. At that time the leaves were ground and pressed into small slices (Cha Bing), which were then dried vigorously over charcoal. Before preparation, the slices were then crumbled and boiled in water with salt and spices. Today, Guzhu Zi Sun is mostly offered loose, but fortunately there are a few producers who also offer the classic version again, which requires a complex and lengthy process.

While Guzhu Zi Sun is hardly available in Europe, it looks even sadder regarding its Cha Bing version. Of course, the loose form is much finer and more delicate, because you cannot expect the greatest finesse out of a finely chopped and pressed tea. Nevertheless, I recommend the Cha Bing in case you happen to get hold of it, as it allows you to immerse yourself in 1,000 years of tea history. À propos "immersion": a bing of roughly 8g is brewed in 250 to 500ml of water at 100°C (sic!), and steeps for anywhere between one and three minutes, preferably in a glass jar. Both the temperature and the infusion time are certainly very unusual for a green tea, but this one can take it. Then you pour a good half of the liquid directly into cups (you do not need a sieve, since the disc practically never falls apart) and leave the rest in the jar. Further infusions can be made throughout the day. Boiling water is poured into the glass again and again, and the jar is never emptied more than to a minimum of one third. I have never drunk another green tea that could be infused so many times. This is a perfect example of how even a very expensive tea can achieve a very decent price/performance ratio. If you leave the slice in the remaining water overnight, the tea is not bitter at all the next day and the bing has still not completely disintegrated. The taste reminds a bit of a yellow tea, showing hay and dark honey notes.

Guzhu Zi Sun in Cha Bing shape

LONG JING 龙井

Dragon Well	
Origin	Meijawu at Westlake or around Longjing, near Hangzhou, Zhejiang
Color	Light green to yellowish, unlike most other green teas a slightly yellowish leaf is by all means a sign of good quality in Long Jing.
Cultivar	Long Jing No. 43, other cultivars are used for variations
Taste	A hint of chestnut and nuts
Harvest time	Ideally before April 5th.
!!!	THE Chinese green tea
Suggested preparation	80°C at 45, 60, 90 seconds

Depending on the transcription from Chinese, the spelling may also be Lung Jing or Lung Ching. Alternatively it is also called Westlake Dragonwell or Xihu (sometimes also Qi Hu) Long Jing. As a Chinese spelling you may encounter the traditional 龍井 or the simplified 龙井. The origin of this tea is the village of Longjing in the Xihu district (Westlake Dragonwell) 西湖 which is located near the famous Dragon Spring or, you guessed it, Dragon Well.

If you are intensively engaged in high-quality teas, you might lose interest in Long Jing after a while. There are at least two obvious reasons for this. Maybe one has not yet found and tasted the highest quality, or one has tasted numerous other spectacular Chinese teas and added them to one's personal hit list, then one may forget about the LJ.

No matter which list of the great Chinese teas you find, it will always contain the Long Jing. Whatever the reason might be, the Long Jing well deserves being on that list. From time immemorial, it has been the reference, the longing, the tea that everyone is craving for in China. In Chinese literature it is permanently mentioned to be a valuable gift or tea for special occasions. It is considered the epitome of luxury, comparable to caviar or champagne which are much sought after elsewhere.

However, this almost mythical adoration is also leading to terrible excesses. Especially in Chinese tourist regions, cheaply produced fakes are offered en masse. Luckily you can get Long Jing in Europe in different qualities and price categories from trustworthy (and experienced) dealers. Pre rain qualities may then cost twice and up to three times as much as later harvests. Street vendors in China baking tea in a wok on the street, aiming at clueless tourists, can safely be accused of being counterfeits, especially when cute looking models wear gloves at the frying pan, because the genuine and high-quality Long Jing is never baked wearing gloves. This way the tea master would lose any feeling for the right temperature during production.

The leaves are usually about 1cm long, quite narrow and pressed flat. The taste is extremely smooth and balanced and shows a light yellowish-green color in the cup. Its aroma is characterized by a very slightly nutty to chestnut-like note, making it easy to identify even in a blind tasting by non-professionals. In this respect it also differs from Anji Baicha, which it resembles somewhat visually; but Long Jing is actually easy to distinguish by its characteristic leaves, which are flattened after heating. The best qualities usually show up much brighter in the infusion than the lesser qualities.

The typical flattened leaves of Long Jing

Very rarely you will also find a red tea called Long Jing, but it is more likely to be found in the trade as Jiuqu Hong Mei. This is a fully oxidized version, which means that the same Long Jing cultivar is processed differently. It tastes delicately floral, with aromas of berries and plums as well as fine nuances of slightly malty chocolate. Interestingly, it does not tolerate as much heat as other red teas, so the water should not exceed 90°C.

Medium quality Long Jing is ideal for beginners and may be purchased at a reasonable price. If you build a tea collection, it should certainly become part of it. As a host you never make a mistake offering Long Jing because it is very well balanced and pleasant to drink, free of bitterness and excessive aroma escapades. You can offer it to almost every guest who has little tea experience or who has had bad experiences with inferior or badly stored or brewed teas before. Nothing can probably go wrong with the tolerant Long Jing. While some sensitive green teas already resent being infused at more than 70°C, a Long Jing is often still pleasantly drinkable after being heavily scalded with boiling water. However, excessive heat certainly does not make it any better.

Specialized dealers who value outstanding quality often keep several variations in their assortment. They then indicate whether the tea tastes rather floral or nutty, whether it was baked normally or rather intensively. An indication of the alternative cultivars creates additional confidence and helps avoid disappointment. Further details worth knowing are shown in the table below.

Some Long Jing variations

Name	中文	Note
Pre-Qingming Long Jing	预清明龙井	Harvest time before the Qingming Festival, naturally produces the smallest and finest leaves.
Xihu Long Jing	西湖龙井	Considered the original, found in the trade as Westlake Long Jing.
Shi Feng Long Jing	狮峰龙井	Place of origin of Long Jing of particularly high quality and also name of the cultivar for the most expensive Long Jing variety. Shi Feng means Lions Peak, it is the mountain with the highest (tea) prestige at Xihu.
Meijiawu Long Jing	梅家坞龙井	Jade green subspecies of Xihu Long Jing.
Zhejiang Long Jing	浙江龙井	Tea grown outside the Xihu district and often cheaper.

MAO FENG 毛峰

Downy Tip, Furry Peak, Hair Peak	
Origin	Zheijiang; Anhui; Henan; Guangxi
Color	Dark green, silvery with white fluff that reminds of snowy mountain peaks
Cultivar	Qun Ti Zhong
Taste	Herbs, breath of mint
Harvest time	Spring (only young shoots, bud and one leaf)
!	Top qualities usually come from the yellow mountain in Anhui and are called Huang Shan Mao Feng 黄山毛峰
Suggested preparation	85°C at 15, 20, 25, ... seconds

Mao Feng

I always face problems with Mao Feng and Mao Jian. Although otherwise master of my senses (or so I believe), some things are difficult for me to remember or to keep apart. For example, I always manage to confuse the two women's names Katja and Tanja, which did not lead to greater popularity on my part with ladies bearing such names. I feel similar with Mao Feng and Mao Jian. Whenever I want to acquire them or even simply drink them, the guesswork starts. Which was which again? Which one did I like better? As I often buy online from

Asian traders, the translation is not always helpful either, as English dealers occasionally also confuse the terms, especially as various (online) dictionaries come up with the same result for both Chinese terms: Downy Tip. This is a rather hairy matter.

Mao Jian is generally considered to be the lower quality of Mao Feng. This does not do justice to Mao Jian, because purely in terms of taste they differ significantly and both can be excellent. The following table briefly lists the main differences:

Mao Feng	Mao Jian
Mostly baked in hot air	Baked in the wok, often by hand
Dark, often larger leaves from second picking	Fine, brighter, spirally curved leaf
Rich spectrum of aromas	Somewhat harsher, tends to be more vegetable, with more umami

Be that as it may, Mao Feng is one of the ten famous teas from China in almost every version of the list. Disrespectfully, I attribute this to various medals won at international exhibitions since the middle of the 19th century. Certainly there are outstanding qualities to be found, in general the Huangshan Maofeng 黄山毛峰 is considered the measure of all things, hailing from the Yellow Mountain in the south of Anhui. However, if the list is limited to ten entries, I personally would favor other champions. But this may be partly due to the fact that under the names Mao Feng and Mao Jian a large quantity of bulk produce from innumerable different cultivars is also being offered, in my opinion the good name suffers from this. The usual way of picking a bud and one leaf only should result in more top quality, but I find many Mao Feng and Mao Jian offered quite arbitrary.

I like to brew Mao Feng a little hotter than other greens and let it steep for quite a short time.

MAO JIAN 毛尖

Downy Tip	
Origin	Xinyang, Henan
Color	Seaweed green (also lighter depending on the time of harvest), with white hairs on the inside of the leaf
Cultivar	Cai Cha
Taste	Sugar cane, vegetables, tender hay and umami, buttery
Harvest time	10 days in spring "before the rain" (bud and a leaf)
!	Top qualities tend to hail from Xinyang and are called Xinyang Mao Jian 信阳毛尖
Suggested preparation	70°C at 30, 45, 60 seconds

Mao Jian

As mentioned above regarding Mao Feng, Mao Jian is often regarded as being of lower quality than the former. Personally I perceive the opposite. Mao Jian for me is a special Chinese green tea, which I like to drink again and again. In a blind tasting, I could almost take him for a (diluted) Japanese tea whose fixation was done with hot steam instead of in a wok. This is because after pouring off the water the still hot leaves almost smell a bit like chicken stock, an indication of its typical, rich umami aroma. However, these typical Japanese aromas are much weaker and more delicate to perceive in Mao Jian than in Japanese tea.

While Mao Feng tends to have a light amber color in the cup due to its light roasting, Mao Jian has a delicate, slightly cloudy yellow color with only a minimal green tinge.

The production method is historically based on that of Long Jing, but for Mao Jian the leaves are lightly rolled in the wok at the end of the baking process and not flattened as is the Long Jing. These two green teas also differ significantly in taste.

While it might be desirable to find a place of origin added to the name (especially Xinyang 信阳 - as a reference to quality), the tea might also be a completely different one if you buy a Beigang Mao Jian 北港毛尖. The latter is a yellow tea from another province, namely Hunan. Unfortunately, I have not yet succeeded in finding one, but one must have some ambitions.

Xinyang Mao Jian

I enjoy drinking Xinyang Mao Jian chilled at 4°C to 7°C, , but brewed at 70°C in the classic way, not as cold brew. Unlike some other teas, it hardly bitters and keeps its rich taste for many hours in the refrigerator.

TAI PING HOU KUI 太平猴魁

Monkey King	
Origin	Taiping, Anhui
Color	Dark to translucent light green
Cultivar	Shi Da Cha
Taste	Extremely mild and subtle, delicately floral, orchid with a touch of citrus freshness
Suggested preparation	At maximum 75°C, served in grandpa style with frequent refills of water

The huge leaves of Tai Ping Huo Kui

Tai Ping Hou Kui immediately appears to be something very special. The huge and almost transparent leaves are plucked when slightly opened, heated and pressed initially by hand and then in a special grid. The whole process reminds of a combination of ironing and running over it with a steamroller. Contrary to many other teas, the leaves are not rolled and thus look as if they were dried inside of books, utilizing blotting paper.

The original TPHK tastes of minerals and is beautifully delicate, although unlike most green teas it is a large leaf tea. When talking to Chinese friends, I do not ask how strong they like it, but only how many leaves they desire. We then simply put hot water into glasses and then add the tea which stays in the glass for the rest of the session. Depending on your preferences you can add water several times..

ZHU CHA 珠茶

Gunpowder	
Origin	Wuxian Taihu, Suzhou City, Jiangsu
Color	Silvery, emerald green
Harvest time	Spring
Suggested preparation	90°C, preferably drunk only in North Africa and with fresh Nana mint ;-)

The green tea originally called Zhu Cha 珠茶 is almost exclusively known by the name Gunpowder around the world. Zhu Cha means pearl tea and this refers to its characteristic form of firmly rolled tea made of the tender and small leaves of the first harvest which is dark green but called Gunpowder none the less.

Unfortunately, I have never come across high-quality Gunpowder so far. Legend has it that the best varieties are internationally available as Pinhead Gunpowder and Temple of Heaven Gunpowder. Personally, I have known it as tolerable at best. To me it is characterized by a powerful aroma without any finesse. It is worth mentioning, however, that it is one of the two ingredients of Thé à la Menthe[121], which is a very popular beverage in North Africa and Arabia, the other ingredient being both dried and fresh Nana mint. This combination produces a deliciously strong drink, both sweet and refreshing.

A combination of Gunpowder and Nana mint is often marketed as Moroccan mint or Tuareg tea, but unfortunately it is sometimes blended with other teas instead of Gunpowder.

BLUE TEA (OOLONG) 烏龍茶

Oolong is one of the most versatile teas, as it covers all degrees of oxidation between green and black tea. The production process is very elaborate and the different varieties vary greatly in appearance, aroma and taste.

The degree of oxidation can be roughly differentiated between lightly oxidized (approx. 20-30%) and strongly oxidized oolong (up to 80+%). Accordingly, oolong is also called semi- or partially oxidized tea, which is in addition more or less strongly roasted or baked.

The strength of the roasting is more important for understanding oolong than for any other tea. The degree of roasting may also defined by a percentage, but usually classified as light, medium and strong. The stronger version is called Nong Xiang (strong aroma), the lighter and more modern version is called Qing Xiang (clear aroma). These Chinese terms are increasingly seen outside of China.

Good dealers should indicate these degrees, which makes it easier for customers to find the desired taste nuances. This is especially important as oolongs are subject to quite significant fashion trends. Some oolongs used to be much more oxidized and roasted in former times and are hardly recognizable nowadays as they are produced more tenderly, flowery and fruity compared to the beginning of the millennium. But who can blame the producers if the demand is as high as it seems?[122]

Oolong roasting levels

English	中文	Pinyin
Lightly oxidized and slightly roasted, very floral	清香	Qing Xiang
Strongly oxidized, slightly roasted	韵香	Yun Xiang
Lightly oxidized, strongly and hot roasted	浓香	Nong Xiang

While the degree of oxidation determines the basic taste characteristics, the degree of roasting defines the power, but also the mildness of the oolong. In contrast to coffee, which can strike delicate stomachs if roasted too strongly, the opposite is true for oolong. Up until now I have only noticed complaints about indigestible oolong in cases where it was too green - although this did not happen very often.

Oolongs that are particularly heavy roasted and baked over charcoal are called Tan Bei 炭焙. The regular rebaking (usually every three years) of stored oolong is called Hong Bei 烘焙. While the former variant produces a distinct and sometimes even a little too strong charcoal aroma (but masters of their trade get exactly the right point), Hong Bei serves on the one hand the durability by removing storage moisture from the tea and on the other hand the aroma often benefits, the oolong becomes more pleasant and even milder.

THE FOUR LEADING OOLONG REGIONS

No rule without exception, but oolong from Anxi nowadays tends to be light to medium roasted. A little more roasting aromas are tastable in many Taiwan oolongs and even more power can be found in Phoenix oolongs. The most heavily roasted oolongs in many cases come from Wuyishan and are called Yancha.

Mainland Chinese oolongs can be divided into three main groups, supplemented by the no less interesting spectrum of oolongs from Taiwan.

Main regions of Chinese oolong

English	中文	Pinyin	Origin
Anxi Oolong	安溪乌龙	Anxi Wulong	Anxi, Southern Fujian
Wuyi Rock Tea, Cliff Tea, Bohea (obsolete)	武夷岩茶	Wuyi Yancha	Wuyi Shan, Nanping, Northern Fujian
Phoenix Mountain Single Bush	凤凰单丛	Fenghuang Dancong	Fenghuang Shan, Chaozhou, Guangdong
Taiwan oolong, High mountain oolong	台湾乌龙 臺灣乌龙	Taiwan Wulong	Taiwan

The first Chinese oolong originated in the Fujian province. The Yancha or Wuyi rock tea (also known as cliff tea) comes from the northern Wuyi Shan mountains, and often develops a mineral and strong roasting aroma.

Nestled in and around the cliffs of a nature reserve, the tea plants there enjoy a unique terroir of mineral-rich soil, limestone rocks, bamboo forests and many rivers.

From Anxi in South Fujian, on the other hand, hails oolong which nowadays tends to be only slightly oxidized and hardly roasted at all and therefore offers a flowery and fresh taste. There are also many classic roasting methods, but due to the contemporary demands of the market, the teas are less roasted and are produced much greener, more flowery and sweeter. Anxi's main tea varieties are the famous Tie Guan Yin, the lesser known Mao Xie and Ben Shan oolongs as well as Huang Jin Gui and the newly developed Jin Guan Yin.

From Fujian the oolong tea then spread further southwest; Fenghuang in Guangdong province is now the biggest traditional growing area. Here the Dancong (literally single shrub) dominates, which can have several definitions. It can mean a single tea tree or uncut shrub instead of a low shrub like in large plantations. Most often, however, it implies the promise that all leaves originate from a single plant, or, more realistically, that all leaves derive from plants that have been cloned from the original. Simply put, these are teas from certain cultivars which all have a Shui Xian as their ancestor. So Dancongs are a subset of the oolongs and the well-known Fenghuang Dancongs are a subset of the Dancongs. They are among more than 100 different oolongs from the north-eastern highlands of Guangdong. There is also a Fenghuang Shan (Phoenix Mountain) in Nantou (Taiwan), where tea is also produced, but no Dancong. Genuine Dancong has always been grown from seeds and comes from older bushes, whose distinct roots, like those of the Yancha, can extract the sought-after minerals from the soil better than young plants grown from cuttings.

Geographical location of important oolong regions and mountains

By no means should you expect a "Phoenix Mountain Single Bush" to be from exactly one single physical bush, which on top of that it said to have historically caused wonder healing or radiates particularly good karma. Things are sometimes different with Pu'er. There, Single Tree really means that a certain tea is supposed to be from one tree only. One may believe this or not, everybody is free to have their own opinion.

Typical Taiwan oolongs are the Oriental Beauty, the high mountain oolong[123] and the honey scent oolongs.

On the following pages I will not provide any preparation suggestions, as they are quite straightforward for all oolongs. Simply use (almost) boiling water, i.e. 95 to 100°C, rinse the tea briefly, and then differentiate the length of the infusion according to assumed oxidation level and degree of roasting. As a rule of thumb, as mentioned earlier, the first infusion should last five to a maximum of 30 seconds, depending on oxidation and roasting.

The lighter (greener) the leaves, the lower the level of oxidation and possible roasting, and the longer the tea may want to steep. This generally refers to Anxi oolongs, but also applies to other green oolongs, no matter from which region.

Likewise, regardless of their origin, strongly oxidized dark (red) oolongs and those with a strong or even charcoal roast should only steep for a very short time.

Some connoisseurs even prefer the so-called flash brewing, where the amount of tea is maximized (the pot or gaiwan is filled almost to the brim) and after about two seconds (the approximate time it takes to put the lid on) the infusion is already poured. Although this method consumes quite a lot of leaf material, it can be used to obtain an extremely large number of infusions. So in terms of cost it does not matter and in terms of taste I prefer this method, provided that thirst and time are in abundance.

The subsequent infusions may each last a few seconds longer, depending on preference. For moderately oxidized teas, simply start with a time between the aforementioned five and 30 seconds.

It would simply not be constructive to suggest more precise infusion times, e.g. for Tie Guan Yin, because there is not "the" TGY, but due to its popularity many combinations of different cultivars, orthodox (strong) oxidation and roasting or the lighter, modern variant. However, as mentioned before, oolongs are rather easy to brew, Japanese green teas demand much more attention.

ANXI OOLONG 安溪乌龙

We will start with Anxi in the south of Fujian and look at the delicate floral to fruity blue teas from this region. They are well suited for beginners who want to take their first steps into the world of oolongs. Internationally, these strongly rolled teas are sometimes called Minnan wulongs, because the region lies south of the river Min. In the global market the Tie Guan Yin outdoes everything else and is therefore widely imitated in other regions, but many other oolongs from Anxi also deserve a mention and a purchase.

BAI YA QI LAN 白芽奇兰

White Bud Remarkable Orchid	
Origin	Pinghe, Zhangzhou, Fujian
Taste	Oily, delicately sweet, fruity

One should not confuse the Bai Ya Qi Lan with the similar sounding Bai Qi Lan, the latter being a Yancha from North Fujian, while the Bai Ya Qi Lan is a cultivar developed in the 90s in Pinghe in South Fujian. Although Pinghe is just under a hundred miles away from Anxi, it is still south of Fujian and thus mentioned in this section. In Taiwan, it is also cultivated in the Nantou area, where it is called Qilan for short.

I am lucky to have a gem from 1993 in my collection, you may read more about it later in the section about aged oolong.

Aged Bai Ya Qi Lan 1993

BEN SHAN 本山

Anxi Ben Shan, Source or Original Mountain	
Origin	Anxi, Fujian
Typical level of oxidation	Light
Typical roasting level	Light
Cultivar	Ben Shan
Taste	Flowery, stronger than TGY, not that subtle
!	Usual suspect in fake TGY

The cultivar Ben Shan as well as the tea named after it resemble Tie Guan Yin in appearance and taste, and genetically there is said to be a very close relationship. In blind tastings[124] a Ben Shan might well be regarded as a somewhat edgier Tie Guan Yin, and thus, similar to Jin Guan Yin, it is often incorrectly sold as the (more expensive) TGY. The Ben Shan has nothing to hide and could proudly stand by his name, but the temptations of the market prevail.

Again similar to TGY, the Ben Shan's spring picking can be distinguished easily from the autumn picking, and those who like the autumnal aromas more will even benefit from a slightly lower price tag.

HUANG JIN GUI 黄金桂

Golden Cassia, Golden Cinnamon (Flower), Golden Osmanthus	
Origin	Anxi, Fujian
Typical level of oxidation	Light
Typical roasting level	Light
Cultivar	Huang Dan, Huang Jin Gui
Taste	Very flowery, slightly reminiscent of osmanthus
!	The name refers to the yellow-gold flower tips of the cultivar. Sometimes osmanthus flowers are added.

JIN GUAN YIN 金观音

Golden Guan Yin, Golden Goddess of Mercy	
Origin	Anxi, Fujian
Typical level of oxidation	Light
Typical roasting level	Light
Cultivar	TGY x Huang Jin Gui
Taste	Slightly more floral and sweeter than TGY, milder, less acidic and mineral
!	JGY is also the name of a Yancha.

Jin Guan Yin

Although Jin Guan Yin may not be the *unloved*, he is certainly the *unknown* stepbrother of Tie Guan Yin. The TGY is far ahead of him in terms of popularity and reputation, and yet the JGY is not necessarily cheaper or less drinkable. It is very similar to its famous relative, but less fine and delicate on the palate, showing a fuller, but also more angular aroma.

Sometimes I tend to resort to this less complex variation if a Tie Guan Yin would feel too flowery-fruity on any given day.

The clearly tastable proximity to Tie Guan Yin results from the fact that the cultivar is a cross between TGY and Huang Jin Gui. TGY branches are grafted onto Huang Jin Gui and after a few years one can harvest a tea with a new aroma.

TIE GUAN YIN 铁观音

Iron Goddess of Mercy, Iron Buddha	
Origin	Xiping, Anxi, Fujian
Typical level of oxidation	Light
Typical roasting level	Varies a lot, traditionally it is strongly roasted. As the roasting requires a lot of experience, the quality in the market fluctuates considerably. Fashionably slightly roasted, it is also offered under the name Jade TGY. A medium roasting degree offers a compromise acceptable to many.
Cultivar	Tie Guan Yin
Taste	Creamy, slightly acidic, mineral, intensely floral to fruity
!	The name originates from Guan Yin, a female Bodhisattva of Mahayana Buddhism, called Goddess of Compassion or Mercy.

Tie Guan Yin[125] among the oolongs is to me what Long Jing is among the greens, kind of a benchmark. After hundreds of oolongs and thousands of cups drunk I fully understand the popularity of this oolong and also the passionate religious wars that are fought over it. Time and again one reads dedicated articles in online forums or tea magazines that TGY is much more pleasant in its just slightly oxidized and roasted modern version than is the classic, darker one. Different methods of production or origin are balanced against each other and it seems as if irreconcilable camps have formed. However, in comparison to actual religious wars, the scourge of our times, this is fortunately just what the British put so beautifully as "a storm in a tea cup". Those who have found their favorite version may enjoy it, regardless of whether it complies with the pure, classical doctrine or whether it may be a newfangled aberration. Personally, I can enjoy almost all variations, whether fresh or aged, green or red, barely or heavily roasted, from spring or autumn harvest. Only the so-called summer and winter TGY I have not yet been able to taste. The latter is rare, because only in very mild winters the leaves will sprout again. From what I have heard, it is rather not worthwhile to buy these qualities, despite their much lower prices.

The village of Gande 感德, located about 50 kilometers north of the origin, seems to be particularly reliable in supplying good quality, even if I choose different quality levels and price ranges for a change. Like elsewhere, small farmers in Gande can choose between the two extremes (maximizing either output or quality), hence it is important to buy from a trader who knows these differences and is not fooled by untrustworthy middlemen. The name Gande alone does not guarantee anything yet, only the experienced buyer or importer makes the value chain really worth our while, because in Gande conditions are almost like in Champagne or Bordeaux, where if possible a winemaker would even grow wine on renatured concrete surfaces or garage roofs, just to be able to produce within the coveted location.

TGY after multiple steepings

But even in Gande the best TGY does not grow on the plain, but outside of the centre, on the slope. The inherently low yielding and slow growing cultivar needs even more time and effort to ripen in the mountainous, rocky terroir, which is noticeable in both taste and wallet.

Still, I also like to drink the Taiwanese Muzha TGY, whose producers were originally inspired by Gande.

Probably no Anxi oolong is faked as often as the TGY, using Ben Shan or Mao Xie[126], which are pretty close to the TGY, but do not quite reach its grandeur.

If you like TGY and plan to deepen your experiences around it, do not miss out on tasting a Jin Guan Yin - especially since some dealers are incorrectly promoting the humble JGY as TGY anyway.

ZHANG PING SHUI XIAN 漳平水仙

Shui Xian from Zhang Ping	
Origin	Zhangping, Longyan, Fujian, China
Typical level of oxidation	Light
Typical roasting level	Light
Cultivar	Shui Xian
Taste	Fresh, full-bodied, variable

This tea is generally considered to be the only oolong which is pressed in the production process. About five to seven grams of high quality Shui Xian are hand-pressed into rectangular wooden blocks slightly smaller than matchboxes. They are then wrapped in paper, completely dried and usually vacuum-packed in foil. Paper wrapping has become a rare form of packaging nowadays. The Taiwanese Pouchong or Baozhong is (or rather was) also traditionally wrapped in paper, but not pressed.

I like the Zhang Ping for two reasons. On the one hand it seems a fact that the producers do not want to dilute the name Zhang Ping with poor quality. Usually the Zhang Ping is of quite high quality and full-bodied with some producers even distinguishing between especially floral and rather fruity varieties. On the other hand, it is perfectly suited for traveling, because of its ready-made serving size.

Technically Zhang Ping is not part of Anxi, but of Longyan, which lies in the south of Fujian only about 100 km away from Anxi, hence the categorization in this section. Also highly recommended is the rare Hong Cha from Zhang Ping, which is likewise wrapped in paper but produced from other oolong cultivars, so it is no descendant of Shui Xian.

Zhang Ping Shui Xian in its characteristic paper wrapping

WUYI YANCHA 武夷岩茶 ROCK TEA

While Minnan (and hence Anxi) is located south of the Min River, the Minbei Wulongs, better known as Wuyi Yancha, can be found north of it. Unlike most oolong from Anxi, they are characteristically not rolled into ball shape.

The name Yancha means rock tea and refers to the volcanic, rocky, mineral notes called Yan Yun 岩韵. This does not only refer to the pure taste, but also to the aftertaste long after the cups have been emptied.

The Wuyi area consists of tea gardens that have been cultivated over decades from a few mother plants which still exist today, being heavily guarded. The more volcanic the soil and the closer a tea garden is to the original plants, the more cherished they are.

Therefore the distinction between three different regions and also quality levels is quite precise:

- Zheng Yan 正岩 or real rock designates the innermost area, over 300 meters of altitude.
- Ban Yan 半岩, half rock, indicates locations between 100 and 300 meters of altitude at the boundaries of the nature reserve.
- Zhou Cha 州茶 or land tea refers to areas far from the inner area but close to the river and has the least appreciation because there is very little influence of volcanic soil left.

Unfortunately, this distinction is unlikely to be found in retail, but outside of China you will hardly be able to purchase the quality from within the inner region anyway. Even visiting the inner area is denied to foreigners. So it can safely be assumed that mainly Ban Yan and Zhou Cha are available in the trade. Whenever merchants are able to get hold of a tea from Zheng Yan, they will emphasize this fact, often with the addition of the name of the exact garden. Should you find trustworthy offers with the following designations of origin you should not hesitate to make a purchase.

- Bi Shi 碧石
- Fo Gu 佛国
- Gui Lin 桂林
- Ma Tou Yan 马头岩
- Hui Yuan 慧苑
- Tao Hua Dong 桃花洞
- Jiu Long Ke 九龙窠
- Tian Xin Yan 天心岩
- San Yang Feng Deng Deng 三仰峰等等
- Shui Lian Dong 水帘洞
- Yan Zi Ke 燕子窠
- Yu Cha Yuan 御茶园
- Yu Hua Dong 玉花洞
- Zhu Ke 竹窠

Yancha are optically characterized by the fact that they are usually rolled into elongated strips and do not look spherical like some other oolongs. Furthermore, the rugged and steep area is not suitable for harvesting, so that one can mostly assume that Yancha are hand-picked.

Also belonging to the Yancha are the Zheng Shan Xiao Zhong and the Jin Jun Mei, but since these are not oolongs but red teas, they have to wait their turn until later.

There are hundreds[127] of different varieties of Yancha, which all have their own names and often sound quite similar, at least for non-chinese.

When I hear or read the names Ye Xia Hong 叶下红 or Ye Xia Qing 叶下青, I cannot say much about them, because I do not know these Yancha. But I know the words Ye, Hong and Qing. Ye is the leaf, Hong means red and Qing can mean green or blue. So are these the variants of the same harvest that are developed into red or blue tea (oolong)? And does Xia refer to the summer (tea) or does it mean "under", so it is a variant of a cultivar? The latter is probably correct, both names refer to cultivars as well as the finished teas made of them.

But you should not get irritated or even discouraged by this. Even for native Chinese speakers this is not easy to understand, if they are not also tea experts for the respective region or variety. And especially Chinese people often baffle me with their ignorance about tea. Yet this can be explained quite easily.

Who outside of Bavaria knows more than a handful of Weißbier (white or wheat beer) varieties that are praised up and down in worldwide advertising? In my opinion, the best wheat beer (I ever had) is called Unertl and comes from Haag in Upper Bavaria. However, even many Bavarians are not aware of this brand, and most Germans or Europeans certainly are none the wiser. And how could they, since they are free to enjoy their regional Pilsner, Alt, Kölsch and whatnot?

Most Chinese will still recognize a Long Jing, Tie Guan Yin or Maofeng, but sometimes this is as far as it goes.

Many people do not even care which mineral water they drink, as long as it tastes neutral and does not make them ill (like tap or well water in some parts of the world). Very few people are interested in the names and details of the water they drink.

So do not let this incredible diversity stop you from consciously drinking your first Yancha.

In the following, I will only list a fraction of the Yancha that I have been able to taste, and I will try to list only those which are widely available in trade. From then on you will certainly feel able to continue your research on your own.

Perhaps you should start with the four most famous and allegedly original cultivars from Wuyi, which can proudly look back at at least 400 years of tradition. While the Shui Xian is regarded as the original cultivar in Dancong, the Yancha

- Bai Ji Guan
- Da Hong Pao
- Shui Jin Gui
- Tie Luo Han

are considered the four famous bushes or Si Da Ming Cong 四大名. Unfortunately, some of their top qualities are extremely expensive and fakes are ubiquitous. But you do not have to worry about that, as other Yancha also offer outstanding flavors and are easily affordable. My favorites here are the Rou Gui and the Fo Shou. These somewhat neglected relatives may be called Qi Zhong 奇种 (strange species) to distinguish them from the Si Da Ming Cong. However, this naming is not meant by any means disrespectful, but merely indicates the further evolved cultivation from the original plants..

BAI JI GUAN 白鸡冠

White Cockscomb	
Origin	Wuyishan
Typical level of oxidation	Light to medium
Typical roasting level	Medium to strong, also charcoal
Cultivar	Bai Ji Guan
Taste	Mineral fruity, sweet quince, bamboo and vanilla
!	Si Da Ming; more lightly oxidized than most other Yancha, optically evident from the whitish yellow color and the shape of the dry leaf that gives the plant its name (No longer visible when roasted strongly, in which case the BJG optically resembles other Yancha).

Bai Ji Guan[128] is not as common in the trade as other Yancha. However, its extraordinary aroma justifies the search efforts.

BU ZHI CHUN 不知春

Not Knowing Springtime	
Origin	Wuyishan
Typical level of oxidation	Light
Typical roasting level	Light to medium
Cultivar	Bu Zhi Chun
Taste	Very light and delicate, like something is missing. However, nothing is amiss, only all its diverse aromas are rather hinted at, even aged notes are often perceptible.
Harvest time	Warm periods in winter
!	Also successfully grown in Taiwan, known there as Dong Pian 冬片 Winter leaf.

The Bu Zhi Chun got its name because it sprouts very early in warm winters and might be harvested before spring. Its full aroma is outstanding, although on some days it appears a bit flat, as if it tries to hide and does not want to be analyzed. Of course, that only makes it more interesting to me. Sometimes I even notice traces of whisky or I get reminded of very young and fine Indian teas. With Bu Zhi Chun one may always discover something new.

Bu Zhi Chun

DA HONG PAO 大红袍

Big Red Robe	
Origin	Wuyishan
Typical level of oxidation	Medium
Typical roasting level	Medium, charcoal
Cultivar	Da Hong Pao
Taste	Dark dried fruit, chocolate, nuts, mineral
!	Si Da Ming

According to legend, the somewhat odd-sounding name "Big Red Robe" originates from a Chinese emperor who, centuries ago when the shrub was first discovered, threw his red cloak over it with sheer enthusiasm in order to mark it and claim it exclusively for himself. Apart from this romantic transfiguration, for many Yancha fans the Da Hong Pao is the highest of emotions - and also the highest of prices.

The Wuyi Da Hong Pao has a very characteristic appearance and a very delicate aroma that can hardly be mistaken. The better qualities feature a gentle, rather fruity character with a sweetish note. Da Hong Pao in fresh or well aged top quality can cost well over one Euro per gram, but one may also get very high-quality leaves for about 60 Cents per gram.

Da Hong Pao

Whenever I tried to make a bargain, however, I was disappointed. Flat, stale infusions, versions roasted too aggressively over charcoal and simple fakes would alternate. Taste usually has its price, but for the DHP this is especially true. It does not seem to be easy to oxidize and roast the two best known cultivars Bei Dou and Qi Dan, either pure or blended (sometimes also with other cultivars), in order to achieve the Yan Yun 岩韵 taste that characterizes the proper Wuyi Yancha.

So if you are not overly wealthy or have outstanding relationships with influential Chinese, you will probably never have drunk a real DHP, at least the one made of the first generation of descendants from the mother plant, in which case it would have been called Bei Dou #1. For the rest of us, it is almost certain that they are imitations trying to get as close as possible to the taste of the original with cultivars like Rou Gui, Shui Xian et al. If customers are being made aware of this fact, then the term fake might be used more forgivingly. Perhaps homage sounds a bit nicer? Personally, I do not look for DHP anymore, because even though I already drank excellent ones, disappointments were also frequent. Yet these can be prevented, as Yancha offers plenty of alternatives.

For the sake of completeness, it should be mentioned that under the name Xiao Hong Pao 小红袍 or Little Red Robe a tea is being offered since the beginning of this millennium, produced from the cultivar Jin Guan Yin No. 204. On top of that, some distributors also refer to their alternative versions of Da Hong Pao as Xiao Hong Pao.

FO SHOU 佛手

Buddhas Hand	
Origin	Yongchun, Wuyishan, Fujian
Typical level of oxidation	Strong
Typical roasting level	Medium
Cultivar	Fo Shou, Beidou
Taste	Charcoal, mineral, slightly floral and almost like scented with citrus fruit

A tasty citrus fruit that even grows in Italy has given this tea its name. The fruit Buddha's hand is a variant of a lemon, more precisely Citrus medica var. sarcodactylis. This fruit resembles a hand with many fingers, and sometimes it is reminiscent of some hand gestures depicted on Buddha statues.

Fo Shou is sometimes also found under the name Xiang Yuan 香橼 or citron, and indeed Fo Shou shows a very characteristic taste of citrus fruit. The taste is characteristic of this cultivar, no aromas are added to the tea, in case you might wonder.

The shape of the citrus fruit resembles such gestures

The Fo Shou cultivar is also grown in Taiwan and is usually green and rolled, while the Wuyi Yancha is darker and not rolled.

Fresh (left) and aged Fo Shou (right)

HUANG GUAN YIN 黃觀音

Yellow Goddess of Mercy	
Origin	Wuyishan (Fujian Tea Research Institute)
Typical level of oxidation	Light
Typical roasting level	Light and over charcoal
Cultivar	Huang Jin Gui x Tie Guan Yin (No. 105)
Taste	Orchid

Huang Guan Yin is a new cross between the two Anxi-cultivars Huang Jin Gui and Tie Guan Yin and offers the characteristics of both teas in one. It is greener and lighter than typical Yancha and sometimes rolled into ball shape, which is untypical for Yancha.

HUANG MEI GUI 黃玫瑰

Yellow Rose	
Origin	Wuyishan (Fujian Tea Research Institute)
Typical level of oxidation	Light
Typical roasting level	Light
Cultivar	Huang Jin Gui x Huang Dan
Taste	Delicate flowers, rose

Huang Mei Gui also is a young cross between two popular cultivars, its name results from the rather yellowish cup and its delicate rose scent. It reminds more of green Taiwan Oolongs than of Yancha.

LAO ZHONG SHUI XIAN 老种水仙

Old Variety Shui Xian, Old Bush Daffodils, Lao Cong Shui Xian	
Origin	Wuyishan and Fenghuangshan
Typical level of oxidation	Varies
Typical roasting level	
Cultivar	Shui Xian
Taste	Fresh wood, mineral
!	Available as both Yancha and Dancong

Lao Zhong (old variety) refers to both tea bushes aged around 100 years and older, and the tea produced from these bushes - at least if those are old, original Shui Xian bushes. Apart from that one hardly encounters the prefix Lao Zhong.

Lao Zhong Shui Xian is offered as Yancha as well as Dancong and then roasted rather strongly (Yancha) or more lightly (Dancong).

Lao Zhong Shui Xian

QI LAN 奇兰

Rare Orchid	
Origin	Wuyishan
Typical level of oxidation	Light to medium
Typical roasting level	Medium to strong
Cultivar	Qi Lan
Taste	Very mild, slightly nutty and sweet
!	Excellent qualities can also be found in Mingjian, Taiwan, and Pinghe, Zhangzhou, in the south of Fujian.

Good qualities are also produced in Mingjian, Taiwan, and Pinghe, Zhangzhou, in the south of Fujian.

ROU GUI XIANG 肉桂香

Cassia Flavour, Cinnamon Flavour, Chinese Cinnamon	
Origin	Anxi
Typical level of oxidation	Strong
Typical roasting level	Medium to strong, possibly charcoal
Cultivar	Rou Gui
Taste	Cassia, cinnamon, spicy, also notes of coffee, dark chocolate and vanilla
!	Rou Gui is also offered as Dancong, then coming from Guangdong and not Fujian.

Rou Gui Xiang, or Rou Gui, for short is one of the leading Yancha. As with many other traditional or particularly popular oolongs it is produced in various regions and more recently in Taiwan, too. Its truly unique scent and taste make it one of my favorites, which is why I have also tasted it frequently both as a Dancong and as a Taiwanese. The Yancha original has totally convinced me. Especially those rare treasures from the inner area, which I was lucky to put my hands on, but also qualities from the outskirts of the Double Breast Mountain are still fascinating.

Sadly, Rou Gui is sometimes also incorrectly offered as the slightly more expensive Da Hong Pao, which it resembles visually, although it mostly comes up a bit brighter. I consider this a stupid approach, because even if DHP is a bit more expensive, a good Rou Gui is by no means inferior. Moreover, Rou Gui shows a strong, unique and distinctive aroma. Rou Gui is certainly one of the teas I would take with me to the proverbial desert island.

Rou Gui

SHUI JIN GUI 水金龟

Golden Water Turtle	
Origin	Wuyishan
Typical level of oxidation	Light to medium
Typical roasting level	Light to medium
Cultivar	Shui Jin Gui
Taste	Powerfully fruity, sweet potato, herbs
!	Si Da Ming

Shui Jin Gui owes its name to the special veining of its leaves, which are said to have reminded the name-giver of a turtle shell. It is usually quite lightly oxidized for a Yancha and looks correspondingly greenish. Despite its good reputation I found it not particularly outstanding the few times I tasted it, maybe I just was not lucky during procurement.

SHUI XIAN 水仙

Daffodil, Water Sprite	
Origin	Shui Xian has been known for almost 1,000 years both in Wuyishan and Fenghuang Shan. Its roots are believed to be in Northern Fujian, but not in Wuyishan.
Typical level of oxidation	Any conceivable variation, noticeably stronger in Wuyishan than elsewhere.
Typical roasting level	
Cultivar	Shui Xian
Taste	Very broad spectrum from floral to fruity, usually very balanced and slightly mineral
!	Similar to Rou Gui, heavily roasted Shui Xian is also misused to fake Da Hong Pao.

Shui Xian (occasionally written Shui Hsien) is a very popular cultivar because of its qualities and richness of variants, thus Taiwanese Shui Xian are also available on the market, not to mention other Chinese regions and Dancongs.

Shui Xian is usually moderately oxidized, with the roasting tending to the stronger side. The infusion therefore shows a golden-brown and a fruity taste. In addition, it can be kept for quite a long time, which also makes it popular with collectors.

Many a famous oolong descends from Shui Xian, for example Da Hong Pao and all Dancong.

If you never drank Yancha or Dancong so far, you should ideally start with a high-quality Shui Xian as a starting point and for reference.

Regrettably, Shui Xian's relative popularity seems to be becoming its downfall. Compared to other Yancha, which need to score with quality, it seems to me that the average quality of Shui Xian offered is distinctly below other Yancha. Nevertheless, a search for high quality is well worth the effort, or else one could quickly write it off as arbitrary and get tired of it.

For a while, this was pretty much what I did, I had almost written it off. I can still remember how I once mentioned to tea friends "I think the world has no need for Shui Xian", and even got approval for that. By this time I must have had too much mediocre Shui Xian, for actually they are all-round talents, which may taste very different depending on the processing by the tea masters. Perhaps the Shui Xian of that time were just too balanced and did not show sufficient specific tastes for my liking? Nowadays I would no longer be judging like that. There certainly is top-class Shui Xian available and it is also the rightful foundation of an incredible number of successful crossbreeds.

TIE LUO HAN 铁罗汉

Iron Wise Man, Iron Monk Arhat	
Origin	Wuyishan
Typical level of oxidation	Medium
Typical roasting level	Medium
Cultivar	Tie Luo Han
Taste	Floral, dried fruit
!	Si Da Ming

Tie Luo Han is considered the most ancient of the Si Da Ming cultivars. According to legend it is named after a monk who is believed to having discovered it centuries ago.

YAN XIANG FEI 岩香妃

Rock Fragrance Imperial Concubine (or Princess)	
Origin	Wuyishan
Taste	Mineral (iron) and yet warm, baked fruit, plum, toasted cereal

As mentioned in the preface, each tea book can only present a limited selection of the wide range of tea on offer from this magnificent plant. Although I have made every effort to mention the most important or most famous ones, I did also state that this is a very personal book with some rather subjective emphasis, so I cannot forego mentioning this extremely rare tea.

Yan Xiang Fei

I only came across it by accident. When I tried a very expensive and delicious Da Hong Pao in an outstanding tea house in Germany (I never had a better one before), I decided to purchase all of it. The price was quite hefty at just under 1.50 Euros per gram, but as we all know, perfection can never be measured in terms of mammon. So I bought all the remaining eleven packages of eight grams each, only to find out when I got home that there had apparently been a mix-up. I had been given the Yan Xiang Fei instead of the DHP by mistake, which would have been even more expensive. I called the tea house and suggested a swap, but luckily they were not keen on that. In the meantime I had also found out that I had not been drinking DHP at the place, but instead this Yan Xiang Fei. I gladly kept it and only drank it on very special occasions.

My research later revealed that the YXF as well as the DHP originated in Wuyishan and is said to have pleased even the emperors in the Qing Dynasty. In the 1980s the local company Rui Qian Tea started to recreate the YXF. To what extent the taste is similar to the original is obviously not known to me and probably most experts would consider it to be a top class DHP. Some Yancha are just very close to each other in taste.

ZI HONG PAO 紫红袍

Purple Red Robe	
Typical level of oxidation	Strong
Typical roasting level	Medium
Cultivar	Jiu Long Pao
Taste	Charcoal, mineral, slightly floral, the aftertaste is somewhat reminiscent of red tea.
!	Buds and young leaves are purple-red, older leaves tend to lose their reddish colouring.

One rarely finds a Zi Hong Pao. In taste and production method it corresponds to a Da Hong Pao, only it is made of a heavily purple colored variety of the tea plant. To Da Hong Pao connoisseurs it is definitely something one would like to taste at least once, although the taste is not quite the same. To me and many of my fellow drinkers it is not that convincing, as it is a tad more bitter and sometimes marginally stronger in floral aromas. At best it leaves the impression of being just a mediocre copy of the original.

FENGHUANG DANCONG 凤凰单丛 PHOENIX OOLONG

Similar to Wuyi, the oolongs in Fenghuang Shan, the Phoenix Mountains, which are about 1,500 meters high, originate from within a defined area. In this case it is Chao'an, a district of the city of Chaozhou in Guangdong province, which boasts some 700 years of selective cultivation. The Fenghuang Shan area rises a few hundred meters above the surrounding peaks, is sparsely populated, but used intensively for tea cultivation.

Dancong 单丛 means single shrub or bush. This translation does not imply that tea comes from one single bush only. It rather means that it descended from a historical mother plant with a very special aroma.

Authentic qualities should derive from one of the famous mother plants (which all originate from Shui Xian). However, these are practically only obtainable in China and in homeopathic quantities and with astronomical price tags. In total, about 100 varieties are known - not as many as with the Yancha, but still impressive. Even though almost all Phoenix oolongs today hail from plantations, the search for top qualities is worthwhile - there are fascinating worlds of taste waiting to be explored.

Like the Yancha, the Dancong are usually not rolled and develop their full flavor accordingly fast when infused. The leaves require little wake-up time and the infusion times should be kept rather short. Dancong are richer than Yancha in floral and fruity aromas with a little more astringency, but are hardly bitter and more forgiving than Yancha in case of too lengthy infusions. High-quality representatives are additionally characterized by a long-lasting aftertaste. The following selection of Dancong is much shorter than the one on Yancha (which I mostly prefer, because they simply offer more oomph than the more delicate, floral Dancong). On the other hand, some of my personal favorites belong to the Dancong category, so my preference for Yancha is not at all disrespectful, but merely subjective.

BA XIAN 八仙

Eight Immortals	
Typical level of oxidation	Light
Typical roasting level	Medium, with charcoal
Cultivar	Ba Xian
Taste	Apricot, sweet potato, some cinnamon

Ba Xian is a very popular Dancong in the fruity to delicately nutty range.

GUI HUA XIANG 桂花香

Osmanthus Fragrance

There is nothing to say against Gui Hua Xiang at first, but if I want to taste strong osmanthus, I prefer to drink a tea flavored with osmanthus blossoms. The natural taste of the GHX has always proven too weak for me during our rare encounters, so I steer clear of it. Presumably my taste buds are just not sensitive enough.

HUANG ZHI XIANG 黄枝香

Gardenia Fragrance	
Typical level of oxidation	Medium
Typical roasting level	Strong
Cultivar	Shui Xian Huangzhi Xiang
Taste	Tropical flowers, apricots, orange blossoms

The Huang Zhi Xiang is one of my personal favorites. What I am looking for in HZX is the scent and taste of orange blossom. Unfortunately not every Huang Zhi Xiang that I have consumed so far was able to offer this aroma, but a good number of them gifted me with this outstanding scent and taste experience. To me, a Huang Zhi Xiang without a distinct orange blossom aroma is something unacceptable, even though I am certainly doing this tea wrong with this opinion. Even the 'without' versions have still been very pleasant and high-quality teas, but once I knew what could be expected, I was hardly satisfied with less any more. At least a strong aroma of fruits is to be expected, purely floral aromas would be really disappointing to me.

It is important not to buy a cheap fake, where orange blossom aroma has been added, either through chemistry or with real blossoms. The latter is quite common and acceptable for some teas, but here the aroma must derive purely from the leaves. An indication of a falsification could be that the tea smells extremely strong of orange even when dry or that the orange blossom dominates the first infusions. Like many oolongs, the Huang Zhi Xiang usually needs several infusions before it fully reveals its special orange blossom aroma.

MI LAN XIANG 蜜兰香

Honey Orchid Fragrance	
Typical level of oxidation	Medium to strong
Typical roasting level	Medium
Cultivar	Shui Xian Mi Lan Xiang
Taste	Flowery, honey, sweet

Depending on the individual taste and smell perception, connoisseurs of Mi Lan Xiang notice strong notes of orchids, hyacinths, gardenias or even osmanthus flowers. But as the name suggests, a hint of honey should always be clearly recognizable. Mi Lan Xiang was one of the first Dancongs I ever drank and I still like it very much. Because of the plentiful supply and the not exactly multifaceted (though distinct) taste it may not seem very exotic, but you can easily find excellent qualities at quite reasonable prices.

Mi Lan Xiang

MO LI XIANG 茉莉香

Jasmine Fragrance

At this point I have to keep a low profile, as I had promised in the introduction to only write about tea that I know well and ideally have tasted several times. I am looking forward to tasting it one day and compare it with a flavored jasmine tea. Therefore, this Dancong which naturally reminds of jasmine shall be mentioned here only for the sake of completeness.

PO TOU XIANG 姜花香

Ginger Flower Fragrance

Unfortunately, I have no experience with the Po Tou either, but I am listing it here, as it is one of the better known original Dancongs. I am aware of the fact that a friend of mine appreciates it very much, so there is a reason to look forward to his next visit. Perhaps you will have better luck than me and discover a competent source first.

SHUI XIAN 水仙

I already discussed Shui Xian and Lao Zhong Shui Xian in the section about Yancha, because Northern Fujian is said to be the ancient origin of this plant. As one of the most original cultivars it is certainly known and cultivated almost everywhere and also brings up decent Dancong, especially as it is considered the Mother of all Dancong, as stated before.

XING REN XIANG 杏仁香

Almond Fragrance	
Typical level of oxidation	Medium
Typical roasting level	Medium to strong
Cultivar	Ju Duo Zai
Taste	Almond, almond, almond, slightly floral with a little apple and occasionally anise
!	Insufficiently roasted, hastily and cheaply produced XRX is being spotted more and more frequently. Caution and testing of small quantities before making a purchase is advisable.

Another one of my personal favorites! Almond fragrance and taste clearly dominates over other secondary aromas. You have to try this oolong - unless you are allergic to almonds. Just kidding…

YA SHI XIANG 鴨屎香

Duck Shit, Duck Feces, Honeysuckle Fragrance	
Typical level of oxidation	Medium
Typical roasting level	Medium
Cultivar	Wu Ye
Taste	Charcoal, mineral, peach, mango, slightly floral
!	An alternative, but widely unknown Chinese name is Yin Hua Xiang 银花香 Honeysuckle fragrance

Duck Shit, also dubbed Duck Sh*t or Duck Feces in politically correct English is called Ya Shi Xiang in China, which means Duck Feces Scent. Is this naming particularly clever or particularly bad marketing? Legend has it that a tea farmer who gave that name to a tea tree intended to scare off thieves or overly eager neighbors by implying that the soil beneath it be rather unpleasant. At least the name has not hurt the popularity of the tea.

Ya Shi Xiang is by no means repulsive, but has a pleasant fruity and floral scent with a slight almond note. It tastes like it smells, but by far not as much of almonds as a Xing Ren Xiang, only a delicate touch of might be recognized.

The very tender almond taste usually disappears with the third infusion and then an explosion of geranium and pear juice taste occurs. From the sixth infusion onward I prefer to extend the infusion time up to 1 minute. The intensity then decreases gradually, but the Hui Gan (sweet or pleasant aftertaste, recurring feeling) fortunately remains.

If you can get hold of it, try a Xue Ya Shi. Xue 雪 or snow denotes a winter harvest. Normally one would not expect much from late picking, but with Ya Shi I was quite pleasantly surprised. The infusions were milder, softer, with less acidity, but therefore tender and well balanced.

Ya Shi Xiang

YOU HUA XIANG 柚花香

Pomelo Flower Fragrance

I also keep it brief with You Hua Xiang, I only drank it once and therefore I cannot really judge it fairly. Its scent promised much more than the cup could keep, so whenever I desire pomelo aroma in my tea, I prefer a You Xiang Hong (red tea flavored with real pomelo blossoms). There might be better You Hua Xiang produced but I am still in search of one..

ZHI LAN XIANG 芝兰香

Orchid Fragrance

Zhi Lan is a Dancong I appreciate less than others. Although I have no objection against floral aromas, I prefer Mi Lan Xiang, whose additional honey notes give it a softer and less perfumed appearance.

TAIWAN OOLONG

The Portuguese sailors who were roaming Taiwan (and Macau) centuries ago had a sixth sense, at least as far as tea was concerned, when they baptized the island with the western name Formosa. Even though Taiwan has not been called that way for a long time, "Ilha Formosa" (beautiful island) is indeed a proper hint for tea lovers, the Taiwan oolongs are among the best of all.

Furthermore, Taiwan[129] is famous for its high mountain teas, called Gao Shan Cha 高山茶. Some excellent teas are also grown at lower altitudes, such as in Mingjian at about 350 meters, the largest tea growing area in Taiwan. In this area mostly simpler teas are harvested by machine.

The first tea plants did not reach Taiwan before the middle of the 17th century, and they did not come alone. They were brought by immigrating tea farmers who cultivated them in their new homeland using tried and tested methods. Certainly of great influence on Taiwan's tea quality was the Cultural Revolution during and after which many a tea master who fled the mainland brought a boost of know-how to the island.

The most important (but not largest) tea regions in Taiwan are Lishan, Dong Ding, Alishan and Wenshan, and the most renowned tea is probably the Oriental Beauty, which is originally called by a different name.

One thing is for certain: if Japan is *the* green tea country, then Taiwan is Oolongland!

ALISHAN 阿里山

Alishan	
Typical level of oxidation	Light
Typical roasting level	Predominantly not up to only slightly roasted
Cultivar	Qing Xin, Jin Xuan, Si Ji Chun
Taste	Floral, also with a touch of herbs; long lasting aftertaste. Based on Jin Xuan rather milkily creamy and slightly sweet, based on Qing Xin more powerful, a bit sweeter and more floral/fruity.
!	Grown at altitudes between 1,000 and 1,400 meters.

Alishan, i.e. the mountain A Li 阿里, does not actually stand for a special tea, but for the most famous high-altitude growing area in Taiwan. Various smaller areas within Alishan produce very similar teas, which are sometimes (especially with high-quality tea) only marketed under their own name, so for example a Shi Zuo or Shan Xi is sold without the indication that it is an Alishan.

The other way round is also possible. Analog to wine, this would be like marketing an Antinori or a Brolio merely as Chianti and concealing the name of the vineyard. Similarly, like certain exceptional Chianti aged in barriques (so-called Supertuscans) such as Sassicaia or Tignanello are not marketed as Chianti (but rather under their own brand name), a decent amount of top-quality high mountain oolongs from Alishan are not being offered under that label. This is determined by the purchasers and middlemen as they see fit. Fortunately, many Alishan taste similarly well, full-bodied and well balanced. If you like one Alishan, you will mostly likely like the others as well, just like, as you may have guessed, with Chianti.

CUI YU 翠玉

Green Jade, Jade Oolong, Yu Oolong	
Typical level of oxidation	Light
Typical roasting level	Medium
Cultivar	TTES #13 Cui Yu
Taste	Fresh, flowery, minty

Like Si Ji Chun and Jin Xuan, Cui Yu is suitable for cultivation in the lowlands and, together with the other two cultivars, is probably one of the most popular in Taiwan. It is usually harvested and processed by machines, and is therefore quite inexpensive to obtain. Good quality smells slightly of jasmine and tastes a tad minty.

DONG DING 凍頂

Tung Ting, Frozen Summit	
Typical level of oxidation	Light to medium
Typical roasting level	Light, traditionally also stronger and with charcoal
Cultivar	Ruan Zhi or Qing Xin
Taste	Roasted grain, slightly nutty and buttery

Genuine Dong Ding hails from the central Taiwanese district of Nantou. It is probably the best known rolled Taiwan oolong. Mainland teas are also offered under that name, so care must be taken when buying if you want to obtain the original. The way the leaves are rolled is particularly characteristic to this tea. They are kneaded and rolled in cloths to form large balls, which are then crumbled apart again.

Dong Ding is cultivated at medium altitudes (at about 700 to 1,000 meters) and is therefore not considered a high mountain Tea. Especially Dong Ding is so well known for its taste that it has created its own style, and similar oolongs from other places are also marketed as Dong Ding, comparable to fake Da Hong Pao or Long Jing.

Dong Ding from 1999

The photo above shows an atypically dark Dong Ding in a plucking that deliberately uses stems. When fresh, the color of the Dong Ding resembles that of the Alishan or Lishan, but here the color gives away the age of that sample, being a 1999 vintage.

DONG FANG MEI REN 東方美人

Bai Hao Oolong, Eastern Beauty, Five Colour Tea, Oriental Beauty, White Tip Oolong	
Origin	Alishan and Zhushan, Taiwan
Color	Brownish
Typical level of oxidation	Strongly wilted and oxidized, approx. 70-75%
Typical roasting level	None
Cultivar	Ruan Zhi or Qing Xin Da Pa, Cui Yu, Jin Xuan, White Hair Monkey
Taste	Very complex: wood, honey, flowers, citrus aromas, lychee, white wine
Harvest time	In summer, when the cicadas swarm
!	Oriental Beauty was initially developed in Taiwan, but is now imitated in mainland China and also in Thailand. In rolled form there is a version called Gui Fei.

Oriental Beauty is the best-known name around the world for this so-called bug bitten tea, an unrolled oolong. Originally called Dong Fang Mei Ren, the literal translation is Oriental Beauty. With its look of dry foliage, the appearance of its leaves is closer to Bancha or Shou Mei than to other oolongs.

Its beauty lies in the taste and which comes from the unique treatment with of cicada bites. Being called Tea Jassids[130], the cicadas take hearty bites and gulps from the sap of the young leaves, the plant then reacts with increased production of polyphenols which add to positive taste and smell (for humans) and also repel the insects. Understandably, the leaves of the best harvests will not look flawless, they even show holes and brown spots (the scars evoked by being bitten). These are however microscopically small and therefore almost only visible in fresh leaves.

Another positive effect of the cicada bites is the fact that they provide evidence of pesticide-free cultivation, because if the tea farmers had sprayed too much, the insects would not have come to work in the first place (due to deaths in their families). However, a completely pesticide-free production is most likely one of the legends spread by traders. At least weeds, fungi and pathogens could still have been controlled by spraying. Fortunately, there are also biological weapons based on chili oil or chrysanthemums available that are considered safe for humans - and cicadas..

GUI FEI 贵妃

Precious Concubine

Gui Fei is a variation of Dong Fang Mei Ren, but rolled into the very typical ball shape of certain oolongs. It is often gently roasted and offers similar sweet honey notes.

JIN XUAN 金萱
NAI XIANG 奶香

Golden Daylily, Milk(y) Oolong, Milk Fragrance	
Typical level of oxidation	Light
Typical roasting level	Light to medium (stronger roasting makes the milk aroma stand out more during the first infusions)
Cultivar	TTES#12 Jin Xuan
Taste	Delicately milky, creamy
!	Also read the upcoming paragraphs on milk oolong.

Jin Xuan is the name of a widely popular (oolong) cultivar, as well as a tea with a strong milky fragrance, soft and pleasant to the tongue. Translated, its name means golden daylily, as the cultivar also offers a floral scent and taste. The name of the tea produced from this cultivar, which is particularly appreciated in Taiwan and Thailand, in China is Nai Xiang or milk scent.

The cultivar Jin Xuan is also used for the production of many other oolongs, it is a true allrounder. Not always is it offered under the name of its cultivar but frequently it is named after the mountain or region from which it derives. It is often cultivated in the lowlands but also well suited for high mountain teas. Jin Xuan guarantees a high yield and is also being flavored with additives (mostly flowers). Rarely Jin Xuan also serves as a basis for red tea.

MILK OOLONG

Milk or milky oolong deserves a special mention, because it is widely available in retail and often misleading stories are entwined around it.

There are two different kinds of milk oolong. The first one is plain Jin Xuan with its natural, soft, mild, light scent like boiling milk or milk powder. If you like that, then buy a high-quality Jin Xuan and enjoy it. It has a very delicate and calming effect in itself, similar to a cup of hot milk with honey, but without actual milk - or honey. A Jin Xuan oolong can certainly be enjoyed, although it often lacks the floral or fruity notes of other high-quality oolongs.

The fun stops with the second version, however. Some merchants spread the myth that the tea was steamed over boiling milk during production or, even more outlandishly, boiled in milk. I would like to see that - or rather not. This variant may be made of Jin Xuan, but the quality is often so despicable that (soy) milk powder is mixed under the leaves. Although this additive is commonly declared, I find the taste unnatural to unpleasant.

Good to excellent qualities do not need any additives, but lesser ones with only a faint inherent fragrance are often flavored. As long as the traders indicate that, this might be acceptable. Currently there seems to be an increased demand for Jin Xuan with additives, dealers also market some of them under the fantasy name Silk Oolong or a bit more fitting as Jin Xuan Nai Cha, thus milk tea.

LISHAN 梨山

Oolong from Lishan (Pear Mountain)	
Typical level of oxidation	Light
Typical roasting level	Light
Cultivar	Qing Xin and others
Taste	Similar but more fruity than other high mountains oolongs
!	Lishan is considered one of the best oolong growing areas in the world.

Like other high altitude regions, Lishan benefits from the cooler mountain air and humid fog. Among Taiwan's three most famous tea mountains or regions, Lishan is the highest with an altitude of 1,600 to 2,600 meters, followed by Alishan and Dong Ding. Correspondingly, and also because of its good reputation regarding quality, slightly higher prices are asked for it, since it is almost as high-altitude as the South Indian Kolukkumalai in Tamil Nadu, probably the highest tea garden in the world.

The same applies to Lishan as does to Alishan and partly also to Dong Ding: particularly precious teas are occasionally marketed under their own name, both with or without mentioning Lishan.

Lishan

MI XIANG 蜜香

Honey Fragrance	
Typical level of oxidation	Light
Typical roasting level	Strong
Taste	Honey, honey and more honey

Mi Xiang is frequently confused with Mi Lan Xiang. However, it does not feature the latter's floral orchid scent, but rather restricts itself quite one-dimensionally to the honey scent and taste and does so almost perfectly. Winnie-the-Pooh would love it!

MUZHA TIE GUAN YIN 木栅铁观音

Muzha Iron Goddess of Mercy	
Origin	Wenshan, Taipei Shi
Typical level of oxidation	Light to medium
Typical roasting level	Medium, charcoal
Cultivar	Ruan Zhi
Taste	More gentle and less complex or fruity than Anxi TGY; honey, spices, caramelized root vegetables

Let me be clear: the best TGY comes from Anxi, China. End of discussion. No matter what other level of quality is produced and offered, nothing comes close to Anxi.

Taiwan TGY tastes noticeably different, which is not only due to the stronger oxidation and roasting, but also due to the local climate and terroir.

In Taiwan the production is much closer to the classic, darker method. I actually like all kinds, classic, modern, or aged. Still I appreciate very much that most dealers clearly distinguish between Anxi and Muzha.

Muzha TGY aged for 20 years

POUCHONG 包种

Bao Zhong	
Origin	Muzha and Pinglin, Wenshan (but originally Anxi, China)
Typical level of oxidation	Less than 10 and up to a maximum of 20%
Cultivar	Qing Xin, Si Ji Chun, Jin Xuan, Cui Yu
Taste	More like a green tea, with green vegetable notes, yeasty, soft
!	Being wrapped in paper during production and also when drying, hence its name "the wrapped one".

Oolong being hand-wrapped in paper (symbolic picture, this is not Pouchong)

Pouchong or Bao Zhong is produced in Fujian province, especially in Anxi, as well as in Taiwan. In Taiwan, it is mainly grown in the north, namely in Wenshan's Pinglin district (lowlands) and in Dong Ding.

Baozhong is, to put it jokingly, a strongly oxidized green tea, which with a little luck might have become an oolong. So it somehow seems like a hybrid, and in my opinion it is not the most tasteful of teas. However, a tea blog recently gave me the idea to chill it after brewing and enjoy it like a cooled white wine. In fact I found it tasting much better that way.

QING XIN 青心

Green Heart	
Origin	Anxi, China
Typical level of oxidation	Varies widely
Typical roasting level	
Cultivar	Ruan Zhi
Taste	Osmanthus, orchids
!	Typical cultivar of many Taiwan oolongs, also Dong Fang Mei Ren and Bao Zhong

Qing Xin is probably the oldest and certainly the most used cultivar in Taiwan, accounting for more than 60% of the country's tea output. It is supposed to either descend from Ruan Zhi 軟枝 or to be identical with it, expert opinions differ on this point. Sometimes it is also transcribed as Luan Ze.

SI JI CHUN 四季春

Four Seasons Springtime, Evergreen	
Origin	Muzha, Wenshan, Taipei Shi
Typical level of oxidation	Light to medium
Typical roasting level	Medium
Cultivar	Si Ji Chun
Taste	Mellow, stone fruit, gardenia, less mineral than other high mountain oolongs.

Si Ji Chun was created by natural crossbreeding, is high-yielding and primarily grows in the Taiwanese lowlands and therefore has a relatively low price. The strong floral scent is often softened by a somewhat stronger oxidation.

The Si Ji Chun owes its name to the fact that it sprouts early and can be harvested all year round in equally decent to good quality.

OTHER REGIONS

On the Chinese mainland, oolong is also produced outside of the large and particularly well-known regions. If you start with some Yancha or Dancong plus some Anxi oolong you have already laid a good foundation.

Each of these areas has a wealth of different teas, which is hard to explore within only one reincarnation. However, if you search outside of these main regions, you will also find a wealth of interesting teas.

I have already smuggled two "foreign" oolongs into the section about Anxi oolongs, namely the Bai Ya Qi Lan and the Zhang Ping Shui Xian, at least they also originate in Southern Fujian. I could alternatively have renamed the section, but the term Anxi oolong is used so ubiquitously, it simply made sense to follow the majority.

There is very little oolong from other countries, only Japan offers a handful representatives of this type worth mentioning. Very rarely you can find oolong from India, but overall there is not much coming after China and a bit of Indochina, namely Thailand.

AGED OOLONG   陳年烏龍

As a tea buyer it is often impossible for me to know whether an older oolong has just been stored or whether it has been actively aged.

Storage is a self-explanatory term: an oolong is packed well and sealed airtight after production and a final, thorough drying, and then sold after 20, 30, or more years. Active aging, on the other hand, means that the oolong is woken up from its ripening sleep approximately every two or three years, to be gently re-roasted and dried again by tea professionals.

Very often dealers were not able to give me a convincing answer as to which method was applied to the produce I had laid my eyes on, but suspiciously often online dealers in particular tell the tale that suddenly/accidentally/unexpectedly they found a sack or a box from the 80s forgotten in a hidden corner of a warehouse and by lucky circumstances (I suspect "good Feng Shui" here) they were able to get hold of this unique treasure. So, if a tea remained unnoticed for 40 years, then of course it cannot have been touched every other year.

This is not to imply anything, but instead of "forgotten", perhaps the attribute "not sellable" would be more appropriate. If a tea did not meet the demands of the market a decade or more ago, then it was probably deliberately stockpiled first and after a few years one would check to see how it had developed or they would have forgotten it completely. After all, the business of most producers is the sale of fresh tea, and thus it is not surprising that the market for aged oolongs is quite small and also somewhat clandestine.

1972 Puli

Hence, it is quite plausible that merchants who actively search for it can still find such forgotten gems. Interestingly enough, these treasures often remain on the shelf or under the counter because there is little demand for them and they are often only available in small quantities. As a result, they are rarely offered online, at least in most European shops. My favorite aged oolongs were actually only available on demand, and some of the best Taiwanese ones were even stored at the retailer in my home country for almost ten years, from the time she acquired them in her home country. Fortunately, she never raised the price either, so I was able to stock up nicely for the next decade.

If you doubt the credibility of the age information, you are free to do so, it is of course not verifiable; but why should traders sugarcoat the age too much when they only have a batch of homeopathic quantities and call for fair prices? Tea traders get rich with other things (if at all), but certainly not with aged oolongs.

With the excellent quality I have been fortunate enough to enjoy, I would not care whether the tea is 20, 30 or 40 years old, as long as it tastes great. Age differences are quite noticeable once you have compared 50, 100, or more aged oolongs, especially if you know your favorites as a fresh, young product and can compare them in different stages of aging.

What I appreciate in terms of credibility is the fact that some dealers only give exact years if they can be sure for themselves. When they like a tea, but cannot determine the age with certainty, they may rather declare it as "from the 80s" etc.

Aged doesn't always have to taste better, but aged oolongs do always taste different than fresh ones. To qualify as aged, an oolong should have matured for at least seven years. The young oolongs that we allow to mature at home for a few more years in a good packaging are by no means to be called aged. Some friends and I prefer to let some fresh, fine, green oolongs mature for a couple of quarters for better taste, but this does not make them aged.

To me aged oolongs are of interest starting at a minimum age of 15 to 20 years, at around 30 years the fun really starts. Most of the seven to ten year old oolongs on offer are actively aged (instead of just stored). Here the popular Tie Guan Yin is frequently promoted, but sadly it seems that the material used there is rather average and roasted far too vigorously over charcoal. In my opinion it is justifiable to pour away the wash and if necessary even do a second rinse, but if the taste is still like licking off a grill grate, the fun stops. Either inferior quality was intentionally covered up or the tea master by the fire was not very masterly. At the latest by the third infusion there has to be a different aroma in the cup but charcoal.

Speaking of aroma, that is what the aged oolongs are all about. Creamy, tender and yet ripe, somehow indescribable, often given away a nice dry fruits aroma. To me real aged oolongs are almost a category of their own, so very different from their younger peers.

Aged Da Hong Pao, which I really appreciate when fresh, has not yet managed to make me overly happy. Like the aforementioned TGY, they were often of rather mediocre quality, roasted way too much, but still quite expensive and hard to find. A well aged DHP with an age of over 30 years would certainly be worth a try but so far I have only been able to get hold of seven to 20 year old ones.

Also a Pouchong from 1978 could not convince me. Quite green by nature, 40 years have done it little good. In general I am not a big friend of Pouchongs anyway, but in this case I even liked the fresh version more. I wonder if the 78 was not produced properly? We could not detect any improper aromas when drinking, but it seems to have been confirmed again that oolongs oxidized too lightly do not gain as much from aging as the redder ones.

Wen Shan Pouchong 1978

Real vintage TGYs have all been produced according to the classic, darker method, like the current favorite in my collection is also a red oolong. It is a 1972 vintage from the rather low-lying city of Puli in central Taiwan, not far from the famous Sun-Moon-Lake.

Dong Ding in its aged version has also always been a pleasure. My 20 to 30 year old collector's items are still in top shape and taste particularly fresh compared to some other vintage tea.

1987 Dong Ding

RED TEA (HONG CHA) 红茶

As mentioned earlier, black tea, or in China red tea, is completely oxidized. During the production process, the leaves have been exposed to a maximum of oxygen and developed correspondingly strong aromas. Nevertheless, the infusions are often still pleasantly mild and floral, only much stronger than other tea types, darker and sometimes malty or with a hint of honey.

There is not much roasting done (as with oolongs), so there is no need to mention the level of oxidation or roasting. In addition, an individual preparation recommendation is practically superfluous, because Hong Cha is always steeped with boiling water up to 100°C. The number of infusions is usually limited between two and five, and the infusion time is typically rather long. 60, 45, 60 and then 90 seconds are a nice rule of thumb, but it is also possible to use considerably more leaf material and reduce the infusion time. However, the fully oxidized leaf requires some time to open up - at least if we are talking about whole leaf tea.

DIAN HONG 云南滇紅

Yunnan Black	
Origin	Jinggu
Color	Black with gold highlights
Cultivar	Yunkang and Da Ye Zhong
Taste	Malt, molasses, delicate floral sweetness
!	Red tea on a large scale has only been produced in Yunnan for about 80 years.

Dian Hong to me is one of the underrated teas or best kept secrets in the world tea market. The term Dian is the short form of the province name Yunnan, and the name itself holds no further secrets. Dian Hong or Red Yunnan may not sound like much and the tea is usually available at a very reasonable price - so what might be expected? Besides the simple, machine-picked and processed varieties, there are also some excellent qualities offered which still provide a very good price-performance ratio. Top-quality offers show the typical golden tips and should have recognizable whole leaves, whereas broken leaves reduce the quality considerably.

Dian Hong

Dian Hong has the typical malty aroma of an Assamica black tea but also has a very fine and floral aroma with very little astringency. Sensitive palates may therefore enjoy it even more than some Indian teas. Its delicate bouquet might taste even more flowery and fine if the same leaf material is used to produce white tea, resulting in the popular Yue Guang Bai or White Moonlight. A so-called Yunnan Black Moonlight is also being offered but in my opinion does not do justice to White Moonlight or decent Dian Hong - at least not from the samples I have been able to try yet. It simply appeared to me like a low-quality Dian Hong which was given a more mundane name for marketing purposes.

A notable Dian Hong is the Da Xue Shan[131] 大雪山, also known as Wild Beauty or Big Snowy Mountain in English. With an altitude of exactly 3,500 meters, this mountain certainly constitutes a regional landmark, but of course the tea is not grown at the mountain's maximum altitude. However, its terroir and microclimate have allowed around 2,000 hectares of large leaf and often wild tea trees to grow, yielding an excellent tea quality that deserves its reputation. The plants are about 50 years of age and thus possess considerably greater age-related qualities than other plantation reds. In addition to the typical aromas of red tea, a hint of cocoa or chocolate can frequently be detected. Good quality is picked and rolled by hand.

HONG YU 红玉

Red Jade, Ruby #18	
Origin	Taiwan
Cultivar	TTES #18 Hong Yu, Assamica #8
Taste	Malty, fruity, honey, cinnamon, sandalwood, mint

Hong Yu

As a Taiwanese proprietary development (hybrid) Hong Yu is characterized by its fresh mouthfeel and simultaneous spiciness.

JIN JUN MEI 金骏眉

Golden Steed Eyebrow	
Origin	Wuyishan, Fujian
Color	Medium brown, caramel
Cultivar	Cai Cha
Taste	Honey, malt, hardly astringent
!	As a rare exception from red teas, JJM prefers to be steeped at just over 80°C. Jin Jun Mei belongs to the category of Mei Cha眉茶, tea in the shape of delicate eyebrows. Commonly, Mei Cha is considered to be green tea like Zhen Mei (also known as Chun Mee) 珍眉, meaning precious eyebrow.

Jin Jun Mei

As previously mentioned in the section on oolongs, two well-known reds are also considered to be Yancha, the Zheng Shan Xiao Zhong following a bit later in this section and this Jin Jun Mei, which are both native to Wuyishan.

Genuine, top-class Jin Jun Mei is made almost exclusively from buds (sometimes also an additional small, first leaf) and tastes correspondingly sweet and fine. The "buds only" plucking and the gentle processing explains its high price. JJM looks rather pale and delicate for a red tea.

JIUQU HONG MEI 九曲紅梅

Nine Bend Red Plum, Long Jing Hongcha, Long Jing Black Tea	
Origin	Meijawu at Westlake or around Longjing, near Hangzhou, Zhejiang
Cultivar	Long Jing No. 43
Taste	Plum, citrus notes and delicate smoke

Considering the fact that the green Long Jing is world famous, it is a little surprising how little the Hong Mei from the same region is known. The late summer harvests of the same fields from which the dragon well tea is produced in spring are now processed for red tea. The larger, stronger leaves tolerate the more vigorous processing more readily and still produce fine teas.

From the many red teas based on Assamica, this small leaf Sinensis stands out favorably. The name is composed of the location Jiuqu (the river with the nine bends), the tea variety (red) and the aroma (plum). Even though it tastes completely different from green LJ, it is a must-try for fans of the original and very hard to get in top quality.

Jiuqu Hong Mei

QI MEN 祁门

Qimen Keemun	
Origin	Qi Men, Anhui
Color	Black
Cultivar	Qimen Zhu Ye, nowadays many other cultivars are also used
Taste	Floral with a touch of red wine(barrel)

Keemun

Keemun hails from the district of the same name in Anhui province and is usually counted among the ten famous teas. It was the first non-green tea produced in Anhui at the end of the 19th century. Keemun tastes a little woody, sometimes in the direction of pine, perhaps also slightly bitter, but it hardly becomes unpleasantly bitter even after being steeped for a long time. It smells mostly floral but tastes more like dark fruit. Its special aroma is attributed to the misty mountain region in which it thrives.

There are many different kinds of Keemun, some of which do not even originate from Anhui. On the one hand, this shows the admiration it receives everywhere, on the other hand it makes it more difficult for the consumer to source decent quality.

A special variant is the Qi Men (Hong) Mao Feng, which despite the addition of the suffix Mao Feng is not a green tea, as you would normally associate with it. Instead, it expresses a special quality level, namely a very early spring picking with many budding tips, traditionally baked over charcoal.

As with many other teas, the search for something special pays off here. The range between modest and outstanding quality of Qi Men is particularly wide, certainly also due to its popularity or fame.

ZHENG SHAN XIAO ZHONG 正山小种

Lapsang Souchong, Bohea Lapsang, Smoke Tea	
Origin	Zheng Shan region of the Wuyi Mountains, Fujian
Color	Black
Cultivar	Tongmu Qi Zhong
Taste	Chocolate, liquorice, rose, longan, (smoke, whisky)
Suggested preparation	As a small leaf tea with quite subtle notes, it should not be infused with fully boiling water, unlike most other black teas. 90° to 95°C usually do suffice.
!	Intentionally very smoky qualities are sometimes indicated by the prefix tarry.

I became aware of at least two teas due to watching certain TV series. The first one was Earl Grey (Star Trek), the other one was Lapsang Souchong (The Mentalist). In almost every episode of The Mentalist the protagonist drank this Yancha (sic!) and it just made me curious. What was that? A smoked black tea? That sounded strange and not really tempting, so I had to give it a try. In addition, the hero drove a "divine" car, the Citroën DS, which increased his coolness factor even more... Luckily I got the tea in quite good quality at my first attempt, maybe because I did not choose the cheapest supplier. In the following years I was not always that lucky, the differences in quality in the market are tremendous.

After a large number of attempts and disappointments, as well as teachings from professionals, I had to recognize that the most-known feature of the ZSXZ usually only occurs when it is marketed as Lapsang Souchong, outside of Asia, and is praised as smoked tea.

Lapsang Souchong in the cup it is a little like Chop Suey on the plate. Nobody in China knows what to do with these supposedly Chinese names, unless they are in the trade or otherwise in contact with Westerners. Whenever I praised an excellent Lapsang Souchong to a Chinese person, I encountered merely uncomprehending faces. It is important to be aware of this fact, if you want to drink or buy such tea in China. Some online shops may offer this tea under the western name, often in the strong Tarry Lapsang Souchong version. Luckily, some retailers meanwhile have understood that there are two completely different types of ZSXZ around and are now doing a good job distinguishing between them.

This red tea originates from the Zheng Shan region of the Wuyi Mountains[132] in Fujian, hence the name. Xiao Zhong simply means small leaf tea or small variant. Its special feature is for it to be smoked over pine wood. This (often) lends it a harsh and smoky taste. Interestingly, the dry leaves of cheaper versions often smell rather unpleasantly of grilled pork rind, but the resulting infusion can still end up being quite mild and tasty. If these barbecue aromas remain in the infusion, I consider this to be a product fault or insinuate that the producer has tried to mask inferior leaf quality by overlaying it with smoky aroma. This almost gives rise to the suspicion that the spice rack was secretly accessed during production. The smoke smell must not taste pungent under any circumstances.

To simplify matters, one can conclude that when we buy Lapsang Souchong outside of Asia we usually get the rather smoky version (in lousy to decent quality). Those who are looking for the original (with only very minimal hints of smoke) should rather ask for Zheng Shan Xiao Zhong. This increases chances to get the authentic one.

ZSXZ is ideally brewed with water almost boiling (90°C+) and, unlike most other Chinese teas, the western method (larger pot, brewing time over two minutes) is working quite well, if you ask me.

Zheng Shan Xiao Zhong

DARK TEA (HEICHA) 黑茶

We are now getting to dark (黑 means dark or black) tea, which is completely different from what the Non-East Asians know as black tea (which the Chinese call Hong Cha, i.e. red tea). Heicha is either naturally or artificially post-fermented and often also aged tea.

Some of these teas undergo the artificial Wodui 渥堆 or heap process, which is done by first inoculating fresh tea with a cocktail of microbes and then further exposing it to humid heat for several weeks. The latter is what I called composting in the section on yellow tea, only for the yellow to be exposed to the moist heat for a much shorter time.

Teas intended to post-ferment without undergoing the accelerated wodui depend on the microorganisms occurring naturally in their region, in order to develop over much longer time. Strictly speaking, they cannot be classified as post-fermented right after production, after a short time the natural fermentation process starts anyway, even if changing color or taste may take years. For the sake of simplicity, all teas that are either marketed as post-fermented or are intended for post-fermentation are summarized here (and by most resellers).

One might wonder about very old (aged) oolongs, does fermentation play a role in their profound change of taste over 20, 30 or more years? Actually not, because whereas heicha is pressed into shape while it is still wet, oolong is dried vigorously at the end of production, which leaves little water for microbial growth. Furthermore, aged oolong is not stored openly like heicha, but sealed, packed airtight, and sometimes even buried in the earth in clay vessels - or frozen, like in Japan. In fact, every now and then oolongs or red (and always the yellow) teas are subjected to a mini-wodui, called Qiang Zhi Wodui Fa Jiao 强制渥堆发酵. But only a very brief fermentation is applied then to release further flavors from the tea, and in contrast to heicha this happens during production and not at the end.

Apart from Shu Pu'er, the following regional heicha, among others, are produced with more or less powerful wodui methods:

- Hua Zhuan (Hunan)
- Liu Bao (Guangxi)
- Liu'an (Anhui)
- Qing Zhuan (Hubei)

By far the best known among all heicha is probably Pu'er, which we will discuss in the section on Yunnan heicha. However, we will also introduce some heicha from other Chinese regions, which are equally worth mentioning. Despite not being in alphabetical order, we will start with Yunnan. Subsequent regions will be presented alphabetically.

SHAPES OF TEA

Heicha is rather rarely[133] offered in loose leave form, at least in Yunnan it is almost always sold in pressed shape. Mostly unfinished Mao Cha, which is later used for the production of pressed teas, is offered loose.

Since I, as already mentioned, do not intend to dive deeply into the history of tea, I will only briefly mention the reasons why heicha was originally compressed. When centuries ago tea was still transported from the tea-growing areas to the consumers by horse or donkey back, saving space was the first priority. However, whereas back then the leaf material was first shredded and later pressed, today, thank Buddha, people prefer whole leaves. Nowadays, pressing is mainly used for conservation and preparation for the lengthy ripening phase.

The following table provides an overview of the most common pressing methods, but by no means claims to be complete.

Most common shapes of pressed tea

English	Pinyin	中文
Cake	Bing Cha	饼茶
Brick	Zhuan Cha	砖茶,
Bird's Nest	Tuo Cha	沱茶
Pumpkin, Golden Melon	Jin Gua	金瓜
Dragon Ball, Dragon Pearl	Long Zhu	龙珠

Bings[134] are usually produced with a weight of 357g, but there are also increasingly larger and especially smaller versions available. They are predominantly used in Yunnan, but other provinces are reacting to the positive response on the international market and have also started offering bings. Yunnan does not limit bings only to heicha, but also offers white tea and Moonlight White in this shape. This makes sense, as the pressing process allows the white tea to mature well from the outside to the inside and gain even more flavor. Red tea in bing form can also be found, but rather infrequently.

Zhuan Cha[135] 砖茶 or brick tea is the most original of the tea forms that used to be traded on the tea routes and usually weighs between 100g and 1kg, with a tendency towards the heavier. Lighter varieties are called Fang Cha 方茶 or square tea. Both varieties can sometimes be found in a shape reminiscent of a chocolate bar, from which portions can be broken off easily. The material used is often much coarser than that of bings.

This convenience, on the other hand, is sought in vain in Tuo Cha 沱茶 (nest tea) or Jin Cha 紧茶 (mushroom tea). While the Tuo really looks like a bird's nest, the Jin features an additional stem and therefore looks similar to a mushroom. These two shapes provide some thrill when it comes to cutting them up or rather breaking off pieces suitable for the pot. I urge caution and, if necessary, the use of a chain glove, just like the one worn when opening oysters, or else the Guild of Hand Surgeons looks forward to spontaneous visits. In the old days, Tuo Cha had a hole in the middle to make it easier to handle and transport, similar to old Chinese money.

Mini bings with only about 5g of weight

Larger than a Tuo and featuring stripes or indentations on the upper side, the shape of the former tribute tea Jin Gua 金瓜 or Golden Melon is rarely seen. Formerly also used for Sheng, today this form is, if at all, almost exclusively used for Shu Pu'er.

Also quite rare in Europe are teas in roll or column shape, which are pressed either into bamboo canes, wickerwork or clay tubes, left to ferment inside of them. The teas are then sold in these same bamboo canes or baskets or even in sturdy cardboard rolls under names such as Dragon Pole, etc. They can be "easily" tackled with a pad saw, as often the Pu'er tea knife does not suffice. This also provides an excellent alternative use for the oyster glove mentioned above.

The Long Zhu 龙珠 or dragon pearl usually weighs only five to eight grams and is ideally suited for single portions or for preparing Gong Yi Cha. Such balls are also available made of white and red teas. Quality and price vary significantly, seven or eight grams can cost anywhere from a few cents to double-digit Euro amounts, and most of them taste just as good as their price is high.

Various dragon pearls of different qualities

As mentioned before, due to the predominance of Pu'er, the overview of the most important heicha does not begin alphabetically with Anhui, but with Yunnan instead. In my opinion, it would be incorrect to call the following section "Pu'er", especially since producers from other regions already started labeling their post-fermented tea as Pu'er, even if they are not even made in China. As is well known, some Asian nations are said to be particularly good counterfeiters, but they themselves see things differently and regard imitations merely as a tribute to the manufacturer of the original. Anyhow, we will now begin with Yunnan Pu'er and then all the rest follows in alphabetical order.

Tuo, the bird's nest

YUNNAN HEICHA 云南 黑茶

In the tea business no one actually talks about Yunnan heicha, rather exclusively the synonym Pu'er is used. The city of Pu'er, which once changed its name to Simao, only to rename itself back to Pu'er because of its tea's great success, is name-giving and formative for practically all Yunnan heicha.

There are usually two variants, the Sheng or raw Pu'er 生普洱 and the Shu[136] or ripe/cooked Pu'er 熟普洱. The distinction between these two variants is technically quite simple.

Tea landscape in Yunnan

SHENG 生 OR SHU 熟, A QUESTION OF PERSONAL PREFERENCE

While Sheng is merely a Mao Cha pressed into discs (bings), i.e. unfinished green tea, for the production of **Shu** the Mao Cha is subjected to an accelerated fermentation or wodui. This is essentially a composting process in which several hundred kilograms of Mao Cha are piled up to a height of about one meter, moistened with water[137] and then "cooked" (giving the Shu its name) under tarpaulins for about 60 days. This process of fermentation must take place at a certain temperature of around 60°C, in order to support exactly the right fungi and bacteria that promise a desirable end result. During this two-month phase, the moist pile is constantly monitored and turned over frequently to ensure even maturation.

Mao Cha piled up for production of Shu Pu'er

Sheng 生 translates to life and health as well as raw. Purists often criticize the classification of fresh, young Sheng into the category heicha, because it has not yet been subjected to fermentation. Whilst this might be technically correct, still the maturation process or post-fermentation begins immediately after pressing the bing, because before pressing the Mao Cha was softened and moulded with water vapor. This moisture, together with the microorganisms present in the air and water of Yunnan, initiates the long-lasting natural ripening process. So we can pragmatically count Sheng Pu'er among the heicha, even though it neither looks nor tastes dark when young. Overly correct, one would only count Lao Sheng 老生, i.e. mature or old Sheng, among the heicha.

At the beginning of the 1970s, the popularity of aged Sheng increased significantly, and so did the prices. Many Chinese climbed the social ladder up into the middle class and more and more demand also came from abroad. Although aging can be accelerated by storing Sheng in a humid environment, it is often at the expense of quality and price, and even the so-called wet storage cannot simply compensate for many years of natural aging. Therefore, the process of wodui 渥堆 mentioned before was applied to Yunnan Mao Cha with the goal to develop an aroma in two months which would have taken 20 years or more if the tea had been allowed to matured naturally.

In my opinion, this plan has failed brilliantly. Shu Pu'er to me is something completely different from Sheng Pu'er, a comparison is almost impossible. But there is something wonderful in this failure, because good Shu offers a whole new range of aromas in addition to Sheng.

Externally, this is already visible in the color of both the leaves and in the cup. Fresh Sheng usually looks more green, whereas Shu typically appears dark brown. Well aged Sheng typically reaches this color only after a decade of aging. The infusion of Sheng is often yellow to amber in color, while Shu produces a reddish-brown, dark cup. Shengs usually taste fresh, fruity and also bitter, whereas Shus taste rather earthy, woody and hardly astringent.

Shu is not always ready to drink right away. Often the tea evaporates the typical smell of wodui for up to two years. Very careful production or a well ventilated storage can shorten the recommended waiting time until consumption. Although decades of storage result in much less aroma development in Shu compared to Sheng, some connoisseurs also prefer to drink Shu that has already been matured for five to ten years, it then tends to taste more creamy and certainly no longer shows any wodui.

PACKAGING AND TRADEMARKS

Producers of Pu'er usually place the Nei Fei 内飞, a small piece of paper with their company logo printed on it, into the mould to make life a little harder for counterfeiters. After pressing, the tea often bonds with the paper and the bing is then usually packed in thin paper. Sometimes another (larger) authentication paper is added as well, called Nei Piao 内票. This may show praise for the tea or the history of the tea factory. Then follows the outer, more sturdy wrapper, on which details of the tea are written. Even if you do not read Chinese, at least the date, the year of production and the factory name might be recognizable and sometimes also the recipe[138], in case it happens to be a so-called number(ed) tea from a larger factory. Factory teas also offer the advantage that additional information[139] may be found on the Internet by using the QS code. Usually the dealer will already provide further details in western languages. Old Pu'er bings may also carry a Tong Piao 筒票, a further marking in the Tongs 筒, i.e. the seven discs held together with bamboo leaves or wrapping paper.

Some Nei Fei and Nei Piao are so appealing that some enthusiasts collect them like stamps.

Bingdao Gushu with Nei Fei and Nei Piao

QUALITY AND ANCIENT TREES

As with all teas, the quality of Pu'er depends on many factors. The most common classification is based on the age of the trees. Wild and/or at least old trees (Gushu 古树) form the pride of creation here, followed by feral (and thus almost renaturalized) plantations. The material of these overgrown bushes (Yefang 野放) can be recognized in the trade by the label Shengtai, which almost corresponds to an organic quality. The bottom end of the scale is characterized by modern plantations, whose bushes 灌木 only produce the quality Taidi 台地 and which were grown from cuttings instead of seeds.[140]

Tea trees

While it is undisputed that older trees tend to produce the better Pu'er (apart from rare exceptions and provided that the work is done by hand), the demand for tea from old trees lures some people into questionable marketing methods. Therefore I will need to make some additional comments on the previous chapter on sourcing, especially regarding Pu'er.

It is commonly accepted that Gushu denotes trees that are more than 300 years old and Dashu means at least 100 years (this is also a matter of some controversy, but we do not want to get into that discussion). According to rules of simplicity, most buyers seem to be convinced that Gushu is better than Dashu and in any case Dashu is better than Taidi. So it is tempting for untrained or unscrupulous traders to call their tea Gushu, no matter how sad it tastes. This is not to put vendors under general suspicion of malice, because incorrect information may have various reasons:

- the tea farmer themself has no precise knowledge of the age of his trees
- the trader has been cheated upon and/or is a bit gullible
- the dealer or intermediary has misunderstood figures
- the trader deliberately acts fraudulently

The situation only becomes annoying when, for any of the above reasons, dealers who have only just begun to offer Pu'er start tossing around Gushu qualities just like this. The age of the trees is sometimes advertised as 1,000 or even more years, with the price per bing (357g) ranging anywhere between 100 to 300 Euros. Every connoisseur knows that tea from such old trees would have to cost a considerable four-digit amount, if sold or exported at all. Some trees that are known to be very old and to produce top qualities are bought by rich Chinese people nowadays, fenced in and only used for private harvests. Realistically, affordable "Gushu" material in the trade comes from trees that are perhaps 100 to 200 years old, and is therefore still Dashu by most estimates.

Other marketers do not participate in this age competition at all, but rather offer their own blends. In other words, blends of different terroirs and qualities, without the customer receiving any further details about the product. If this means that their most expensive teas will taste best, this might be a reasonable approach. Personally, I would like to know more, so this approach is not to my liking - how can I increase my level of expertise if I practically always taste blindly?

In my opinion the best approach at Pu'er is to order a yet unknown tea in small sample quantities (breaks off a bing) and compare them thoroughly. What does the leaf material look like, how does the tea taste? Only then do I order entire bings of teas that were previously unknown to me.

TWO WAYS TO GET STARTED

Now, as a beginner, how do you start if you want to get to know Pu'er? On the one hand, you can confide in a dealer who specializes in Pu'er and/or heicha. Not just one who offers a handful of teas and has little more to tell about them, but one who stocks this type of tea predominantly in their portfolio. Calling or visiting such dealers aight bring a lot of useful information, or at least visiting their website.

If you do not (yet) know such a trader, you may orientate yourself in two directions. Either you may purchase tea of one or more factories, or you may start by getting some samples from different regions. Let's have a look at the regional approach first.

REGIONS

If I wanted to list all the tea mountains and villages of Yunnan, I would certainly need more than one book. If I wanted to taste all of them, I would probably need more than one lifetime. That is why I deliberately simplify a lot by stating the following:

There are three prefectures in Yunnan worthy of special attention regarding Pu'er: Lincang[141], Pu'er and Xishuangbanna (and partly Baoshan, too).

When I look at my private inventory of more than 100 Pu'er, these are mostly teas from Xishuangbanna and not that many from Lincang and the Pu'er prefecture itself.

If this is not a coincidence, Xishuangbanna seems to be the measure of all things. In fact, there are many tea mountains west and east of the Lancang River (better known to us as the Mekong).

The following table lists the most popular areas. Their names (in the left column) usually denote mountains[142] or mountainous regions, but sometimes they just stand for individual villages that have acquired a special reputation. The often mentioned "Six famous tea mountains" are also listed here. I have not listed them separately, because meanwhile there are already two areas claiming the name Six famous tea mountains[143], the classic and the modern ones, in which some mountains even overlap. I do not want to add to this confusion. Recently, advertisers have been trying to actively promote seven mountains, so I rather stay out of this game.

The most popular tea mountains and regions in Yunnan

Area	Region	Note
Ailao	Zhenyuan, Pu'er	Many peaks above 3000m, real high mountain tea. According to the prevailing opinion, the teas are strongest in the north and become increasingly milder towards the south.
Bada	Menghai, Xishuangbanna	Located on the border to Myanmar, this is probably the largest and oldest area with wild tea trees.
Banpen	Menghai, Xishuangbanna	Very close to Lao Banzhang and so appreciated that its material is already offered under its own name. Full-bodied, but somewhat more reserved than LBZ or Lao Man E.
Bangwei	Lancang, Pu'er	Very small area.
Banzhang	Menghai, Xishuangbanna	Belonging to Bulang, known for the famous Lao Banzhang, the undisputed "King of Pu'er Teas".
Baoshan	Baoshan	Bordering Fengqing and Yongde.
Bingdao	Shuangjiang, Lincang	Also known as the "Queen of Pu'er", analogous to Lao Banzhang.
Bulang	Menghai, Xishuangbanna	Famous for Banzhang, Lao Banzhang, Jiliang, Lao Man E, Mannuo, Padian and many more.
Da Mengsong	Menghai, Xishuangbanna	Only a few old trees and many new plantings. Naka is the most renowned part within Da Mengsong.
Da Xue Shan	Shuangjiang, Lincang	Also known for outstanding Dian Hong.

Area	Region	Note
Dehong	Yunnan	Dehong is located northwest of Lincang on the southwest border of China to Myanmar, virtually bypassing Myanmar from three sides. Large supply of loose (not pressed) Ye Sheng (Wild Purple).
Gedeng	Mengla, Xishuangbanna	Small area with few old trees, many recent plantings.
Fengqing	Linxiang, Lincang	Fengqing is also known for first class Dian Hong.
Hekai	Menghai, Xishuangbanna	Large, old and partly wild tea gardens.
Jiangcheng	Jiangcheng, Pu'er	Bordering on Laos, many new plantations are emerging in this area.
Jingdong	Jingdong, Pu'er	Includes Ai Lao and Wuliang.
Jinggu	Jinggu, Pu'er	Situated in the southwest of Wuliangshan. Known for good balance between sweetness and bitterness as well as a large amount of Gushu.
Jingmai	Lancang, Pu'er	Known for particularly many wild tea trees in the forest between other trees. This results in deep shading and very organic quality. Jingmai borders on Menghai.
Kunlu	Ning'er, Pu'er	Largest number of old and wild trees in Pu'er. Legend has it that in the past the tea was shipped exclusively to the imperial court and the trees were guarded by the army.
Lao Man E	Menghai, Xishuangbanna	Belongs to Bulang, with over 75% old tea gardens.
Lao Mansa	Mengla, Xishuangbanna	Part of Yiwu.
Mangzhi	Mengla, Xishuangbanna	Very few old trees, many replantings. Rather average qualities. Located between Gedeng, Manzhuang and Yibang.
Mannuo	Menghai, Xishuangbanna	Bordering on Lancang with only a few old trees left. Belongs to Bulang.
Manzhuan	Mengla, Xishuangbanna	Many young growing areas with large plantations.
Mengku	Lincang	Largest number of old and wild trees in Lincang.

Area	Region	Note
Mengsong	Menghai, Xishuangbanna	Many young growing areas. Bordering on Myanmar and there is a certain assumption that material from there is declared as Pu'er from Mengsong. Known for both particularly sweet and particularly bitter varieties.
Nannuo	Menghai, Xishuangbanna	Weather divide between Menghai and Linghong.
Pasha	Menghai, Xishuangbanna	Located between Nannuo and Bulang, belongs to Nannuo.
Wuliang	Pu'er	Wuliang stretches up to Dali in the north and features a broad spectrum of terroirs, so individual teas can vary greatly. Mainly wild plants.
Xiao Mengsong	Jinghong, Xishuangbanna	With a maximum altitude of 1.500m relatively low-lying and known for its unconventional taste.
Yibang	Mengla, Xishuangbanna	Mainly old trees of various cultivars.
Yongde	Lincang	Da Xue Shan (Big Snow Mountain) is probably the most famous peak in Yongde. The region claims more than 1,000 trees with an age of more than 1,000 years, which grow in veritable forests.
Youle	Jinghong, Xishuangbanna	Also known as Jinuo.
Yiwu	Mengla, Xishuangbanna	Very well known and popular region. Includes the Mansa area.
Zhenyuan	Pu'er	Bordered by the Ailao and Wuliang Mountains in the southwest.

Now how to use this table? After all, it only gives very little detail about differences in taste! So if you intend to explore Pu'er by starting with a select region, you may simply pick some samples from their different areas first, as by now you already know the most important ones. Still, you may not be able to relate most teas on the market directly to a region. By the way, do you remember the chapter on deciphering tea names earlier in the book?

Well, I could name some differences in taste that I have noticed myself, but there are a few reasons for not doing so:

- many teas taste quite similar
- the teas from different areas within a region may taste very differently
- one may never know for sure whether the material in question is in fact coming from a neighboring region

And yet I cannot refrain from stating my personal preferences. After I had gotten my hands on a lot of Pu'er from Yiwu by coincidence in the beginning, I generally thought Pu'er was a little weak in aroma. Some of the ladies in our tea circle swear by Yiwus, perhaps they have a more sensitive nose and palate than some carriers of the Y chromosome. Indeed, there are also very aromatic and stronger Yiwu, but I tend to stick to my personal judgement.

For me, it was the Bulangs that really hit home, with their enormous power or Cha Qi and also their special bitterness, together with their unmatched Hui Gan.

Many Jingmais are much milder and softer, but still far more substantial in my opinion than most Yiwus. At first I had underestimated Jingmai, so I had to literally drink myself into it and soon realized that Shengs that were too young often needed some time to develop. Often after six to twelve months the beginning fermentation had shown its first subtle effects. I was particularly impressed by representatives from Gulan, Mangjong and Nanzuo. In general, I was practically never disappointed by Jingmais.

Different bings in two sizes (Bulang 100g and Jingmai 357g)

The other extreme among my favorites, the Bulangs I even drink very fresh, but then I know what to expect. I have already mentioned more about this in the chapter on Tea tasting.

Among the Bulangs, the Lao Banzhang is undoubtedly the most popular, powerful and aromatic. However, when you realize that even as a young tea in China, this tea is traded in the high three-digit to medium four-digit range (for Gushu) per bing, you wonder how authentic the product can be on the western market, when offered at lower prices.

For me and many others, second place goes to Lao Man E, less well known but still very expensive. It is less subtle, but even stronger and more bitter. For me, the price vs. performance ratio in the high-quality range feels more than appropriate. I also enjoy particularly pleasant Bulangs from Jiliang or Padian, for example.

Bingdaos I often got to know as slightly minty-fresh and pleasant. I always found tea from Mansa boring, but I felt the same with Ailao, until I was allowed to taste an Ao Ne Me from Ailao, which showed me a completely different, pleasant side of the Ailao mountains.

I enjoy the search for Pu'er from my favorite areas, but also the discovery of new areas. So please take the previous statements for what they are: a personal preference, nothing more and nothing less. I am sure that in almost every region mentioned in the table, you will find top quality teas.

The orientation by tea factory instead of region can be no less exciting, so just read on.

TEA FACTORIES

One might assume that the market for Pu'er would be more transparent than the market for loose leaf tea. Heicha are almost always marketed pressed, often clearly marked by the printed front and rear sides of the wrappers. Unfortunately this is not quite so.

State and private tea factories, both big and small, buy freshly harvested leaves or Mao Cha from farmers in their region and (hopefully) their circle of trust, then sort and blend this material and finally press and market it under their own name. The big factories in turn own numerous smaller factories or distribute under special labels, so that it is not always easy to see exactly which tea comes wherefrom.

That said, whose products are most suitable for purchase? How can you make sure that you consistently receive the same great quality? With heicha and especially Pu'er this is done quite easily, thanks to the tea factories that are very common here, apart from the aforementioned danger of counterfeiting.

Many factories try to produce an annual version that is comparable to the previous year's tea. This is particularly evident in the case of the so-called number teas, which are brought onto the market each year. To a lesser extent, this also applies to teas without numbers, which are offered much more frequently. Brands from CNNP or Dayi are particularly well-known. In addition to the numbered factories (or rather companies, as they often include several smaller factories), Yunnan Xishuangbanna Yiwu Zhengshan, Mengku Shuangjiang, Fuhai, Jixing or Yunnan Changtai are also worth mentioning.

But also small factories do have their special charm, for example Farmerleaf. Originally, they only marketed material from their own (family) gardens, but in recent years, they have selectively bought material from friends in nearby locations and pressed and/or marketed it as well. If you like, you can find online information about the exact villages where the material comes from, when it was harvested and occasionally even the first name of the tea farmer. This would not be possible in such detail with larger factories.

The following table shows some of the better known factories, which in the past were simply numbered[144].

Names of the classic tea factories (fourth digit in the recipe name)

#	Factory	Note
1	Kunming Tea Factory	Founded in 1938 as a subsidiary of CNNP. Today marketed almost exclusively as CNNP or Zhong Cha.
2	Menghai Tea Factory	Founded in 1940 as Fo Hai Tea Factory, renamed in the 50s, since 1996 operating under the Taetea and Dayi brands.
3	Xiaguan Tea Factory	Established in 1941 and belonging to CNNP. Especially known for their hard pressed Tuo-forms and their strong and occasionally smoky teas. Often quite inexpensive.
4	Lancang Tea Factory or Fengqing Tea Factory	Reopened in 1996.
5	Pu'er Tea Factory	Founded in 1958, since 2003 also used by the Jing-Gu White Dragon Tea Factory.
6	Six Famous Tea Mountain Factory (6FTM)	Established in 2002.
8	Haiwan Tea Factory or Longsheng Tea Factory	Sometimes identified as Anning according to the location of the factory.
9	Menghai Langhe Tea Factory	Established in 1995.

But Pu'er does not necessarily have to come from factories, every tea farmer or buyer can have his Mao Cha pressed and provided with their own wrappers on a contract basis, so that the same material may actually be available under different branding.

As already mentioned, a Sheng starts its life as an unfinished green tea (Mao Cha), sometimes it is freshly pressed into bings, and sometimes it is stored in loose form for several years first.

Maliciously put, one moistens it, presses it into bings and then hopes for the best. Unfortunately, most of the time it is not that simple. Many (big) producers or factories blend Mao Cha of different qualities to achieve different goals. Either they want to increase the value of low-quality Mao Cha by mixing in as little high-quality material as possible, or they try to stretch expensive material hoping to get away with it. But it does not always have to be one of these two extremes. If they have a reputation and a well-known brand, they are simply trying to create blends that taste harmonic. Powerful but rather bitter basic substance can thus be turned into a full-bodied and tasty tea by adding selected finer material.

NUMBER TEAS

The major factories in particular developed their own recipes early on, in other words, blends that are intended to ensure the same taste year after year. A high percentage of their teas were then given four-digit numbers, representing the recipe of a particular blend and processing (humidity, temperature, etc.).

So if a tea is marketed as **7542 2018 <1801> 357g**, for example, you know pretty much what to expect. Namely, a bing from the Menghai Tea Factory based on the recipe from 1975, which was pressed in 2018 (the Mao Cha used may sometimes be substantially older) and comes from the first batch, i.e. the first pressing. It is also a standard weight bing, sometimes (as with the 7542) variants with less weight are made. There is a simple logic behind the digits as follows:

- Digits #1 and #2: Year of recipe creation
- Digit #3: Average leaf degree or quality of the blend
- Digit #4: Factory number[145]

The year of production is usually only found on the back of the wrapper, and with large factories, the batch number is also often given. For buyers and collectors of older teas in particular, the "correct" batch number can mean significant price differences depending on the popularity of the tea.

The leaf grades (i.e. the third digit of the recipe number) should not be taken too literally. In general, the smallest number expresses the highest quality. Not only because of the fact that the materials are blended (after all, the same taste is to be guaranteed every year), but also because sometimes more beautiful leaves are used at the top than on the underside and sometimes more breakage goes in the center - it is not always possible to speak of uniform leaf quality. Let us therefore consider the third digit as an indication of the overall quality of the raw leaves in this respective blend, according to the following table.[146]

Leaf grades of Mao Cha

Grade	Quality
0	Extremely rare selection
1-3	Strong proportion of buds
4-6	Upper leaves with some buds
7-9	Hardly any or no buds and lower leaves of the branch
10	Coarse leaves and stems

Some factories adhere very strongly to this graduation, others less so. Some also phrase the leaf quality rather creatively, for example as follows:

- Jin Si (Golden Ribbon), highest quality level at Xiaguan factory, actually only consisting of buds
- Gong Ting, royal or tribute quality with the smallest and most delicate leaves
- Te Ji, superior grade, one level below Gong Ting
- Jia Ji, A-grade
- Yi Ji, First Grade
- FT, not a factory grading, but somewhat non-specific higher export quality for the Taiwanese importer Fei Tai Hao (specialized in Menghai and Xiaguan)

It should be noted that higher leaf quality usually mean a higher price, but not necessarily. Neither can a better taste be inferred from higher prices, but in any case a different taste. A Shu with a low quality digit will offer many buds, tender leaves and a great aroma, but may in return taste more similar to a Hong Cha, while lower grades tend to show the typical Shu aroma of forest soil and old foliage.

The following table presents a number of the best known Pu'er number teas, offers a distinction between Sheng and Shu (one can easily get confused there as the numbers do NOT provide any regarding that subject), highlights digit #3 (the leaf quality) for easier readability and finally tells the shape and producer.

Selected number teas

Recipe/Year	Type	Material	Shape	Factory
1972				
7262	Shu	6	Bing	Menghai
1974				
7432	Sheng	3	Bing	Menghai
7452	Shu	5	Bing	Menghai
1975				
7532	Sheng	3	Bing	Menghai
7536	Sheng	3	Bing	Fuhai
7542	Sheng	4	Bing	Menghai
7543	Sheng	4	Bing	XiaGuan
7548	Sheng	4	Bing	Haiwan
7552	Shu	5	Bing	Menghai
7562	Shu	6	Brick	Menghai
7572	Shu	7	Bing	Menghai
7576	Shu	7	Bing	Fuhai
7578	Shu	7	Bing	Haiwan
7581	Shu	8	Brick	Kunming
7582	Sheng	8	Bing	Menghai
7592	Shu	9	Bing	Menghai
1976				
7632	Shu	3	Bing	Menghai
7663	Shu	6	Tuo	XiaGuan
7672	Shu	7	Bing	Menghai
7692	Shu	9	Bing	Menghai

Recipe/Year	Type	Material	Shape	Factory
1977				
7742	Sheng	4	Bing	Menghai
7752	Shu	5	Bing	Menghai
1980				
8001	Sheng	0	Bing	Kunming
1985				
8542	Sheng	4	Bing	Menghai
8562	Shu	6	Bing	Menghai
8582	Sheng	8	Bing	Menghai
8592	Shu	9	Bing	Menghai
1986				
8653	Sheng	5	Bing	XiaGuan
8663	Shu	6	Bing	XiaGuan
1988				
8853	Sheng	5	Brick	XiaGuan
8891	Sheng	9	Bing	Kunming
1989				
8972	Sheng	7	Brick	Menghai
1990				
9016	Shu	1	Tuo	Kunming
1995				
9559	Shu	5	Bing	Langhe
9579	Shu	7	Bing	Langhe
9599	Shu	9	Bing	Langhe
1999				

Recipe/Year	Type	Material	Shape	Factory
9948	Sheng	4	Bing	Haiwan
9978	Shu	7	Bing	Haiwan
2005				
0502	Sheng	?	Bing	Lancang
0532	Shu	3	Bing	Menghai
0562	Shu	6	Bing	Menghai
V93	Shu	Not specified	Tuo	DaYi
2006				
0622	Sheng	2	Bing	Menghai
2007				
0712	Sheng	1	Bing	Menghai
0752	Sheng	5	Bing	Menghai
0772	Sheng	7	Bing	Menghai
2008				
0821	Sheng	2	Bing	Menghai Liming Xinghuo
2009				
968	Shu	6	Tuo	Haiwan
99 Square	Shu	Not specified	Brick	DaYi
2014				
1401	Sheng	Not specified	Tuo	Menghai

The table above also contains some inconsistencies, which shall be addressed here. For example, the 9016 ends with the figure 6 and not with the 1, which would be correct, as it comes from the Kunming Tea Factory. The 0502 should end with the digit 4, but it does not, and furthermore I do not agree with leaf grade 0.

The 0821 has a similar issue, the producing Menghai Liming Xinghuo company owns no "official" digit at all. So in both cases, the work is "creative", which might lead to misunderstandings if you take the fourth digit (or any numbers in this business) too seriously.

A 0821 from the year 2014, already quite dark

Similarly, the 7536 and 7576 come from the Fuhai Tea Factory, formerly a part of Menghai, which was split off in 1998. The number 6 as the fourth digit is therefore not in line with the classic factory number system. The 7536 is often compared to the 7542, but in my opinion it offers a clearer and more precise aroma, albeit being slightly more bitter. The 7532 is also preferable to the 7542, but less common. Although rather average (and extremely low-priced), the 7542 is nevertheless simply THE reference or benchmark. Everyone knows it and knows how to rate it, and so it is practically the starting point for many research trips or at least conversations throughout the tea community. Not very aromatic as a young bing, somewhat flat and clearly too smoky, it develops into a more than acceptable daily drinker from the age of 15 years onwards, but no spectacular heights are ever to be expected.

7542 150g Mini bing from 2014

7542 in the 357g standard size

These anomalies do not make the table obsolete. For about a quarter of a century, there has been a lot of development in the tea industry and the network of relationships between companies. Today, more and more factories assign numbers as they please, even the historical numbers of other factories are not always respected. In Germany you would certainly get a problem if you, being not the owner of the brand, wanted to launch any product with the name 4711 into the market, whereas the numbering system of Pu'er is seemingly not that rigid.

The omission of a digit can also be irritating, as with the 968. Here, only the leading digit 0 has been omitted, so the recipe is from the year 2009. Also conspicuous is V93, in this case it is a 2005 remake of a recipe from 1993, the V meaning vintage. The 99Square to me is not a number tea at all, but rather a curiosity. It weighs 81 grams (nine times nine) and was pressed in the shape of a square chocolate with nine tiles.

Unfortunately, the digits in the number teas are not only often inconsistent, they also do not provide any further information. It would be nice if a non-professional could already tell by the number how much a Shu has been subjected to the wodui, i.e. how little or heavily it has been artificially fermented. This is especially interesting to know if you want to acquire Shu that will continue to increase in taste over the years. You already guessed it, this only happens if the wodui was very mild. Lightly fermented Shu are for example

- 7581
- 8592
- V93

The 7572 and the 7262 are known to be stronger, i.e. somewhat more heavily fermented, and the 7572 is particularly noteworthy here. Originally, before pressing, about 70% Shu was mixed with 30% Sheng, which was beneficial for the ripening potential. This is still said to be the case with the 7581 today. However, such mixtures are now rare and the factories keep quiet about details.

Number teas also exist outside of Yunnan, for example the 0307 Liu Bao, to name but one. The 6740 from the vicinity of the mountain Meili Xue Shan did not make it into the table either. Strictly speaking, this is not a number tea at all, because the number only indicates the height of the mountain of 6,740 meters.

At the end of the section on Yunnan heicha we have a look at some exotic or special types that should be known, not because they are so outstanding, but because they round off the segment (mostly downwards).

CHA GAO 茶膏

Cha Gao is the name of an instant variant of Pu'er, a concentrate of already brewed tea. It means tea paste and is offered pressed into the shape of tiny individual bricks; made of both Sheng or Shu, visually reminiscent of malt candies, but unfortunately not as delicious. And this brings us to the topic of taste, or rather its non-existence.

At best Cha Gao is an ad-hoc remedy, a tea-to-go, which may even be dissolved in cold water. Its taste is rather remotely reminiscent of Pu'er, but at least the water will take on its usual color. In general, however, I prefer a tea-to-sit.

Chunks of Cha Gao only weigh a few grams and sometimes even less. Approximately one gram per 100 to 200ml of water is needed. It is not possible to give any exact recommendations because the strength of the Cha Gao may from factory to factory and in the end it all depends on the drinker's preference anyway.

Fun fact: similar to Matcha, Cha Gao only allows for a single infusion.

Two different types of Cha Gao

HUANG PIAN 黄片 YELLOW LEAVES

Yellow leaves, which either were not carefully avoided during plucking or (mostly) got too much heat during the production of the Mao Cha and look quite brown, are sorted out from the Mao Cha before the pressing of premium teas.

Huang Pian[147] is clearly a reject of the tea production, and one may smirk when it is marketed as a rare specialty, sometimes with the story that tea farmers would reserve it for themselves because it is so delicious. It is more likely that (the poorer) tea farmers drink it because they prefer to rather sell the superior qualities.

However, it needs to be mentioned that this scrap can sometimes taste quite excellent. Dry and brown, it has little astringency and bitterness, but it can be very digestible, has a pleasant smell and a very mild taste. It sometimes reminds me a little of the Japanese batabatacha, which is also post-fermented, but tastes more acidic and much less like wood. The better qualities may well be in the elevated price segment and are sometimes suitable for long term maturation. The oldest Huang Pian in my collection is said to be 60 years old and is simply unparalleled, but also hard to find.

Huang Pian is also offered from other tea varieties, especially oolong. Those are missing quite a bit, but due to their simplicity they are also particularly suitable for beginners.

Huang Pian from 1960

LAO CHA TUO 老茶头 OLD TEA NUGGET

Lao Cha Tuo is scarcely available on the market. It translates to old tea lump or nugget and some reseller also offer it under tea name tea fossils.

Similar to Cha Gao it also is a rejection of production, but solely of Shu Pu'er. It consists of the clumped chunks that solidify during production and are sorted out or sieved before the pressing of bings. In contrast to Cha Gao, its quality can be equivalent to the optically more beautiful material of the pressed bing, and the unwanted wodui may evaporate faster, since it is not pressed, thus it might be savored earlier.

Besides loose lumps, somewhat visually more appealing versions are also marketed in brick shape. One brand even offers a square 100 grams bar which is reminiscent of a famous chocolate brand, bearing similar ridges for easy portioning.

Loose Lao Cha Tuo (above) and brick version (below)

PANG XIE JIAO 螃蟹脚 CRAB LEGS

Crab legs are very different plants than Camellia sinensis, yet often found on Pu'er trees.

Pang Xie Jiao is a parasite from the mistletoe family (Viscum in Latin), which grows on tea trees, among other plants. The "legs" are harvested, dried and sold separately from the tea. Their infusion smells pleasantly plummy, is bright and tastes sweetish. Unfortunately, I could not notice a potion-like effect similar to that found in the potion of a well known Gaulish village brewed by the druid Getafix - probably the Chinese tea farmers do not harvest them with the golden sickles required. However, the taste reminds of tea, probably corresponding chemicals from the tea tree get into the symbiotically living mistletoe and thus into the cup.

In TCM, Pang Xie Jiao is regarded as a medicine against stomach pain and diabetes. However, one should probably enjoy it without sugar for it to have a positive effect. They are brewed pure or mixed with Sheng, one simply adds some pieces of them to the leaves.

Pang Xie Jiao

Crab legs ready for brewing

ANHUI HEICHA   安徽 黑茶

LIU'AN HEICHA   六安黑茶

Liu'an heicha (sometimes transcribed "Lu'an") is certainly the most famous representative of his regional guild. When shopping, you should not confuse him with L(i)u'an Gua Pian, a green tea native to the area. Originally (you might have guessed) it comes from Liu'an, but today it is often produced in Qimen, thus remaining an Anhui heicha. Both are Liu'an Cha, but only the former is a heicha.

I appreciate Anhui for its yellow tea, Qi Men (Keemun) and also the famous Monkey King, but Liu'an heicha I only drank a few times (but very willingly).

To make Liu'an heicha, red tea is fermented (or composted) with a method similar to Shu Pu'er, and then matured in willow or bamboo baskets with bamboo or cardboard inlays for many years. It is even sold in these baskets[148], as well as in the shape of bricks. In terms of taste it is usually sweeter than Shu Pu'er, but its infusion shows a similar beautiful copper red color.

Depending on your preferences, you can also add bamboo pieces of the packaging to the infusion, but its flavor should have already been absorbed by the tea during the maturation process anyway. Liu'an heicha is definitely recommended for friends of this variant. While it does not offer overly complex aromas, it is very reasonably priced and a decent value for money.

Liu'an heicha with basket chunks

GUANGXI HEICHA 广西黑茶

LIU BAO CHA 六堡茶

The raw material used for Liu Bao is often coarse, large-leaved and may contain many stems. Liu Bao is named after the city of the same name in Guangxi, and is traditionally moistened after production and put into woven wicker baskets with very light pressure. These baskets can hold from 500 grams to several kilograms of material. After two months of post-fermentation, the tea is ready for sale, but the ancient treasures stored for a long time are especially sought-after. The manufacturing process was the reference point for the production of Shu Pu'er, but there is a greater distinction between light, medium and strong fermentation. Recently, more and more lightly fermented versions are coming onto the market and it is increasingly packed in paper bags only (without basket).

Loose Liu Bao in a paper bag

Liu Bao is also available in the shape of bings or bricks. As with Pu'er, good qualities have been matured loosely for several years before pressing. A more lightly fermented bing is 0307, whereas the 0207 bing, like the loose 2503, is heavily fermented, i.e. it has undergone the wet piling more often or for a longer time. Numbers similar to Pu'er are also found here, but the recipe names may be three, four or even five digits and are difficult to understand, some seem to simply mark batches.

0307 Liu Bao Mini Cake

Liu Bao is one of the teas in which a certain type of mould growth is not only harmless, but even particularly desirable. The Aspergillus Eurotium Cristatus or Jin Hua 金花 (Golden flower) is inoculated into the moist tea during production and shows itself in tiny yellowish spots all over the tea. Jin Hua is particularly popular in Hunan, where it is often found in Fu Zhuan. Liu Bao was historically brought to Malaysia by Chinese guest workers and was considered a simple daily drinker for these miners until the 80s of the last century. Today, 30 to 60 year old tea comes home to China at boutique prices.

I like drinking Liu Bao, but only qualities aged 20 to 30 years can really delight me. Aromas such as damp wood, moss, and sometimes even slight mintiness can be experienced therein, paired with a pleasant acidity, especially when Jin Hua is involved. As with Shu Pu'er, one starts with very brief infusions of just a few seconds, increasing the duration very gently. Unlike many Shu Pu'er, Liu Bao on average tastes a bit milder and more delicate, simply more subtle.

CHONG SHI CHA 虫屎茶

Chong Shi Cha is not only but most notably produced in Guangxi. You already know the Chinese character Shi 屎 from the oolong Ya Shi Xiang, in English duck feces scent. As mentioned, the Ya Shi Xiang has nothing to do with excrements of any kind, but the Chong Shi Cha definitely does.

Chong Shi Sha

Chong Shi Cha 虫屎茶, in short Chong Cha 虫茶 or euphemistically Dragon Pearl Tea 龙珠茶, means worm (feces or poop) tea. In shops you may also find it under the name Insect Droppings Tea

However, it is not worms, but caterpillars of moths which feed on openly stored Liu Bao in which their mothers did lay their eggs. The tea leaves pass through the moths' digestive tracts, and what comes out at the end is collected and consists of undigested leaf parts and just the usual digestive residues. Now that does not sound very appetizing, but perhaps it might help if you compare it to fresh, high-quality compost. In this case it is really worms, earthworms and their relatives, which produce valuable humus from plant waste with its essential nutrients which in turn enables new plant growth and thus gives life.

Do the Chinese drink this tea because of its taste, or because it is in TCM attributed with having healing effects (e.g. for stomach aches and digestive problems)? Sometimes other medicinal herbs are added to Liu Bao, which are then also digested by the caterpillars. Pure Chong Shi Sha, which is visually reminiscent of African CTC tea, does not seem to be very popular, as once dried, it is usually first roasted in a wok together with tea and honey and brewed later on. The infusion is therefore considered rather a medicine than a drink.

I prefer to prepare my vintage Chong Shi Cha straight, for about 20 seconds with boiling water; one gram is enough for 100 milliliters of water. From the third infusion onwards the taste diminishes considerably. The smell is, unsurprisingly, humus-like, like damp earth. In terms of taste, the Chong Shi Cha also shows the flavor of Liu Bao, enriched with notes of mint, camphor or licorice. All in all, a tasty, refreshing drink, there is nothing disgusting about it, perhaps with the exception of its name.

HUBEI HEICHA 湖北黑茶

Brick tea is characteristic for Hubei. It is extremely inexpensive, sometimes even below the price level of a Kang Brick (more about this in the following section on Sichuan) and, like the Kang, is traditionally produced for people who live at high altitudes and whose diet consists mainly of animal fats. Perhaps these teas would also be suitable for my fellow citizens in the European Alps?

There are two main versions of this tea on the market:

- Qing Zhuan 青砖 Green brick
- Mi Zhuan 米砖 Black brick

The name refers to the differing raw material, on the one hand a green Mao Cha and on the other hand one that almost became a red tea.

Hubei heicha is truly not the ultimate of sensations, but offers an unmatched price/performance ratio. It tastes like a mouthful of cotton candy, just not as sweet, slightly sour and if you let it steep too long you can feel a slight tingling on your tongue, but it hardly gets bitter.

Qing Zhuan

HUNAN HEICHA 湖南黑茶

As mentioned with the Liu Bao, the tradition of cultivating Jin Hua (a non-toxic aspergillus) on tea originates from Hunan. It not only indicates high quality, but is also a flavoring agent. As a warning it should be mentioned that the golden flowers (the yellow mould) may have been contaminated with wheat flour in the tea factory for better development, so tea with Jin Hua should, as a precaution, be avoided by people with severe gluten-related allergies or celiac disease!

FU ZHUAN 茯砖 FU BRICK

Fu Zhuan is part of the (long) list of my favorite teas. Although not very subtle, but sourly aromatic I enjoy drinking it very much, especially if it is sprinkled with Jin Hua 金花, the aforementioned golden flowers. For them I am always willing to shell out extra dough.

Golden flowers in Fu Zhuan

The same applies to Fu as to most other heicha. What already tastes great when young may increase significantly over the years. My oldest Fu dates back to 1991 and is simply delicious, but even one that is only a few years old can be very tasty.

Fu Zhuan from 1991

In Fu I sense a distinct proximity to the Japanese Goishicha, which is also post-fermented and has a nice sour note. Goishicha is even more aromatic than Fu, but Fu therefore tastes more full-bodied.

Fu is usually produced in the form of bricks and often weighs 400 or 800 grams and in some cases even one or more kilograms. The leaf quality appears higher than that of many other heicha, containing more delicate leaves from early harvests, but of course there is a whole range of qualities.

The cup should be light brown to amber in color. The taste suggests sour dried fruit, hay and sometimes even malt or mushrooms. The earthy and woody flavor of many other heicha is missing here, not least because the wodui process is only light to medium.

Fu is steeped more like a Sheng, it can tolerate a somewhat longer infusion time well and hardly ever turns bitter. Unlike Shu, where a few seconds too much may already shift the taste towards bitterness.

HUA JUAN CHA 花卷茶

Another Hunan speciality comes from the Anhua region and stands out for its characteristic shape. Hua Juan Cha is mainly pressed into clay or bamboo tubes, which traditionally weigh between 100 grams and several dozen kilograms.

Shi Liang Cha

These teas are also available in the form of smaller pieces and often simply wrapped in paper. They are frequently named after the classical Chinese weight unit Tael (approx. 37g) and referred to as:

- Shi Liang Cha 十两茶 Ten tael tea
- Bai Liang Cha 百两茶 Hundred tael tea
- Qian Liang Cha 千两茶 Thousand tael tea

Although a Shi Liang Cha should weigh just under 370 grams, dealers also offer variations with slightly different weights under this name.

As much as I appreciate the Fu from Hunan, I cannot get enthusiastic about Hua Juan Cha. Like Hubei heicha, these teas to me are at most tolerable as daily drinkers, and even if they taste smooth and rounded, they are not particularly aromatic. I think its most exciting aspect is the fancy shape.

Qian Liang Cha

SICHUAN HEICHA 四川黑茶

LU BIAN CHA 路边茶 BORDER TEA

Very early on, Sichuan (but also Hunan) exported coarse, simple teas to neighboring provinces. Because the tea crossed borders, these products were called border teas in the West. The Chinese word for it is much more profane and means tea by the roadside. These heicha have been and are still going to Tibet (Xizang), Mongolia or Xinjiang and are all of a humble nature, twigs are processed completely with stem and stalk, thus a high level of tannin is guaranteed.

KANG ZHUAN 康砖 KANG BRICK

The tea brick called Kang is produced in Sichuan and also in Guizhou and is mainly sold into Tibet. In history this tea had a very high value (not least because its name implies wellness) and was even the official currency at times. It is classically boiled for hours, salted and then mashed with yak butter, a quite pleasant drink, which is called butter tea[149] in Tibet.

Instant-version of butter tea (not recommended)

I do not churn the tea at home like a monk does in his monastery, but rather mix the tea leaves with the yak butter by hand and then put the lumps into boiling water, allowing it to boil for about 20 to 30 minutes. Then I salt to taste, add just a pinch of sugar (to round off the taste, not to sweeten), sieve and serve it hot.

Yak butter

This tea is quite popular, at least in parts of China, so there is also an instant version available, which only needs to be infused with hot water. This variety tastes more like a Masala

Chai without spices, the real stuff in contrast offers a lot of taste (and fat-based calories) for little money, because Kang-bricks are amazingly cheap and are not really exciting in their pure version, that is without the butter. I try to always avee a little yak butter at hand (the actual cost factor), which keeps well in the fridge and is produced in in modern factories in Tibet and Mongolia. Using butter made from cow milk simple does not come close to the real deal.

The Kang brick matures similar to a Sheng over the years (and decades), but because of its rather plain material you cannot expect a great delicacy. In Tibet, enjoyment was also rather secondary in the daily diet, more important were and are the valuable ingredients that make tea the basis of the daily food intake, even today. Kang offers a good opportunity to experience a spicy-medicinal aroma at low cost, even 30-year-old bricks are still available for little money.

PURPLE TEA (ZI CHA) 紫茶

There is no purple tea. At least not in the sense of the six tea colors which are known to stand for the six basic production methods. Purple tea therefore always has to be subsumed under one of these six colors. The unique feature of purple tea is the use of a special variety of Camellia sinensis. Purple tea is mostly a product of Camellia sinensis var. Dehongensis, whose leaf tips are characterized by a purple or lilac shimmer.

In order not to make things too easy, there are at least three different cultivars, and eager researchers in China are also busy developing crosses between varieties from Yunnan and Fujian.

The main differentiation is between the original Ye Sheng or Wild Purple, the extremely rare and wild Zi Cha (also an Assamica large-leaf variety), and the cultivated form Zi Juan (also seen under the name Purple Beauty).

Originally processed into Mao Cha and then into Pu'er or white tea, Ye Sheng is nowadays also used to produce Hong Cha. Similar to many Yunnan heicha, it is initially a tad bitter, but develops more complex aromas and body over time.

Purple tea is certainly interesting for explorers, but often it cannot satisfy my personal taste. Maybe in a few decades it will be dismissed as a fad, we shall see. It certainly offers new nuances and alternatives to traditional teas made from classic leaf varieties, but as long as it is not significantly better, I will keep watching this alternative with very limited attention. Even very good Zi Hong Pao oolongs never came close to the quality of real Da Hong Pao during my studies. Anyhow, when it is about personal taste preferences, you should always try for yourself before judging. In the end, curiosity may win out, and that's just as well...

Jingmai Purple Bud Pu'er

FLAVORED TEAS

At the beginning of this section I would like to clarify once more that I despise artificially flavored teas. Creamy Strawberry Black Tea or Tropical Magic Green Tea with dried fruit chunks usually put me off. Truly good tea needs no additives whatsoever, but sometimes I make exceptions, as long as natural ingredients are used.

In China, there are two categories of flavored tea worth mentioning, flower tea or Hua Cha 花茶 and crafted tea or Gong Yi Cha 工艺茶. Hua Cha refers to teas or tisanes produced *from* or *with added* flowers, while Gong Yi Cha refers to Hua Cha which is especially shaped during production in order to also take on a flower-like form when infused.

Crafted tea is supposed to look particularly beautiful, i.e. it should unfold from simple balls into optical works of art, preferably in glass pots. Flowers are skillfully sewn into mostly green tea and reveal their full splendor under the influence of hot water.

Personally, I have rarely had pleasant taste experiences with such tea, it mostly tasted unpleasantly bitter or almost like perfumed. Since my primary goal is not to look at tea but to drink and taste it, I prefer the humble Hua Cha. Accordingly, I consider crafted tea a subcategory of Hua Cha.

Purists often also avoid Jasmin tea or similar products with added blossoms, and for a good reason. All too often, low-cost leaves from large plantations or poorly processed tea which is no longer sellable is embellished with flowers or fruits.

In general, I understand and agree with this purist view, especially since high-quality tea by nature offers such incredibly rich aromas that additives should be more than superfluous, but every now and then a desire for change is tempting me, and then I also like to reach for one or the other scented tea.

BAMBOO

Bamboo, botanically a grass, occurs in different varieties of which several may be found in tea products.

Bamboo leaves for the solo infusion (tisane)

On the one hand, bamboo was historically used as a transport vessel for tea. Even today some heicha are still pressed into bamboo tubes and then marketed under the English term pillar or pole, sometimes still contained in the bamboo and sometimes only in a pressed shape, already sliced into convenient discs. In the past, these tea columns were quite large for transportation purposes and could weigh more than 30kg.

Apart from pure shipping purposes, bamboo is also used as a tasteful flavor. One either adds a few leaves of the bamboo basket to the heicha during the steeping, or the tea is already roasted by the producers in a young, thin bamboo cane, sawn into handy portions before selling.

White tea roasted in bamboo

The latter option provides a rather tasty alternative aroma and adds a fleeting sweetness and the typical mild, unobtrusive bamboo scent to the infusion. I have tried this kind of bamboo with white, red and Pu'er tea and I like to drink it every now and then for a change.

Furthermore, fresh, loose bamboo leaves are offered, which in dry form smell like cocoa powder. Unfortunately, when infused, they only offer a taste of hay and distant camomile, there is no trace of chocolate, even the fleeting sweetness cannot do much good.

Bamboo infusion are nicely drinkable, but in my opinion, the bamboo track does not lead to specific culinary heights. This is one of the many reasons why pandas should rather not be envied .

BITTER MELON

Oolong aged in bitter melon

Visually, the tea ripened or aged in bitter melons (also called bitter apple, bitter gourd, bitter squash, karela etc.)[150] is certainly not a highlight, and in terms of taste, I do not think the cucumber is the ideal container to store tea in. Up until now I never had the luck to find a high quality content in the cucumber, but it was not really bad either. The bitter melon from Anxi is well known, filled with Tie Guan Yin. It makes it possible to cheaply approach aged oolongs and is not to be sneezed at under this aspect. The price/performance ratio never disappoints.

Similar to the pomelo (mentioned later on), the bitter melon is also attributed various powers in traditional Chinese medicine or TCM, called Ku Gua[151] 苦瓜 there. However, since in this book we are only interested in the taste aspects, we shall not elaborate any further. If you are interested in tasting it, try adding some of the melon skin to your tea, just like with bamboo or citrus flavored teas.

CHRYSANTHEMUM

Ju Hua in full bloom

Having already been disloyal to my intention to write about Camellia sinensis exclusively when it came to the bamboo leaves, I may as well continue with this inconsistency. The chrysanthemum blossoms or in Chinese Ju Hua 菊花 (Kikka in Japanese) certainly appeal to me. I know of two types, the white-yellow and the larger purely yellow one. The former looks like daisies, while the latter resembles dandelions. Both variants taste pleasantly mild and sweet, slightly like camomile and very delicate. I infuse the smaller kind in bulk, while the large yellow one is so aromatic that usually a single blossom is sufficient. As with most good teas, several infusions are possible without problems.

Chrysanthemum is sometimes added to plain Pu'er teas by factories in order to complement or round off sweetness and aroma.

JASMINE TEA

Jasmine tea or (Mo Li Hua Cha) 茉莉花茶 is mostly made predominantly in Fujian and with red or green tea. It can be found in many Chinese restaurants around the world, which is quite understandable, as waiters may simply pour new boiling water over the leaves in order to re-steep when passing by. In case of green tea this may require a little more attention, as one should take care of a decent temperature there. In the hectic routine of a restaurant with hundreds of numbers on the menu card, there might be little time for this. On second thought, even the green might tolerate boiling water, given its supposed quality level…

Jasmine Pearls

This is not to say that the green tea necessarily has to result in a better taste, but high quality versions mostly utilize green tea. Occasionally you may also find good alternatives based on white tea, for example made with Yinzhen (Silver Needles).

A popular variant of Jasmine tea are the Jasmine Pearls, where the bud and leaves are rolled in an elaborate process to create a beautiful product. However, the taste does not depend on the beauty, but on the type of flavoring.

For high-quality aromatization, fresh jasmine blossoms are mixed into the finished tea base four to eight times, left in for 24 hours each time and then sorted out again. The final product then no longer contains any jasmine blossoms, but the exquisite fragrance has been transferred to the tea.

Paradoxically, however, some consumers demand that blossoms be visible in the end product; otherwise they doubt the natural flavoring and suspect added artificial flavors. This skepticism is perfectly understandable, but unfortunately Jasmine tea with visible blossoms is not the finest. The blossoms will have transferred their aroma almost completely over to the tea and do not contribute to the taste any longer, in the worst case they even lead to a slightly bitter or even soapy note. If you like flavored tea but find jasmine too dominant, you might consider looking for tea flavored with osmanthus. And if you can trust your vendor, ask them about the exact production method and you might be able to conjure a fine, delicate fragrance out of your cup.

ROSE OOLONG

While pure Jin Xuan can taste pleasantly soft it is, like a few other oolongs, sometimes spiced up with rose petals. This actually does not taste as weird as it sounds, and so every once in a while even this tea finds its way into my cup.

I always strive for certified pesticide-free quality, since flowers are often heavily exposed to the blessings of the chemical industry.

However, after drinking this scented diversion, I may not be willing to smell any perfume for a few weeks…

Oolong refined with rose petals in 8g aroma pack, accompanied by a moisture protection pouch

CITRUS FRUIT

EARL AND LADY GREY

The legendary English Earl Grey is credited with the questionable accomplishment of having added the oil of the bergamot orange to tea which was considered spoiled after a long sea voyage in order to make it marketable. Formerly made exclusively from Chinese tea, it is now brought onto the market using black tea of any origin. Alternatively, lemon scent is added instead of bergamot, then known as Lady Grey. Unfortunately, nowadays the Greys are almost only available with artificial flavoring and inexpensive raw tea.

To make it look more appealing, pieces of orange peel or cornflower blossoms are occasionally added. I have drunk many unpleasant and some less unpleasant Earl Greys; unfortunately, none of them has impressed me much until today.[152]

Cornflowers will not improve the taste either

ORANGE, TANGERINE, ET AL

Especially from Taiwan an oolong is offered which has been supplemented with more or less peel of the bergamot orange. It must not be confused with the Earl Grey mentioned above. Personally, I have not yet had the chance to enjoy it, but if you like this flavor in general, you might even want to complement high-quality tea from your own collection with high-quality peels.

Unless it does not necessarily have to be bergamot, tangerine peels might be an even better option. They also contain strong but somewhat less obtrusive essential oils and are offered under their Chinese name Chen Pi 陈皮. They are either added to the tea in the pot or first stored for a few months, blended with the tea. The best quality is generally considered to be (aged) peels from Xinhui 新会 in Guangdong.

Different types and sizes of citrus fruits filled with white tea or Shu Pu'er

Shu Pu'er is also frequently and very cheaply offered stuffed in tangerines and such, for example under the name Xiao Qing Gan 小青柑, literally small green mandarin. Personally, I like to drink this tea whenever I have the feeling that a sore throat or a cold is approaching. Tangerine filled with heicha also comes from Guangxi, but then rather stuffed with Liu Bao and not Shu Pu'er.

While silver brewing or drinking vessels are easier to clean than open-pored earthenware, silver is not at all suitable for teas with citrus ingredients, not even for Earl Grey. Glass or porcelain is the material of choice in this case. The unique taste silver adds when drinking out of it does not get along well with acidic flavors.

Silver is pretty on the eye, but not tasteless

POMELO

There are again two different options to consider with Pomelo. The first one is a hollowed out fruit, usually filled with oolong or Shu Pu'er, which is dried after filling and sometimes also roasted or even smoked.

Although visually not very appealing, I can certainly enjoy the Fuxi Pomelo oolong from Zhangzhou, Fujian. The one pictured here was filled with lightly oxidized oolong, then baked for many hours over wood fire and finally kept underground in ceramic pots for several years, during which it was allowed to mature. And this is supposed to taste delicious? In fact, it is. It will certainly not win gourmet accolades but it should not be despised either.

Much tastier than it might seem: pomelo stuffed with oolong

After scraping or breaking the tea out of the opening and adding a few small fragments of peel to the pot, brew it with boiling water for a maximum of one minute, or even shorter if more material is used. It offers at least five decent infusions and tastes like a mixture of aged oolong (not surprisingly), mildly earthy Shu Pu'er and smoky red tea. The smoked smell is stronger than the resulting taste in the cup. The hint of citrus fruit decreases with each infusion, a fresh and slightly tingling sensation in the front of the mouth and on the tip of the tongue lasts for quite some time.

A completely different option is the You Xiang Hong 柚香红 or pomelo fragrant red tea from Pinghe, Zhangzhou, Fujian. It may also be available from other areas, but the tea from Pinghe (based on the Jin Mudan cultivar) is the only one I have been able to buy and drink repeatedly so far. It should not be confused with the Dancong called You Hua Xiang 柚花香 or pomelo flower fragrance oolong. In the Dancong, the aroma of pomelo blossoms derives naturally from the tea leaf. You Xiang Hong, on the other hand, is produced in a similar way as a high-quality Jasmine tea, often flavored with fresh pomelo blossoms, none of which, however, remain in the final product. Thus, the resulting tea has the dry look of a fine Hong Cha and only the nose reveals what it has in store. On the palate, of course, one experiences the pomelo blossoms, paired with a sweet hint of chestnut honey and some elusive chocolate. This is my favorite among all flavored teas - just in case anyone would like to know.

GONG YI CHA 工艺茶

Crafted tea, Art tea	
Origin	Huang Shan, Anhui; Fujian; Sichuan
Basic tea	Green or white tea, Huang Shan Mao Feng
Taste	Depending on the added blossoms

Due to the abundance of crafted tea, I have decided to dedicate a few lines to it at the end of this chapter on China, even though I have unfortunately not yet found any high-quality teas of this type.

Green or white and only slightly oxidized tea is carefully handcrafted for Gong Yi Cha together with chrysanthemums, jasmine, lilies, cloves or snow lotus.

The purpose of the teas, which are usually offered as compact balls (very similar in appearance to Pu'er Dragonballs), is to unfold magnificently in the water over several minutes when infused. While this often turn out very nicely, this method of brewing contradicts everything I appreciate. Basically, these teas can only be infused western style or according to the grandpa method, and this does not produce the most delicious tea. Often the long infusion time results in an unpleasant bitterness.

I do not primarily want to look at tea, but rather drink it, and as much as I like to infuse chrysanthemum blossoms now and then, I am not attracted to this kind of tea. Ju Hua 菊花, the chrysanthemum, tastes much too good on its own for me to mix it with tea. Some producers of simple Pu'er Bings, however, like to do so, as the flower gives a lot of sweetness and a flavor reminiscent of camomile. Again, one has to ask the question if sub-standard tea material is just supposed to be pimped.

Those who are better acquainted with this type of tea may call me ignorant, but until proven otherwise, I consider it a show or gift tea, from and for people who do not know any better. In all fairness I have to add that I do happen to know a few people who actually like Gong Yi Cha, but taste is always subjective. So if you want to give it a try, look for terms like Mo Li Hua Cha 茉莉花茶, that is jasmine flower tea or Mei Gui Hua Cha 玫瑰花茶, a crafted tea made of roses.

JAPAN 日本

At first glance, Japan's tea landscape seems more comprehensible than China's. This may be due to the fact that often only green tea from Japan is known, which is just one of the six colors or types. It is all too easy to be fooled by this, because if the well-known expression "40 shades of green" is not nearly enough for Ireland, it certainly is not sufficient for Japan.

Japan is a green tea country. Period. All other colors are very rare and not as dreamlike as many of its green teas. Every now and then you find a black tea or an oolong, so we will also look at these rarer ones, including some post-fermented teas, because they deserve mentioning.

The classification of Japanese tea is practically a classification of green tea, everything else is rather secondary in Japan. We will now take a closer look at the following criteria:

- Cultivation methods
- Harvest time and methods
- Processing of raw tea
- Further processing, sorting, post-treatment

At first we will start with the cultivation and harvesting, the processing will be considered individually and later in this chapter because the final produce will be very diverse.

GROWING METHOD

Japanese tea is mainly grown in plantations where the plants are arranged in orderly rows. Euphemistically called tea gardens, these plantations are often still family-owned and usually smaller than in other countries. Nevertheless, automation is pretty advanced. Japan is an industrialized country, the labor and living costs are enormously high and thus only very little is picked by hand; only the finest teas are given this treatment. Fortunately, despite the often brutal harvest using motorized hedge shears, very decent qualities are produced and Japan is therefore ranked second for me as a tea country, right after China.

Other than in China, almost all Japanese teas are made from bushes, which usually do not get older than 30 years, this is similar to the methods used in India, for example. Old trees are practically non-existent but in just a few centuries many cultivars have been hybridized, optimized to suit the Japanese terroir, climate and regional taste preferences.

SHADED TEA - JAPAN'S UNIQUE CULTIVATION METHOD

In Japan, we must first differentiate between the normally tea grown tea and the so-called shaded tea, which is covered for a few days or weeks before harvesting and thus develops the special aromas that only these Japanese teas offer.

Traditionally, this is done using bamboo mats known as Kabuse 被せ, while modern production uses simple black nets or foil. The shading reduces bitter substances and stimulates chlorophyll production in the tea plant. This way aromas are developing like nowhere else in the world. For more details, see the green tea section of this chapter. There you will also find the table called "Shading, roasting and steaming in common Japanese green teas".

A preliminary categorization of Japanese teas is therefore the distinction between the type of plantation. Two different kinds are to be found here:

- Roten'en 露天園
- Oishita'en 覆下園

Type of plantation does not really nail it, although Roten'en means open or open-air garden and Oishita'en is best translated as covered garden. But because the Oishita'en is also in the open air and does not mean a greenhouse, this translation is also a little misleading. Oishita'en, in contrast to Roten'en, only means that there are devices available which enable the tea farmers to cover the tea before harvesting for a varying period of time in order to provide shade. These days this is usually done with dark foil, nets or more traditionally with bamboo mats.

It is not necessary to remember these two terms, but the distinction between regular tea and shaded tea is important, because the former is usually processed into Sencha or Bancha and is much cheaper to produce than the shaded tea from the Oishita'en. The costs for the shades and also the increased workload in the Oishita'en are reflected in the price, but the varieties Gyokuro, Matcha or Kabusecha produced are also regarded as much superior.

Kabusecha is also a fitting cue for the two important terms you might want to remember:

- Roji Saibai
- Kabuse Saibai

Simply put, Roji Saibai (unshaded cultivation) is the method of a Roten'en and Kabuse Saibai (shaded cultivation) is the method of the Oishita'en.

TIME AND TYPE OF HARVEST

In Japan the tea year begins with the first harvest in the spring. In general, the various harvest times[153] are referred to as follows:

Harvest periods in Japan

Harvest	Duration	Period	Kanji
First flush (Shincha)	10 March - 31 May	Ichibancha	一番茶
Second flush	1 June - 31 July	Nibancha	二番茶
Summer harvest	1 August - 10 September There is no 3rd harvest in the Kyoto/Uji area	Sanbancha	三番茶
Autumn harvest	11 September - 20 October	Yonbancha	四番茶
Winter harvest	21 October - 31 December	Shutobancha	秋冬番茶
Winter/spring harvest	1 January - 9 March	Toshunbancha	冬春番茶

The first four harvest periods in Japan are thus numbered consecutively, similar to the flushes in India: Ichi, Ni, San, Yon. Within this basic scheme, additional specific characteristics are being distinguished.

Instead of being marketed as Ichibancha[154], particularly high-quality tea is also marketed as Shincha 新茶. Usually a special Sencha is meant by this, but also Gyokuro or Kabusecha may be declared as Shincha.

Also traditionally popular is the first tea plucking 88 days after the beginning of spring (Risshun 立春) in the Japanese lunar calendar, usually on February 3rd or 4th. This event is called 88 nights (Hachijyuhachiya 八十八夜) and falls into the first week of May. This tea promises good luck and health for the year (eight is a lucky number in most of Asia).

Marketeers sometimes surpass themselves with further superlatives. Now and then you may come across the terms hashiri, o-hashiri, or hatsutsumi.

Hashiri 走り means running and o-hashiri 大走り translates into big run, both implying a particularly early harvest. To use an analogy with wine for a change, this reminds me of the cleverly marketed race for Beaujolais Primeur, which was not made better by this, but at least more popular. Japanese producers, however, aspire to high quality and have a reputation to lose, they should be careful not to use these terms too carelessly. Consequently, teas with these additions to the name can be expected to be of a significantly superior quality.

Hatsutsumi 初摘み on the other hand more or less[155] means first (hand) plucking and thus already raises the bar. Even if the tea garden in principle harvests mechanically, a first hand harvest is particularly emphasized.

The harvesting period not only significantly determines the quality and price of the tea, but also its name. The first two harvests in Roten'en are used for Sencha, later harvests are processed into Bancha or Hojicha. An exception is the Bancha Yanagi 柳. Excessively large leaves of the early Sencha harvests are selected for this particular tea.

The early harvests in the Roten'en are acknowledged to yield the best qualities, because the tea bush has gathered nutrients in winter and can now offer them to the connoisseur. Caffeine, catechin and amino acids (teanine) that influence taste are particularly abundant in young leaves. With time, the content decreases and consequently the quality and price of the later harvests also drop. The latter also produce higher yields simply because the leaves have grown larger later in the year.

In Oishita'en, where the raw material for Tencha or Gyokuro grows, a single harvest is often all that is done. Afterwards the bushes are cut down and allowed to regain strength for the next year. This renouncement of multiple harvests also explains the significantly higher price of shaded teas.

Another aspect that buyers should be aware of is the picking method. One can distinguish between mechanical harvesting, semi-manual (with scissors) and pure hand picking. If no method is specified, the use of machines can almost always be assumed in Japan.

WHITE TEA (SHIROCHA) 白茶

Japanese white tea, Shirocha 白茶, is extremely rare. It is produced in a similar way to other growing areas on this planet, but there are hardly any offerings.

Personally, I have never drunk a white tea from Japan and can therefore only report from hearsay that there are some that are well worth drinking. One of them is from the cultivar Zairai, but it is said that it is by far not as suitable for storing or aging as for example Chinese white tea. I am looking forward to check this out during my next visit to Japan. The price is on a higher level than for white teas of other origins, but this does not come as a surprise when it concerns Japan.

GREEN TEA (RYOKUCHA) 緑茶

Japanese green teas are in general completely different from their Chinese siblings. Even though they are all Camellia sinensis, Japanese tea farmers have created numerous cultivars in roughly 1,300 years which are more in tune with the taste of a fish-eating nation.

As a result, it is usually easy to distinguish high-grade Japanese green tea from its Chinese relatives, even in blind tastings. This is due to the fact that most Chinese green teas are roasted in a pan or wok, but almost all Japanese teas are steamed instead. The pan-roasted green Japanese teas are called Kamairicha and are almost irrelevant in the market.

Shading, roasting and steaming in common Japanese green teas

Tea		Steaming	Roasting	Shading
Aracha		Yes	None	Varies
Bancha		Yes	Varies	None
Demono	Karigane	Yes	None	Medium to heavy
Demono	Konacha	Yes	None	Varies
Demono	Kukicha	Yes	None	None
Demono	Mecha	Yes	None	None
Genmaicha		Yes	Only the rice is roasted	None
Gyukuro		Yes	None	Heavy
Houjicha		Yes	After steaming	None
Kabusecha		Yes	Varies	Light
Kamairicha		None	Instead of steaming	None
Matcha		Yes	None	Heavy
Sencha	Asamushi	Light	None	None
Sencha	Chumushi	Medium	None	None
Sencha	Fukamushi	Deep	None	None
Tamaryokucha		Varies	Varies	Varies
Tencha		Yes	None	Heavy

The table above provides you with a basic overview but for the sake of clarity omits the important process of rolling, which is mentioned in the description of the individual teas if necessary. Some teas are rolled into long needles like Sencha or curled like Tamaryokucha, while some teas remain unrolled, mostly Bancha types.

The table still seems to be quite comprehensible, yet it gets considerably more complex due to the huge amount of different cultivars, which often provide significantly different taste nuances. Other than in China, the cultivar used is promoted much more actively and is often part of the tea's name. The connoisseur for instance will not simply buy a Sencha but rather a Sencha Okumidori. The cultivar Yabukita is rarely mentioned, however. There is nothing wrong with this cultivar, after all it is the most popular cultivar in Japan with a share of over 70% of the total production, so it is hardly ever necessary to mention it.

If one intended to classify Japanese teas in terms of quality, Bancha would probably be quite far down, way below Sencha, Gyokuro or Matcha, the king of Japanese teas. However, a top Bancha can be far superior to a poorly produced Sencha.

ARACHA 荒茶

Tea Garden	Oishita'en
Heating	Steaming
Shading	Varies depending on the desired end-product

Ara 荒 means crude or rough, a tea in the state immediately after the first processing, up to the point when it is dried[156]. From here, leaf stalks, broken leaf parts or dust are separated out and the leaves are selected to produce particularly fine delicacies. Whether from the Roten'en or the Oishita'en, Aracha is the preliminary stage of production after heating, be it by steaming or pan roasting, as well as rolling and drying, comparable to the Mao Cha in China. If Aracha has already been roasted, but not yet finally sorted into Sencha or Gyokuro, it is called Seicha, to be more precise.

Aracha rarely comes to the market, but lately it seems to be fashionable to market it as a speciality. Therefore it is by no means rare, so if you want to give it a try, you may buy and enjoy it without worries.

By sorting and blending Aracha the final products like Bancha, Sencha or Tencha are being defined. The parts that are frequently sorted out in this process are called Demono 出物 (2nd choice) and are divided into the following three or four tea types:

- Konacha
- Kukicha und Karigane
- Mecha

These varieties can be very tasty. Especially Kukicha has a very individual fandom, which is well deserved. Therefore, I compare Demono with the Chinese Huang Pian, which is also sorted out and still has its raison d'être. If you prefer it a bit stronger, slightly more bitter and do not expect too much in terms of aroma, then Demono might be to your liking.

One may ask if the final sorting of the Aracha could possibly be avoided by better selection during the harvest, but this would require hand picking, which as mentioned earlier is very rare in Japan. Even in the countries with a high amount of manual harvesting, sorting is often done at the end of production, because otherwise the time saved on sorting would have to be paid for by a correspondingly longer time needed for harvesting. Sorting can be done later in peace and quiet, whereas time is often in short supply during the harvesting season. The best time for picking is early in the morning and only in dry weather, so the window of opportunity for harvesting is much smaller than for sorting, which can easily be done indoors.

BANCHA 番茶

Tea Garden	Roten'en
Heating	Steaming
Shading	None
!	Often an inexpensive Sencha variation from a late harvest with its own distinctive taste and little caffeine.

Bancha is translated as work or shift tea, but coarse tea is also a valid meaning. The name may seem a little disrespectful, but actually it is very precise. Bancha is harvested from the same plants as Sencha, only later in the year, and therefore its leaves are larger and more coarse, and because of its lower average price it has established itself as a daily drinker. However, a carefully produced Bancha may still be a top tea.

Also Bancha often lacks catechin, which makes the Sencha plucked earlier more popular. Bancha is also often used to make simple Hojicha or Genmaicha.

In general, it gives off less umami, bitterness or sweetness than Sencha from the same bush, but a little more astringency. People who are sensitive to caffeine appreciate Bancha from the autumn or winter harvest for its particularly low content of the same, so it is often sipped as an evening tea.

The qualities of Bancha range from very simple to quite high. In addition, many varieties are on offer. Most of them play a marginal commercial role, but are often worth discovering and tasting.

AKI BANCHA 秋番茶

Akibancha usually comes from the last harvest of a year (Yonbancha) and takes pride in its special feature that stems are not sorted. Thus it receives more tannic acids than a pure Yonbancha, which consists of leaves only.

HAKUTA BANCHA 伯太番茶

Bancha from the city of Hakuta (Shimane region) is harvested as a speciality all year round. It tastes very mild and is subject to a slightly different processing than ordinary Bancha, it rather resembles a Kyobancha. It is heavily steamed, dried in the sun, roasted, but not rolled, making it look like dark autumn foliage.

KAGEBOSHI BANCHA 陰干し番茶

Unlike the Hakuta, Kageboshi is a shadow-dried Bancha, for this is how its name is translated. Alternatively it is called Hikage (daylight shadow) Bancha 日陰番茶.

Although it is produced in a few other areas except the Shimane region, it is not produced all year round, making it a rarity. Depending on the place of production it is treated slightly differently, sometimes even hung up to dry. This is possible because it is often produced semi-privately in very small batches. People who have old, half feral bushes in their garden harvest whole branches and process them in one piece.

KANCHA 寒茶

Bancha harvested in winter is also called Kancha, cold tea. Despite its rather low quality it is rare and therefore not necessarily easy to obtain. Originating mainly from the regions of Aichi and Tokushima, it is also one of the rare Japanese teas picked from older bushes or trees. Unlike the Kageboshi, however, the branches are removed and the leaves are dried in the sun. In the city of Shishikui (Tokushima) it is rolled by hand at the end and - you guessed it - gets its own name again: it is then called Shishikui Kancha 宍喰寒茶.

Winter teas often lack freshness and aroma, but offer a lot of sweetness to compensate, as does the Kancha.

KYOBANCHA 京番茶

Roasted Bancha from Kyoto is referred to as Kyobancha. The roasting often gives it a slightly smoky flavor, and unlike Hojicha, it is not rolled and thus takes on more roasted aromas. It is also called Iribancha (roasted Bancha) いり番茶. Kyobancha is basically a Toshun Bancha, as it is harvested at the beginning of the calendar year, when the tea bushes are pruned to ensure a uniform first harvest a few months later.

It tastes tender, sweet and fresh, and like most Bancha has little caffeine (roasting is also beneficial) and is therefore considered an Akachan Bancha or Bancha for babies, something you can provide your children with to make them appreciate the taste early on... ;-)

Kyobancha

YOSHINO NIKKAN BANCHA 吉野日干番茶

This Bancha, in English sun-dried Bancha, hails from Yoshino in the Nara Prefecture. It is dried in the sun after steaming and roasted with the aid of hot sand. This sounds a bit like Houjicha, which is also roasted. However, despite the roasting, it is not Houjicha. Houjicha is made from unrolled Bancha (or Kukicha) and provides a different taste.

DEMONO 出物

Demono means second choice. When stems, buds or flakes are sorted from Aracha during the production of high-quality Sencha or Gyokuro, the still delicious "rejects" are marketed under different names. Since these products are not truly considered rejects, they form their own categories and will be honored in the following sections of this chapter: Karigane, Konacha, Kukicha and Mecha. The higher the quality of the final product, the better the quality of the Demono. My personal favorite among the Demono is a well-tended Kukicha.

GENMAICHA 玄米茶

Tea Garden	Roten'en
Heating	Steaming
Shading	None
!	Bancha or Sencha with puffed rice, occasionally with added Matcha.

By adding puffed rice[157] to Bancha[158] you may create Genmaicha[159]. This tea speciality rightly deserves a prominent place on the tea shelf, as it offers a unique taste. Even tea of a rather average quality can clearly benefit from the slightly malty roasting flavors of the rice. Although still a tea, a Genmaicha almost feels like a small snack, even if the rice does not really offer any significant saturation. Another positive aspect is that Genmaicha is quite attractively priced due to the low cost rice additive, which historically is said to have been the motivation for this blend.

A rare variety is called Matcha Iri Genmaicha 抹茶入り玄米茶, which is further enriched with Matcha powder. It can be recognized by the characteristic green color of the puffed rice, because the Matcha gets stuck in its pores.

Genmaicha is also offered in powder form, but in contrast to Matcha or Kabuse powder I had no luck with my choices so far, which makes me doubt whether Genmaicha should be offered in an instant version at all.

Genmaicha

GYOKURO 玉露

Tea Garden	Oishita'en
Heating	Steaming
Shading	Heavy

Certainly most steamed Japanese teas taste somehow typically Japanese, but the Gyokuro 玉露 or jade dew towers above everything. It is the prime example for Japanese flavor, as the umami is the most outstanding part of it - provided that it is correctly prepared.

It got its name from the striking green color in the cup, and like rare dewdrops it is only enjoyed in small quantities. It is also the shaded tea par excellence, because no other Japanese tea is shaded for as long or as much[160] as this one. During these three weeks the content of caffeine and aroma-giving amino acids increases, while the bittering agent catechin is reduced. In addition to the umami, Gyukuro is therefore characterized by a special sweetness and intensity.

While Sencha is often made of the cultivar Yabukita, Gyokuro is mostly made of rarer cultivars such as Asahi, Asatsuyu, Okumidori, Yamakai or Saemidori. This is another reason why it stands out from Sencha, but primarily because of the shading.

Gyokuro

HOUJICHA　焙じ茶

Tea Garden	Roten'en
Heating	Steaming
Shading	None
!	Roasted Bancha, rarely Sencha.

Charcoal-roasted green tea, usually made from Bancha quality raw material, is generally called Hojicha (roasted tea) or Houjicha. The Japanese spelling is 焙じ茶 or ほうじ茶. Tasting sweet, mild, and slightly smoky it also reminds a bit of chocolate or bread.

Personally, I have had mixed experiences with Houjicha. From some I could not get enough and from others I could not get away fast enough. This is noteworthy because I practically never had to drink other bad Japanese teas, even simple qualities are at least always tolerable. The unpleasant Houjicha were always made from Kukicha, which I have avoided ever since. Those who generally like their tea stronger, choose a Houjicha based on Sencha instead of Bancha.

KABUSECHA　被せ茶

Tea Garden	Oishita'en
Heating	Steaming
Shading	Light
!	Similar to Matcha, high-quality Kabusecha is also offered in powder form.

Kabusecha (literally covered tea) is also known as penumbra tea. It is covered[161] less long than Tencha or Gyokuro before harvesting, usually only for one or at most two weeks.

Thus, Kabusecha lies between Sencha, which is not covered at all, and the above-mentioned teas, some of which remain in the shade three times as long. Kabusecha led a shadowy existence in the metaphorical sense for a long time, as it was mainly considered a tea for blends that made Sencha or Gyokuro appear more valuable. Since it combines a combination of both extremes (no shading vs. full shading), it has gained a loyal fan base.

Kabusecha has a finer taste than Sencha[162], is less bitter, but has a certain freshness and often already shows the soft sweetness of Gyokuro. It is less expensive than Gyokuro and therefore a popular alternative for those on a budget.

KAMAIRICHA 釜炒り茶

Tea Garden	Roten'en
Heating	Pan roasting
Shading	None
!	Rather comparable to Chinese green teas because of the roasting.

Pan-roasted green Japanese teas are called Kamairicha[163], which makes them taste more like Chinese teas[164], less bitter, but also they lack the sweetness or umami of the classic Japanese teas. Instead, Kamairicha reveals a slightly nutty roasted flavor.

KARIGANE 雁音

See Kukicha.

KONACHA 粉茶

Tea Garden	Oishita'en
Heating	Steaming
Shading	Medium to heavy
!	Flakes that have been sorted out during the production of Sencha or Gyokuro
Preparation	>= 90°C hot water. Yields a maximum of two infusions.

Konacha or powder tea is a variation of the Demono teas. While tea leaves are rolled during Sencha[165] production, plenty of small and medium sized flakes as well as, depending on the cultivar or leaf quality, fine hairs break off the leaves and are sieved out of the aracha. The substance that is obtained by this process is called Konacha[166] in Japan.

When it comes to Konacha, opinions differ. Often used for tea bags and the free tea in sushi restaurants (called Agari there)[167], it can be rather tasty when the quality is top-notch. However, it is usually more pleasing to the eye than to the palate, as its fine particles pass easily through many filters and therefore give the infusion a strong green hue. On any international tea exchange it would usually not be classified as Dust, but as Fannings (smallest pieces still recognizable).

So Konacha is usually a rather insignificant tea, which is also used for many ready-made teas. As it is comparatively cheap, it can also be used instead of cooking Matcha, e.g. in pastries, if color is more important than authentic Matcha quality. But in this case it is probably more advisable to use Funmatsucha.

FUNMATSUCHA 粉末茶

Funmatsuryokucha 粉末緑茶 (powdered green tea), or Funmatsucha[168] for short, is manufactured from the whole leaf, similar to Matcha. However, it is made from a much simpler raw material, be it Sencha or Hojicha, whatever comes cheap - but certainly not from high-quality Tencha. Therefore it is very attractive in price, but less in taste.

KOKEICHA 固形茶

Kokeicha (solid tea) is a soluble or instant tea that looks similar to the cheap, sugared lemon "tea" pellets from supermarkets or the Turkish instant apple tea.

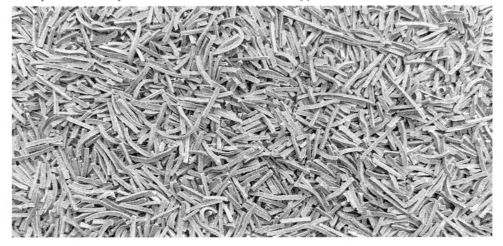

Kokeicha

Unlike the aforementioned analogies, it is produced from Konacha, only without sugar or artificial flavorings, but every line written about it is almost one too much, because here tea powder is mixed with rice flour and then stirred with water into a paste. It is then given its shape in an industrial extruder process, comparable to cutting spaghetti into short, very thin pieces that are remotely reminiscent of fir needles. 15 to 30 seconds at around 70°C are recommended and several infusions are possible, provided that you still want to continue drinking after the first infusion. The "needles" dissolve very slowly and unevenly, so stirring may be required. Alternatively, you can let it steep longer, after all this delays the time until you have to drink it again. With that, everything worth mentioning about its taste has been said.

KUKICHA 茎茶

Tea Garden	Oishita'en
Heating	Steaming
Shading	Medium to heavy
!	Stems sorted out during green tea production

Kuki 茎 means stem in English, and Kukicha is therefore made from leaf veins, stems, stalks and small twigs, making it one of the three Demono assortments. It is offered both roasted (recognizable by its darker color) and unroasted.

In case a particularly large number of stems and fewer leaf veins etc. are used, one also speaks of Bocha[169] 棒茶, although it can hardly be found in the trade under this name. The visual appearance alone is enough to tell you which quality level you are dealing with. If you see practically only stems, then it is a Bocha, even if not declared as such.

Kukicha

Kukicha collected during the production of Gyokuro or Top Sencha is also called Karigane 雁ヶ音[170] or Shiraore 白折[171], in order to particularly ennoble it.

Depending on taste and quality, Kukicha is steeped at 70 to 90°C for a maximum of one minute and should be re-steeped several times. It is considered to be low in caffeine, but contains a particularly high amount of L-theanine, which makes it pleasantly sweet. Kukicha is by no means a waste product of the tea production, but offers a very special charm and taste.

MATCHA 抹茶

Tea Garden	Oishita'en
Heating	Steaming
Shading	Heavy

As already mentioned elsewhere, it is difficult to find a tea that contains more caffeine than Matcha (ground tea), since one consumes the whole leaf of a Tencha. This shaded tea is not rolled after drying, only the stalks and leaf veins are removed before the leaf is carefully ground into powder. For higher qualities this is done in slowly rotating granite mills, for more industrial use the material is handled less sophisticated as it is not economical to produce only 300 or 400 grams per day.

The price of Matcha is therefore not only determined by the quality of the Tencha used, but also depends on how meticulously it is ground. Usually the best material is milled using traditional granite equipment.

In the chapter on preparing tea I already mentioned the two different kinds of Matcha: Usucha (thin tea) and Koicha (thick or concentrated tea). The basic difference is the limited amount of powder used in the Usucha, but also the fact that Koicha is whipped very little.

Considering that whipping or foaming with the bamboo whisk[172] improves the texture and mouthfeel due to the air mixed in, one might wonder why the Koicha does not receive this treatment, especially since there are people recommending to not only beat one but several minutes when preparing Usucha.

The reason for beating the Usucha is said to be that the Tencha used for it comes from rather young plants which contain a lot of bitter substances and thus more or less require the Matcha to be aired well in order to achieve the best possible taste. The Tencha used for Koicha, on the other hand, is said to come from somewhat older bushes and to contain even more carefully picked leaves, thus making strong foaming quite unnecessary.

Since tea bushes gradually start oseing their strong umami after about 20 years, the age of the leaves should only make a small difference here, but proper fertilization, type and length of shading and the final sorting will be more relevant.

My rule of thumb is: in case the Matcha tastes too bitter - next time wiggle the broom for a bit longer!

Dealers specialized in Matcha and their suppliers specify the kind of grinding and the intended use more precisely than e.g. shops that only offer random Matcha (which might even be for cooking purposes[173]) to supplement their product range. Some specialists add the suffix *no mukashi* to Koicha which is supposed to express traditional high quality. These qualities will then start at prices of 1.50 Euro per gram upwards. More rarely, Usucha is supplemented with the suffix *no shiro* which suggests exceptional freshness.

This freshness is the reason why Matcha should be drunk young and always kept chilled. If you do not reside in Japan, this is already the first obstacle. Powdered tea becomes unsightly and loses its aroma much faster than whole leaf tea, especially if it is not constantly chilled but rather travels around the world for weeks. That's why my passion for collecting tea is non-existent when it comes to Matcha, I only ever keep a maximum of two or three different ones in small quantities in the fridge and drink them within short time.

Trade is often creative in decorating its Matcha with authentic or alleged quality levels, be it gold/silver/bronze or premium/imperial. I do not even bother trying to get behind the individual definitions but rather seek advice or, when buying offline, I may even go by color, if possible. A strong (but not too lightly) shining jade green is preferable, pale green indicates rather low quality and any deviation into yellowish or brownish is to be avoided.

Miscellaneous Matcha qualities (descending from left to right) from KEIKO

In order to accommodate the short half-life of Matcha powder, Shimodozono International is even grinding KEIKO Tencha freshly in Germany for retail and selected gastronomy, using granite mills for almost all of their products worldwide. The fact that the company is so serious about freshness and granite is also proven by the fact that it even offers Matcha machines which grind the Tencha leaf in individual portions prior to brewing and dispense the fresh Matcha similar to fully automatic coffee machines.

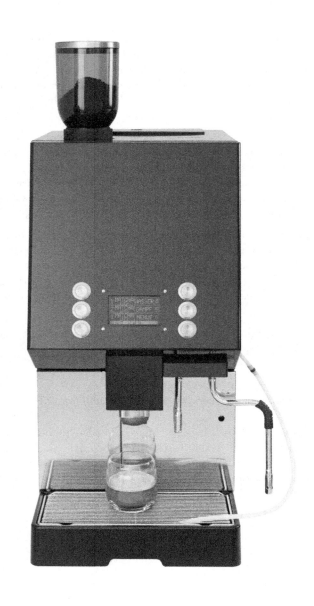

CHADO Mark 1 Matcha Dispenser from KEIKO

MECHA 芽茶

Tea Garden	Oishita'en
Heating	Steaming
Shading	Medium to heavy
!	Buds sorted out during the production of Sencha or Gyokuro

Mecha, bud tea, is one of the three Demono, i.e. the buds and leaf tips of second choice and are therefore sorted out of Aracha during the Sencha or Gyokuro production.

As Mecha is the reject of the high quality spring harvest, it offers high quality at mostly low prices.

Although Mecha is usually called Demono, top quality is also available, in which case it is made from first choice buds. Intense and somewhat bitter, it can be almost equated with good Sencha.

SENCHA 煎茶

Tea Garden	Roten'en
Heating	Steaming
Shading	None
!	Accounts for about 70% of Japanese green tea production.

Sencha is a fine tea in many ways. Visually appealing, medium to dark green and rolled into beautiful needles, olfactorically pleasing in the nose and tasty on the palate, there is no way around it. Starting with Sencha, the world of Japanese teas may ideally be explored.

Sencha means steamed tea and is the classic Japanese tea par excellence, from which most variations originate. Sometimes Sencha may appear a bit boring, as it accounts for roughly three-quarters of the Japanese tea volume, including the cultivar Yabukita, which is the most commonly used. But this does not do him justice, what is boring about almost always providing decent quality? Of course it offers little variety if you drink it exclusively, but nobody is forced to do so. It tastes quite balanced and fresh, but also possesses a certain power.

Since Sencha dominates the market so much, it makes sense to know some classifications to get a better overview.

I have already discussed the names of the harvest periods earlier, the following table shall provide you with a brief overview of some of the quality grades commonly used in Japan.

Sencha grades

Name	Kanji	Meaning
Temomi	手揉み	Hand-rolled Sencha. Previously very common, nowadays only rarely produced for outstanding teas, e.g. for competitions.
Gokujo Sencha	極上煎茶	Best Sencha
Tokujo Sencha	特上煎茶	Special or extra fine Sencha, in general the second highest quality grade.
Jo Sencha	上煎茶	Fine Sencha
Hachiju Hachiya	八十八夜	Harvested 88 nights after the beginning of spring

As with Matcha, dealers are also creative with the Sencha grading system. Only trial and error (which we all love to do) brings us closer to the truth. Or a trustworthy vendor, of course!

VARIATIONS OF THE STEAMING PROCESS

In Sencha production, steaming times of about 30-90 seconds (Chumushi) are common, while Fukamushicha steams for about 120 seconds. This method originally comes from Shizuoka, but is meanwhile used in other regions as well. Because the tea leaves in Shizuoka are thicker than in other regions such as Kagoshima due to the cooler climate, the ingredients do not dissolve as well and the tea also tastes more bitter. The intensive steaming applied causes the cell walls of the tea leaves to open, which results in a strong green color when infused and makes the tea taste milder. Due to the long steaming time of Fukamushicha, it is recommended to choose a lower water temperature and shorter infusion times.

Normally **Chumushi** is not advertised as such, as this is the standard variation. Sencha without an additional name should therefore be Chumushi. Donbukashi (a local variant from Shizuoka) is also quite rare, while **Asamushi** and **Fukamushi** are quite popular variations.

Fukamushicha (深蒸し茶), literally deep steamed tea, also is a general term for Japanese green tea which has been subjected to a non-standard (meaning longer) steaming process. Sencha, Gyokuro, Kabusecha or Bancha can be used for this purpose. Fukamushi is then placed as a prefix in front of the respective tea variety.

Shincha 新茶 or new tea, is secretly considered the best Sencha. It is the tea of the first Sencha plucking. Only the fresh, tender young leaves are plucked, therefore this tea has a very mild, sweet taste with little bitterness. Shincha is very popular in Japan and is only available for a short time. Meanwhile good varieties are also available in many places, but like in Japan they sell out quickly.

Steaming times of Sencha

Type	English	Kanji	Duration in seconds
Asamushi	Light steaming	浅蒸し	10-30
Chumushi	Medium steaming	中蒸し	30-90
Fukamushi	Deep steaming	深蒸し	90-120
Donbukashi	Extreme steaming	どんぶかし	up to 180

SHIRAORE 白折

See Kukicha.

SHINCHA 新茶

Shincha

Instead of Ichibancha (First flush), particularly high-quality tea is also marketed under the term Shincha. Usually a special Sencha is being referred to, but also Gyokuro or Kabusecha can be declared as Shincha. Shincha normally does not undergo the final baking of the leaves, so that it tastes even fresher and greener, but this also makes it less durable before it loses quality.

TAMACHA 玉茶

Tamacha (ball tea) is a kind of lumpy Kamairi Tamaryokucha, offered in the form of small chunks or balls.

TAMARYOKUCHA 玉緑茶

Tamaryokucha, or ball green tea, is baked in a wok after steaming, which makes the leaves smaller and rounder, hence the prefix Tama (ball). Thus no needles are produced, it looks rather curly and is therefore also called Guricha (curly tea). It is not rolled at the end of production.

If it is not produced like a Sencha, i.e. without steaming, it is called Kamairi Tamaryokucha 釜炒り玉緑茶, since it tastes more like Chinese green tea.

Not only does the absence of rolling result in a different appearance, the tea also tastes more sour, fruity, a little bit like berries compared to its rolled varieties. The Kamairi Tamaryokucha also often tastes a little bit more vegetable or slightly nutty. The typical grassy aroma is almost completely missing.

Tamaryokucha is mainly produced on the island of Kyushu, mostly in the Ureshino region of Saga Prefecture. This makes it very rare and not exactly cheap.

Tamaryokucha

TENCHA 碾茶

Tea Garden	Oishita'en
Heating	Steaming
Shading	Heavy
!	Raw product for Matcha

Tencha 碾茶 is the name given to the preliminary stage of Matcha, the leaves not yet ground. It is a shaded tea like Gyokuro, but it is not rolled during drying. For Tencha, compared to Gyokuro, two additional leaves are harvested per branch. After drying, the leaves are broken into flakes and left to grind. In this state they can even be exported and ground in the destination country, as for example KEIKO does in Germany. At least the consumer has the choice of buying the genuine product from Japan or choosing local grinding instead.

YANAGICHA 柳茶

Yanagi (willow) is made from leaves of the so-called post-harvest, i.e. a harvest shortly after the first or second flush. While in the main harvest only the noble and young shoots are picked, for the Yanagi they also harvest older leaves in a generous manner. The fact that these look like willow leaves gives the tea its name. It has a less strong taste than Sencha, but still attracts its fans.

OOLONG (URON-CHA) 烏竜茶

Japanese oolong (pronounced like Uron-cha) is rare, hard to find and (who would have thought) rather expensive, but I must clearly admit to being quite a fan, even though Japanese oolongs may seem rather disappointing at first, lacking many facets of the rich Chinese offerings. But in the niche where it is in terms of taste, Japanese oolong offers outstanding quality and taste nuances that are hard to describe.

They are manufactured according to the same principles as other oolongs, apart from a few local deviations. And yet they are different - thanks of course to the different raw material, terroir and microclimate. Visually and production-wise they may mainly be compared to the red oolongs, i.e. the rather strongly oxidized ones, and moreover they are lightly roasted.

Up to now I could only acquire and taste a rather manageable amount of Japanese oolongs. All of them impressed me positively and made me want more. Besides the fresh and up to only a few years old representatives in organic quality, two aged oolongs have particularly impressed me.

The first one is an Aki (autumn) oolong of indefinite age from Kumamoto, whose aging took place in cooling chambers at -20°C, which gave it its very special aroma. This is only surpassed by a 30 year old oolong from Shizuoka, which was also stored frozen. This form of cold aging brings out notes that are simply incomparable. The fact that both teas were produced in certified organic quality was certainly not detrimental to their exquisite taste and justifies the very high price of these well-aged teas.

Organic Shizuoka oolong, 1991 Limited Reserve

RED (BLACK) TEA (KOCHA) 紅茶

Kocha[174] are more familiar to me than Japanese oolongs, but unfortunately I am less enthusiastic about them than about reds from other regions. I try them, usually find them pleasant and well done, but I do not buy them in large quantities. Although there was never anything wrong with them, they rather seemed a bit boring to me. I think Japan has more interesting things to offer, and red teas are often produced better in other regions of the world.

In spite of my penchant for aged teas, even purposefully matured red teas could not knock me off my feet.

But what I often remember positively is the high quality of smoked Kocha. Whoever appreciates subtle smoke in red tea, whoever finds a strongly smoked Lapsang Souchong too strong and a Zheng Shan Xiao Zhong not smoky enough, may enjoy trying the Japanese smoked red tea or Kunsei Kocha 燻製紅茶. As with good ZSXZ, pine wood is also commonly used here, but I was particularly taken with a type that claims to have been smoked over the (oak) wood of old whisky casks. That was a really great experience I will hardly forget.

Kocha

POST-FERMENTED TEA

Dark or post-fermented teas are very rare in Japan and for this reason alone cannot match the incredibly wide range of varieties and flavors of the Chinese heicha. But what Japan has to offer is really extraordinary and can hardly be compared to post-fermented teas from other countries, in fact they complement the spectrum of dark teas wonderfully. They are often made by ethnic minorities in small quantities and by hand, and yet they are quite affordable. Technically, they are initially green teas, like most Chinese heicha. In trade they are also called Folk Tea. What they all have in common is being very tolerant towards extended infusion times, even several minutes do not make them significantly bitter. Nevertheless, two or more brewing processes are mostly possible.

AWABANCHA 阿波番茶

Awabancha is a postfermented Bancha from the Tokushima or Fukuoka regions and usually harvested in July. Unlike Chinese heicha, the raw Bancha is first cooked, then pressed for weeks in a moist state and finally dried. During the moist pressing process, lactic acid fermentation takes place. This is somewhat similar to the Shu Pu'er, but the Shu is not pressed during the fermentation phase and left to ferment for twice as long. Also, different microorganisms are used in the fermentation of the Shu, so that the result tastes completely different. Awabancha tastes distinctly acidic and is very refreshing.

BATABATACHA バタバタ茶

Batabatacha is native to the Toyama region and used for ritual ceremonies such as weddings. Its harvest takes place at the beginning of August. Unlike the Awabancha, the Batabatacha is not pressed, but stored in moist wooden boxes where it slowly ferments.

I like to drink it very much, it visually reminds me a little bit of old loose leaf Huang Pian from China, but it tastes more fresh and sour, therefore lacking the typical wood and forest elements of Huang Pian. Unfortunately I have not yet managed to correctly whip it with its special whisk in the traditional way, but that does ont harm its taste.

GOISHICHA 碁石茶

Goishicha is most likely the rarest representative in the category of post-fermented Japanese tea. It comes from the Kochi prefecture and its name means Go-stone tea, because its appearance is said to resemble the dark stones of the popular game Go.

In terms of taste, I consider Goishicha to be at the top of this category. Its scent reminds of licorice and plums, its taste of strongly oxidized tea with a little bit of citrus fruit.

Like Awabancha, the material for Goishicha is harvested in July and steamed in hot vapor for several hours. It then rests in moist conditions for a good week, during which a first fermentation starts. It is then layered in barrels, similar to sauerkraut, and doused with its own juice from the initial steaming. Afterwards it is weighed down with stones, i.e. pressed. Here too, lactic acid fermentation takes place over a period of about three weeks. Then the leaves are formed into their typical shape and dried.

Goishicha is prepared in two different ways. It is common to boil a piece (usually only 2 to 3g) for about 10 minutes in 1l or even more water, allowing for one more steeping. This method brings out all the aromas in the tea.

More infusions are possible if you brew the same amount with only a third of the water and let it steep for just a few minutes. After the fourth infusion, the tea will slowly yield. This method produces a cup with emphasis on the sour notes, also very delicious, but different.

This is a tea that lives up to its high production standards, and anyone buying a post-fermented Japanese tea for the first time is safe to start with this, it does not get much better.

Goishicha

MIMASAKACHA 美作番茶

Mimasakacha or Mimasaka Bancha, on the other hand, is a lightly fermented tea which, like Awabancha, is first boiled and then dried in the sun. It is sprinkled several times with its own cooking water to keep it moist, whereby a light fermentation process begins. Like Goishicha, it also offers a clearly different result depending on the method of preparation (long boiling versus shorter brewing). It hails from the Okayama region, better known as Mimasaka.

Mimasaka Bancha

KOREA 한국

Between China and Japan we not only have the Korean peninsula, but there is also a big gap in my knowledge. I have perhaps drunk a few dozen Korean[175] teas to date and there are not even ten of them in my current stock. Even when I was still buying rather indiscriminately, Korean teas rarely found their way into my shopping basket. Was this due to my ignorance, or more to the fact that the local trade was holding back with a broader range of offers? Well, even in Korea itself, coffee and other infusions are seemingly more popular than tea.

Of course, the moderate production volume is also responsible for the small supply. Korea produces only one percent of the tea produced in Turkey or Vietnam, and even only one per mille of the quantity produced in China. Japan produces about 33 times more tea than Korea, so it does not come as a surprise that not a lot of tea is exported from Korea. Also, tea is unlikely to be one of the strategic export products in comparison to cars or electronics in this wealthy country.

Well-known growing areas are Boseong (largest) and Hadong (oldest). However, in the last 30 years, especially on the island of Jeju, many plantations of organic qualities have been established which are export-oriented. The production is mainly based on Japanese methods, which also means that for the international market the teas are called Matcha, Sencha, etc.

Let us first take a look at the somewhat different tea types that one should be familiar with. Before we do so, however, we must first look at the term Balhyocha, as this sometimes leads to confusion.

In Korea there are basically two categories of tea, the non-oxidized tea and the oxidized tea or Balhyocha 발효차.

Simply put, in Korea everything that is not green tea is called Balhyocha. This means that yellow, oolong and red teas, but also post-fermented ones, fall under this term.

GREEN TEA (NOKCHA) 녹차

Green tea is classified according to harvest time and leaf grades, similar to China, where the earlier harvest is generally considered to be the highest quality in terms of pricing. The following brief table lists them together with the differing romanized spellings commonly used.

If you are familiar with the harvest times and the regions mentioned, you only also need to know some of the best known producers or tea farms and can then decode the names of many Korean teas. The names of the teas on offer are usually made up of these three components, the variety, the harvest time and the origin.

Naming of Korean harvest periods

Period	한국어	Meaning
Teuk Ujeon	특우전	March pluckings are very rare and buds only. Usually they are not found in the trade, but regular Ujeon seems to be euphemistically renamed to Teuk Ujeon. Purchase with caution.
Ujeon Woojeon	우전	First flush, harvested before the first spring rain. Usually two leaves and a bud. Similar to Japanese Shincha or Chinese pre rain.
Sejak Dumul Cha Jaksul Cha	세작 두물차 작설차	Second flush (may be first flush in case no Ujeon has been made before), harvested after the rain. Typically three leaves and a bud.
Joongjak Jungjak Semul Cha	중작 세물차	Late second flush, harvested from late April to end of May. Three leaves and a bud.
Daejak	대작	Third or even forth Flush, more or less summer harvest, big leaves.
Yeop Cha	엽차	Lowest grade, may contain broken leaves and stems, supermarket quality.

Ujeon harvested just a bit too late and thus not allowed to be called that name in Korean trade may be offered as a bargain. Look out for the term Cheonmul Cha 첫물차, which also means first flush.

Woojeon

I brew high end Ujeon almost like I do with Japanese Gyokuro (50°C and below) as the usual 70°C mostly produced a rather unpleasant soapy taste. The temperature may later be increased for the second and third infusion. I keep the initial infusion time a bit shorter than for Gyokuro or Sencha, but as always please try it for yourself and make up your own mind. Later harvests (Sejak, Joongjak, Daejak) may even tolerate more than 70°C, go get everything out of those leaves!

Excellent first flush Sejak qualities are also marketed as Jaksul, or Sparrow's Tongue, because the delicate and still partly unopened shoots supposedly remind of their shape.

Jeungje Cha 증제차 is the Korean term for green tea (of any harvest period) which is steamed like Japanese Sencha and sometimes it is (incorrectly) marketed as such.

YELLOW TEA (HWANGCHA) 황차

Considering Hwangcha to be simply synonymous with Chinese yellow tea would be incorrect. Hwangcha technically resembles an oolong to some extent, because it is partially oxidized. However, there is also a brief fermentation or composting process similar to that of Chinese yellow tea, but without the preceding kill-green process[176]. Without kill-green, the raw material is more likely to be considered white and not green tea, which is used for yellow tea production in China. Hence, the Korean Hwangcha tea is not identical to the Chinese Huang Cha, because kill-green only occurs after the processing is completed, during the final drying process.

Some experts also categorize Hwangcha as slightly oxidized red tea, but since the latter is defined as fully oxidized, there is actually no such thing as slightly oxidized red tea. Nor is it a dark or red oolong, as explained above. So the only thing left to do is to accept Korean yellow tea as a speciality that cannot be forcible squeezed into the classical Chinese color scheme.

RED (BLACK) TEA (HONGCHA) 홍차

Hongcha is called the same as in China. Unfortunately, the few times I had Korean Hongcha in my cup did not leave a lasting impression, but of course they were not truly representative either.

Only a slightly post-fermented Hongcha called Deong i Cha was able to impress me so far. When a tea friend brought it to me, I had only considered it as red tea first, judging by its appearance. At first I was not aware that it was in fact not a fully dried red tea, instead it ripened in a high-quality wooden box for one year before it was moistened and pressed into balls for further ripening. Nevertheless, a smelling test soon made me curious to find out more about all the details. When dry, it had a pleasant smell like a mixture of Shu Pu'er, Liu Bao and dark cocoa.

Deong i Cha

YUJA-CHA (YUZU TEA) 유자차

In Korea, hot infusions are made from an overwhelming amount of substances, not only from herbs and flowers, but also from seeds, sprouts and shoots, roots and barks, grains, beans, algae and fungi. So it comes as little surprise that "tea" is also produced from fruits.

Of course, all the materials mentioned above have nothing to do with Camellia sinensis, I simply took the liberty of mentioning a personal favorite here. And is fruit "tea" not a popular choice around the world, even if it is often made from dried fruits enhanced with aromatic substances?

I enjoy Yuja-cha as an alternative to hot lemon, the freshly squeezed lemon juice that is poured over hot water and simply sweetened with honey or sugar. The yuzu fruit or Yuja 유자 in Korean simply gives off a much finer and more complex aroma than regular lemons. Unfortunately, the yuzu is hard to find outside of Asia, and mandarins are no substitute in terms of taste. The disadvantage of ready-to-drink Yuja-cha is that no fresh vitamins get into the cup, as it is basically nothing but citrus jam, prepared with hot or cold water, similar to British marmalade which also contains thin zests or peel. But if the body does crave for sugar, why not try to combine it with as much flavor as possible?

CONCLUSION

Despite my very modest experience with Korean tea, I am happy to state that not only the location between China and Japan, but also the different influences from both countries (cultivars, production methods, etc.) brings out some interesting facets, especially when Japanese steaming is combined with Chinese roasting. From time to time Korean teas will certainly find their way into my pots again for a change, however, in general they simply do not offer me enough genuine personality and distinctiveness.

INDIAN SUBCONTINENT

Whereas my personal tea focus is on East Asia, I know many people who like to spend a lot of money for the best teas from India and its neighboring countries. First flush by air and hand-picked leaves require a certain financial commitment and offer exciting experiences for the palate.

While not trying to evangelize them, I occasionally offer an overview of the tea specialties of Eastern Asia to friends with rather Indian tea experience. The inherent natural curiosity of mankind should make for plenty of interest in such a voyage of discovery - at least one would think so. Sometimes, however, the enthusiasm of those invited is rather moderate. Whether it is because they believe that they have already found the perfect treat or whether they are put off by the tea quality of the common Chinese restaurant is beyond my knowledge. If these people are happy with their tea, then I am sincerely happy for them and it is just as well.

Nevertheless, this chapter is much less detailed than the one on China, even though the subcontinent includes Bangladesh, Bhutan, Nepal, Pakistan and Sri Lanka, in addition to India. For me personally, the teas from India and the surrounding countries are simply not as versatile or multifaceted as those from further east.

While the chapter on China was sorted by color, I prefer to classify the Indian subcontinent by growing area. Even if white, green or oolong teas are sporadically produced, the subcontinent is still a black tea region. Indian picking standards and leaf qualities have already been discussed in previous chapters.

Since the 19th century, India has been among the world's main suppliers of tea, producing almost one third of the entire world's demand for (black) tea.

Although as far as I know I have never drunk tea from Bangladesh, at least in blends it will have curdled over my tongue.

INDIA भारत

In India there are two very well-known and several lesser known tea growing areas. Assam and Darjeeling are those two that almost everyone will have heard of. And even though I know about other Indian tea areas, I humbly refrain from talking about them because the teas from smaller areas such as Dooars, Terai or Kangra are so rarely found in my vicinity that I can hardly get hold of them. Not much better is my knowledge of the Southern Indian Nilgiri. However, with Assam and Darjeeling the majority of the Indian tea offered on the world market is mostly covered.

Assam and Darjeeling are not only East Indian tea growing regions, but also a federal state (Assam) or a district (Darjeeling, in the state of West Bengal). The most important distinguishing features of the two regions are summarized in this tiny table:

State	Tea production area	Elevation	Dominant variety
Assam	Assam	Lowlands	Assamica
West-Bengal	Darjeeling	High mountain	Sinensis

ASSAM असम

Assam, huh, now, what do I have to say about Assam? Countless cups drunk, perceived in countless blends, accepted as strong and drinkable and more or less written off. I usually drink Assams in Indian restaurants together with my meals, but even when the restaurant offers loose leaf tea I tend to ask for Ceylon tea.

Tea has been cultivated in Assam since the 1830s, for which purpose the native, wild Assamica[177] plants were crossed with Sinensis imported from China, thus achieving more taste and particularly higher yields. Unlike Darjeeling, Assam hardly produces any green tea, although Assam is said to be the world's largest single tea-growing region. Unlike the highlands of Darjeeling and Nilgiri, Assam tea is grown in the lowlands.

High quality SFTGFOP Assam

Assam usually sees two harvests a year, the very early first and the second flush, with the local peculiarity that the second flush usually has more leaf buds or tips and is sweeter, which is expressed by the suffix T for tippy.

Assam is (with some exceptions) a rather malty, often quite bitter tea. Unfortunately its bitterness is of a kind that does not make it easy for many people to enjoy in its pure form. Assam (single-estate) is often also a bit one-dimensional, simply put, either too weak or too bitter. And so they are frequently used in blends, which are then marketed as English Breakfast (often blends from Assam, Sri Lanka and Kenya), Irish Breakfast (mainly Assam), Scottish Breakfast, Welsh Breakfast or the well-known East Frisian blend. The main ingredient of all these breakfast teas are Assams, which can handle hard water much better than more subtle varieties. At an early stage, importers began to take into account the varying regional preferences (and water qualities) available to their customers and started blending these particular regional teas.

Even if I do not envy the professional tea tasters in their Hanseatic or British offices for their job, I cannot help but respect them for their achievements. To create a blend from umpteen different raw teas year after year, and to consistently reproduce the well-known taste of their respective brands is certainly a challenging task.

According to my observation, "breakfast" means that most consumers drink these teas at least with sugar and often also with milk, which can taste quite appealing. There is little to be said against this combination if you desire a sweetened drink.

As with most teas from India and Sri Lanka, I prefer to purchase once again from tea gardens or regions that have already attracted my attention. My urge for research and discovery of new tea is not as strong here as it is with Chinese teas.

DARJEELING दार्जिलिंग

At the beginning of the first chapter I wrote about my first experiences with black teas, and just now I expressed ambivalence towards Assam. Although I am aware today that the cheap black teas of that time did not come from India most of the time, in later years I still often had reservations about Indian teas, but never about Darjeeling. Of course, there are charmless plantations there as well, allowing only for a boring infusion to be made. But I have rarely had completely awful experiences, even with tea bags. It goes without saying that even Darjeeling bags never gave me the greatest pleasure.

Darjeeling is completely dedicated to the cultivation and modification of the famous Darjeeling tea. Due to the different sites in which the tea is grown, about a dozen variations of Darjeeling are available. These depend on the date and type of harvest, climate, position of the slope towards the sun plus a number of other factors. There is the first flush, in-between flush, second flush, monsoon flush, third flush, and even white and green Darjeeling. Even a lonesome oolong might sometimes find its route to market.

Admittedly, I did compare some aspects of wine and tea in the preface. Still, I do not know why some advertisers, retailers or authors always declare Darjeeling (or alternatively Oriental Beauty oolong) as the champagne among the teas. Let us completely disregard the fact that champagne is made from Pinot and Chardonnay wines from a very small growing area (around 33,000 hectares) and let us also assume that champagne is the highest of feelings when it comes to sparkling wine. Darjeeling in contrast is a vast growing region, where countless mediocre plantations and less often excellent farms produce their daily crop. To lump them all together is way too simple, even for marketing purposes. But on the other hand, in some delicate teas, such as the highest quality Darjeelings, one can certainly perceive notes that are slightly reminiscent of white or sparkling wine, but this is also true for Chinese white teas, especially the aged ones.

Darjeelings are less tolerant towards hard water than Assam and Ceylon teas, which in return contain more tannic acid. Thus, depending on the regional water, a delicate Darjeeling can even taste unpleasantly chlorous or at least bland.

Unlike in Assam, in Darjeeling the first flush is always the top of the crop, and it is here where the better qualities and higher prices are obtained.

First flush black Darjeeling, looking very bright and covered with soft fluff

The very first first flush from Darjeeling (which the Japanese would call Shincha) is often expedited by air. Darjeeling enthusiasts used to look forward to receiving their first crop fresh off the plane every year, but the popularity of those teas seems to be declining a bit at the moment. On the one hand, the hype around them has brought the harvesting date forward, which did not help the quality, and then in recent years frequent strikes of the struggling pickers, demanding fair pay, have also made planning difficult.

Not so much out of concern for the environment, but simply because black tea (and that's how Darjeeling is usually produced) does not perish fast and transport by ship is acceptable, I consider air transport for black tea relatively superfluous. In any case, I have been able to find enough first-class and fresh Darjeelings that were not flown in.

Flying in pineapples or mangos makes more sense to me because those are allowed to complete their natural ripening process unlike their cousins harvested prematurely, resulting in quality loss. While I completely support premium air mail for fresh green Japanese teas, I do not get it regarding black teas. Not to mention the carbon footprint this evokes…

Second flush and autumnal Darjeeling (the autumn picking) also have their raison d'être, not only for simple factory blends, but they are also preferred by enthusiasts who favor a somewhat stronger brew. Even price sensitive buyers can still find top-notch and delicately aromatic qualities there.

For some time now, white teas from India have also been appearing on the market, resembling Chinese teas. In the trade, they are for instance offered as Indian White Peony and are definitely an alternative to the Chinese whites, even if their typical Darjeeling aroma cannot be denied. Somewhat stronger in aroma are the rare Darjeeling greens, very close to the common blacks, but lacking in sweetness. In return they taste more refreshing while still being typical Darjeelings.

Green Darjeeling from the Steinthal plantation

I cannot help the impression (and the color of the leaves seems to confirm my suspicions) that some (black) first flush Darjeelings are not fully oxidized teas, so the difference in taste to green Darjeelings is sometimes rather small. Second flushes, on the other hand, are always completely oxidized, showing full black leaves. They are also darker and more mineral and earthy in the cup, less floral and more reminiscent of white wine.

As far as I can remember, I have only drunk a handful Darjeeling teas declared as oolongs, but it is obvious that not all black teas from Darjeeling have always been fully oxidized. Even though they might have been handpicked and skillfully produced, these teas declared to be oolongs did not tempt me to try more of their siblings. Darjeeling should rather, if I had a say in the matter, continue to concentrate on black and also green and white teas.

For Darjeeling fans who have only drunk the black ones so far, the white and green teas might manifest an excellent alternative.

Darjeeling oolong

Top Darjeelings I got to know from the tea gardens of Gopaldhara, Jungpana, Maharani Hills, Makaibari, Margaret's Hope, Pasabong, Phoobsering, Pussimbing, Puttabong, Risheehat and Steinthal, but you will certainly find many more proper offerings. I have to thank Margaret's Hope for some of my best Darjeeling memories, but please go and discover for yourself. Remember to choose the better qualities according to your financial capabilities, considering the overall low price of tea this should yield positive results for most people.

MASALA CHAI मसाला चाय

Masala is usually known as Garam or Tandoori Masala, powdery mixtures of roasted spices, darker and stronger than the typical curry powder popular in the West. Masala simply means spice and is ubiquitous on the entire subcontinent. For the sake of simplicity, however, Masala Chai is included under India in this book.

A masala also exists for tea purposes, a blend of different ingredients (not in powder form) in both traditional and enhanced quality. A selection of spices such as anise, black pepper, **cardamom, cinnamon, cloves**[178], fennel, **ginger, laurel**, mace, nutmeg, star anise, vanilla, or even chili are cooked together with black Indian tea (preferably Assam or the inexpensive Monsoon Darjeeling) for several minutes and results in a powerfully spicy and yet refreshing drink. Modern, western adaptations also add vanilla or cocoa beans to the spice blend. To be avoided are blends in ground form, their flavors are not pleasant in this form.

Masala Chai blend

It is however the milk which is the special ingredient in this Indian delight. Depending on your preferences, milk, more or less diluted, is boiled for about a quarter of an hour with the mix of tea and spices, sieved, and then generously sweetened with sugar or honey. The finished drink is called Masala Chai, which simply means spiced tea. It is often served free of charge after a meal in restaurants and therefore it is, for Indian restaurateurs around the world, the equivalent to the grappa, raki or ouzo of the Italian, Turkish or Greek restaurants.

Masala Chai may, if prepared well, taste very impressive, but it is often served as a rather loveless extra, so most of the times, I decline the free offer.

NEPAL नेपाल

Geographically, Nepal only partly belongs to the Indian subcontinent and could therefore also fall under Other Asian countries, but due to the rather Indian-influenced tea cultivation it is included here. After all, Nepal borders Darjeeling in the east, so there is no shortage of cross-border exchange of experience and tea among these high mountain regions.

The tea garden Jun Chiyabari is known especially, producing outstanding qualities not only in terms of taste, but also visually appealing teas. About 50 kilometers to the south, a feeder river to the Ganges has its source and tea gardens such as Aishwarya cultivate good qualities of white, green and black teas. Smaller farms also sell their material to factories such as Himalayan Shangri-La Tea Producers, which then ends up in blends, but is also worthy of attention.

White organic Shangri La 2nd Flush

Black Aishwarya first flush

SRI LANKA ශ්‍රී ලංකා இலங்கை

Despite being renamed in 1972 to its current country name, many teas produced in Sri Lanka (the third largest tea producing country in the world) still bear the old country name "Ceylon". Maybe that is because the term "Sri Lankan tea" or "Tea from Sri Lanka" does not roll off our tongues as smoothly as "Ceylon tea".

Silver needles from Sri Lanka

The country offers many different kinds of tea, which are grown in seven different regions in the southern part of the island. In general, these are black and green tea varieties, with the former being the dominant kind.

Like I already mentioned in the section about Assam, tea from Sri Lanka simply appeals more to me. In addition to the dominant maltiness, I recognize more aroma diversity and finesse. On the other hand, this preference may also be due to the fact that I have mostly come across single estate teas from there more often, i.e. teas whose material originates from a single tea garden and which has not been blended at factories using tea from different origins.

Tea regions of Sri Lanka

Region	Altitude	Comments
Nuwara Eliya	Almost 2,000 meters	Highest region, most delicate tea
Dimbula	Over 1,250 meters	Mild and refreshing
Uva	900 to 1,500 meters	Monsoon region with a unique, mild aroma
Uda Pussellawa	950 to 1,600 meters	Neighbouring region to Nuwara Eliya, but fuller and more spicy
Kandy	650 to 1,300 meters	Different aromas depending on the altitude, very aromatic and full-bodied
Ruhuna	Below 600 meters	Strong, dark cup
Sabaragamuwa	Sea level up to almost 800 meters	Similar to Ruhuna, but sweeter or more caramel and milder

Whenever I have the choice when it comes to Ceylon tea, I request (black) Nuwara Eliya, because these teas have always tasted delicious to me without exception (as always, I am only talking about loose leaf quality), but I also had very good Silver Needles from there. Black tea from Ratnapura (Sabaragamuwa) will also positively remain in my memory.

Teas from Sri Lanka make me crave for more, so this country, alongside Colombia, is at the top of my list of upcoming travel destinations. As with Colombia, I would especially like to taste green teas on-site in Sri Lanka.

OTHER ASIAN COUNTRIES

While a Lao Wai 老外 (foreigner)[179] can never have a complete understanding of the range of Chinese, Indian or Japanese teas on offer, it is however available in abundance and good quality around the world. Less frequently and not always as well, teas from other Asian countries are also available. While it is certainly a bit strenuous to acquire Korean tea in Europe, there are countries which, rightly or wrongly, make themselves even more scarce. Still, at least we want to take a quick look at them.

Russia will not get its own section here, even if the country is well known among the tea-loving nations because of the samovar or drinking from the saucer. It should be mentioned, however, that the Russian caravan tea is not a domestic product, but a blend from China, mostly made of Qi Men, Dian Hong and for the hint of smokiness also some Lapsang Souchong. In former times, these teas were transported on camel backs over thousands of kilometers towards the West.

GEORGIA საქართველო

Honestly, I know exactly two teas from Georgia, the country between the Black Sea and the Caspian Sea in the north of Eastern Turkey. I got both of them from a dear tea friend who brought them to me from a shop in her home country.

Before the Soviet Union disintegrated, Georgia was one of the world's leading producers of simple teas for the mass market, which were produced in huge factories. With the end of the USSR, the market collapsed and the plantations lay abandoned. Georgian tea production declined massively and local farmers kept producing tea for their own consumption only.

For a few years now, committed young Balts have been working with the company Renegade Tea Estate to revive some of the old areas to produce new tea, and are already exporting their first products, which originate from their own gardens and those of befriended farmers. According to their own information no pesticides are used, so that the quality from those locations in the province of Imereti should be more or less comparable to the Chinese heicha Shengtai.

I have this producer on my bucket list, but the two teas I mentioned in the beginning came from a producer in the neighboring province Guria. In the English speaking trade those black teas can be found as Georgian Old Lady and Georgian Caravan from Naghobilevi.

Both floral and earthy, the Old Lady is a very positive surprise, and the smoked Caravan also leaves pleasant memories. One should keep an eye on Georgia, at least as long as tea continues to be produced there with the same care and craftsmanship as it currently appears to be.

Georgian Caravan

INDONESIA

The islands of Sumatra and Java produce the lion's share of Indonesian tea and make the nation the fifth largest tea producer in the world. While Indonesia is a beautiful country and produces excellent coffee[180], I cannot say much positive when it comes to tea from that region. Whenever I drink Indonesian teas, my mood goes south fast.

For research purposes and in order to be fair we recently sat together again in a small group and tasted three fresh teas from Java, one green and two black teas. The first Javanese, a black Orange Pekoe from the north of Bandung was just trivial, arbitrary and slightly smoky. To spend more words about this unloving mass product would be a waste of paper - or pixels. At a price of around 2 Euros for 100g, however, nothing much could have been expected.

Straight away, we increased the stakes and brewed up the second black, which after all had the attribute honey prominently in its name and was much more expensive. And in fact, a natural honey note was detectable, even accompanied by a milky note in the second infusion. Sadly the leathery and weak-looking leaves did not yield any more taste, we just could not take the third infusion seriously any more.

Finally, a green Pekoe Souchong from the Purwakarta region reconciled us a little. We brewed it with almost 70°C and tasted tamarind, ginger and a slight smokiness, but it was also quite watery, despite an infusion time of 45 seconds. Courageously the second infusion was then carried out at 100°C and was allowed to infuse for 75 seconds, so that we could squeeze everything out of the leaves. Unfortunately, nothing really came out of them. Admittedly, the leaf grade was not the finest and the price more than fair, but I do not like to waste any lifetime drinking such teas. Of course, these samples are not representative, and nothing would please me more than to be proven wrong. However, I already spent one month in Indonesia and whenever possible I rather drank coffee for a reason. Personally I am done with Indonesian tea and I have filed this country as a producer of bulk tea for good.

25 years ago, one of the IT reference books I wrote at the time was translated into the national language Bahasa Indonesia, but because of my thoughts on Indonesian teas, I would rather not have this actual book translated…

LAOS   ປະເທດລາວ

For a long time I have not had Laos on my tea radar, having only been able to get hold of some sad green teas from there a long time ago. The northern province of Phongsaly borders on China, more precisely on Yunnan province, offering a similar terroir. Due to the low wages in Laos compared to China and the annually increasing prices of heicha from Yunnan, more and more tea Chinese farmers have started buying material from Laos and pressing it either locally or in China, then marketing it through their distribution channels. As long as the origin is clearly stated, there is nothing to oppose this approach. This way, an economic exchange and knowledge transfer may take place from which the entire region might benefit.

Although Laos has ancient tea trees of its own and many workers and pickers have been working in China for a long time, the quality is not yet fully competitive with Chinese teas. The leaf material is quite decent, but the tea masters still seem to need some more training. More and more tea is becoming available, however, and the quality development in Laos should be monitored very closely in the long term. The only irritating fact to me is heicha from Burma or Laos often being offered in the trade as Pu'er tea (and sometimes even with fake Chinese provenance) and not as Burmese or Laotian dark tea. It would be similarly strange if Spanish cava or Italian spumante were sold as champagne instead. I do not wish to accuse any vendor of malicious intent, especially when a non-chinese origin of the tea in question is not known to them, but the already little-informed global market will not get any smarter from this.

Chunk of a young Sheng from Phongsaly

MYANMAR မြန်မာ

The Chinese province Yunnan borders on Myanmar, Laos and Vietnam, and accordingly the climatic and soil conditions, the ethnic groups and languages, and their affinity to tea are relatively similar.

Formerly called Burma, the country was almost completely isolated from the outside world for about 50 years and has only been opening up cautiously in the past decade or so.

In eastern Myanmar lies the region known as Shan State, which borders Laos to the east, Thailand to the south and Yunnan to the northeast. At the very northeast of Shan State lies the Kokang Autonomous Region, Chinese Guogan 果敢, which is predominantly inhabited by ethnic Han Chinese. There, the conditions for the tea business are similar to those in

Laos and the Burmese farmers have begun to position some of their products on the international market as well. I have not yet seen truly great teas from there but they are very mild and balanced, somewhat resembling a characteristic Jingmai.

Like in Laos, Chinese tea farmers are also active, and the first Sheng heicha are already finding their way onto the world market and are already quite promising, especially for tea enthusiasts on a budget. Again, like with tea from Laos, various traders do not yet understand that Burmese Sheng is not Chinese tea, so buyers beware.

Sheng of the Sen Zhi Kui factory from Kokang

THAILAND ประเทศไทย

Thailand has been growing tea for a considerable time. Oolongs are probably the best known, but in recent years more and more post-fermented tea from Thailand has been coming into the trade. This is quite understandable and welcome, because even if Thailand does not directly border on China like Myanmar (in the southwest), Laos (in the south) or Vietnam (in the southeast), the northern mountainous region of Thailand is only 100 kilometers away from the south of Yunnan. And there, in the provinces of Mae Hong Son, Chiang Mai and Chiang Rai, just south of the border to Myanmar, the main tea growing areas are located.

Since the transfer of knowledge in the oolong field is often done by Taiwanese experts, it is not surprising to find Taiwanese cultivars and clones of the Taiwanese Greatest Hits there, mostly labelled with the TTES numbers, just like in Taiwan. The fact that Thailand does not share a common border with China may also benefit the prosperous cooperation with Taiwan. Apart from the omnipresent cultivar Jin Xuan, especially Dong Ding, Ruan Zhi and Si Ji Chun have become popular.

NANG NGAM นาง งาม

The world famous Taiwanese oolong Dong Fang Mei Ren (Oriental Beauty) is also imitated in Thailand, where they call it Nang Ngam or Beauty Queen.

CHA KHAO HOM ชา ข้าว หอม STICKY RICE TEA

Those who know and appreciate rice in its natural form, and not the rather strange parboiled (non-sticky) variant, may also enjoy the Thai tea called sticky rice.

It should not be confused with Japanese Genmaicha, which is known to contain puffed rice, the Cha Khao Hom offers a rather remotely related scent. Cha Khao Hom tastes like sticky rice smells, which sometimes seems to me to be slightly fried or burnt, but in a very pleasant way.

This special taste is achieved by two components, on the one hand the Jin Xuan (Milk oolong) and on the other hand an herb visually resembling peppermint, bearing the botanical name Semnostachya menglaensis H. P. Tsui. It is endemic to southern Yunnan, parts of Myanmar and northern Thailand and gives off this typical sticky rice flavor.

Despite the usually quite unpretentious oolong quality used for Cha Khao Hom, I like to drink this flavored tea, which might partly be due to the fact that rice is also my preferred source of carbohydrates.

The Chinese call the herb Nuo Mi Xiang 糯米香, which simply means sticky rice fragrance or taste. Now and then some Pu'er, Sheng as well as Shu, are also flavored with Nuo Mi Xiang in China. I am not sure what to think about that and I have not yet been tempted to taste such material. Such teas are sold as Xiang Mi Cha 香米茶.

Sticky rice oolong

TURKEY

A small part of Turkey is geographically located in Europe, but the rest of Anatolia is located in Asia, so I categorize Turkey under Asia. Turkey is certainly a great country with an old tea culture, but the quality of tea and the excitement it brings to me seems rather limited. Maybe I am merely ignorant and have always bought the wrong teas or sat in the wrong tea houses. But no matter whether on the ferry across the Bosporus, in the shop of a carpet dealer in Istanbul, in simple or upscale restaurants in Germany or Turkey, or in the homes of Turkish friends, I have never been able to perceive big differences in Turkish tea. Admittedly, Çay is almost always drunk with sugar, so one does not taste much else anyway.

In other words: I enjoy drinking Turkish tea, but I do not expect top gastronomic quality. It is rather the people who drink with me that determine the quality of Turkish tea. They make the tea pleasantly sweet, whether drunk with or without sugar.

My home country Germany is considered to be the largest importer of Turkish tea, which is certainly because of the vast number of our Ottoman[181]-born fellow citizens; of the approximately 500 tons that are exported annually, about a quarter goes to Germany. Tea cultivation in Turkey only began about 150 years ago. The Black Sea region around Rize, where the first tea factory was founded in 1947 and which is still the hub of the Turkish tea trade as of today, accounts for more than 5% of the world's tea production with half of it going into export. In the supermarkets, one mostly looks for Rize Çay when in need and basically always gets a coal-black small-leaf tea in practical pounds or kilo packets at incredibly low prices.

Turkish tea is also available in bags, but then the whole flair goes missing

While tea from Turkish factories certainly does not arouse enthusiasm (they also often origin from abroad, e.g. Sri Lanka), for many people they are pleasant, simple and inexpensive daily drinkers who do not have to hide behind so-called breakfast blends at all. There are certainly people who do not care that much about huge assortment and top quality and who just want to drink something warm (and sweet) all day long. And here Turkish tea is at its best, especially when its preparation takes place in the authentic Çaydanlık, or also in the better known samovar.

The Çaydanlık consists of two metal pots stacked on top of each other; the lower, lidless pot contains hot water and the upper one an ultra-strong brew of tea. The samovar is basically a metal hot water boiler in the form of a table-top appliance from which hot water can be drawn at any time by means of a tap. On top of the samovar sits a smaller metal pot in which a concentrated tea brew can be kept warm all day long. This brew is practically a much too strong tea, which is prepared in the morning and then put into tea glasses in small quantities and gets thinned with the hot water. The ratio of this concentrated tea to water varies according to taste. Those who like it to be mild demand an Açık Çay, the stronger infusion (with less water added) is called Demli Çay.

I do not have much more to say about Turkish tea, in by all means possible I prefer a good Turkish mocha instead.

It is said that there is quite acceptable white tea from Turkish production, but I have not come across it yet.

VIETNAM   VIỆT NAM

Vietnamese tea scarcely appears in trade, or at least can hardly be identified as such. At present, I am not aware of any high quality examples, and it is probably no coincidence that the country itself seems to prefer flavored teas of all sorts, e.g. with added jasmine or lotus.

Vietnamese GABA-oolong

Also popular in Vietnam[182] is the Kudingcha, Chinese 苦丁茶, which is made with the leaves of either a wax tree or a holly species and has nothing to do with Camellia Sinensis. I drink it very seldom, but then rather as a medicine. Its bitterness is unparalleled, even topping the mightiest fresh Shengs from Bulang.

Fish Hook

Even though I am not a fan of GABA teas, I keep stumbling upon quite acceptable GABA oolongs from Vietnam, which are almost ridiculously cheap, often made of Jin Xuan (TTES #12), rather green and only slightly roasted. For sure the altitude of the southern cultivation region Lâm Đ`ông (over 1,000 meters) contributes to the aroma.

A nice curiosity for me is a tea from the northern Vietnamese province Thái Nguyên. The green tea with the charming English trade name Fish Hook is considered a traditional Vietnamese tea and carries its name for obvious reasons. It needs to be brewed at well below 70°C, and I even prefer to choose only 50°C for the first infusion, the second one may be a tad hotter. Also the infusion time is unusually short, more than 15 seconds is not advisable. Whether this is due to the regional cultivar Ta or to the production process is beyond my knowledge, but whoever wants to get to know this exotic tea should treat it with care. It grants a creamy taste of grass and cereals, somewhat reminiscent of yellow tea and cooked soybeans.

The tea served by our friendly Vietnamese neighborhood restaurant cannot score plus points either, but that is no different in many Chinese restaurants.

However, as with the other non-chinese tea-growing regions adjacent to Yunnan, it is safe to assume that the quality of Sheng Pu'er imitations will continue to increase in Vietnam and that in five to ten years' time we might be offered cheap and appealing competitors from there. Unfortunately, the samples I have tasted so far are not yet at a level that I consider recommendable.

Kuding "tea"

AFRICA

Tea in Africa is mainly produced in the five East African countries, which are discussed in the following. Often South Africa is added to this list because of rooibos, but first of all this is not tea (yes, I am repeating myself here), and secondly I personally do not know any real teas from South Africa, so it just does not have a place here. The same applies to Cameroon, Mauritius, Zimbabwe and further countries from which I have not tasted any teas so far.

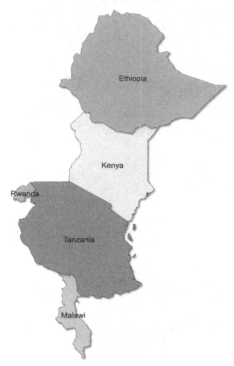

ETHIOPIA ኢትዮጵያ

So what was I thinking when buying tea in Ethiopia? As far as I remember the reason was a drink I had on the streets of Addis Ababa which excited me and then made me go search for more. This drink is called Bunna Sprice and is a mixture of tea and coffee. When it was first offered to me, I almost refused to taste it - but what would I have missed!?

Bunna Sprice

Bunna Sprice is a strong (spiced) coffee that floats on top of tea, both dividing the glass into halves. Already visually appealing, Bunna Sprice also has an interesting taste and offers a convincing result. Whether you simply drink it from top to bottom or stirred is up to you, I opted for stirring.

Unfortunately I wasted some time in this amazing coffee country in an attempt to find decent loose leaf tea. Unfortunately, the herbs and weeds which were offered to me for tea were so dreadful in look and taste that I soon decided to put them to better use as fertilizers in my garden.

Ethiopian tea bag

Of course, a few random samples are not enough for a verdict, but thanks to the excellent coffee in Ethiopia (when in Rome…), one can get along very well without tea there.

TANZANIA

On holiday in Zanzibar, which is situated in the Indian Ocean off the coast of Tanzania and politically affiliated to it, they always offered tea in the morning, but mostly from Kenya, if identifiable at all.

At home, I have mostly only found CTC quality from Tanzania, which is not worth mentioning. Only one black tea from the Usambara region has been able to positively surprise me with its delicate acidity, mild honey sweetness and pleasant creamy texture. So it is possible to source decent quality from Tanzania, especially since this one on was only a second flush. Produced carefully, the high mountains there certainly have the potential to deliver quality which is also quite acceptable in terms of price.

CTC from Tanzania

KENYA

This African country is the second largest tea exporter in the world and produces roughly eight percent of the world's tea supply. Large plantations predominate and provide material for mostly simple teas. The quality of the Kenyan teas served in Zanzibar was accordingly of limited quality, but one should probably not come to conclusions about an entire country based on some bags. The latest tea I deliberately bought from Kenya is currently being offered by several traders, at least in Europe, probably thanks to a single importer, as is often the case. It is an orthodox, i.e. hand-picked GFOP. Here the first infusion was an acceptable one, not very aromatic, but halfway pleasantly metallic. However, this tea did not yield a satisfactory second infusion.

Black tea from Kenya

MALAWI

Especially from Malawi, I know some very pleasantly tasting African white teas. In analogy to the Chinese model they call themselves Peony, even if the cultivars used are (hard to believe!) supposedly endemic (some of them leaning more in the Sinensis and some more in the Assamica direction), and thus not comparable on a 1:1 basis with Chinese tea.

The former British colony Malawi is located south of Tanzania, embedded between Zambia and Mozambique. More than a fifth of the country's surface is taken up by Lake Malawi, and in its south the Shire-Highlands (up to 2,000 meters) are located, with the oldest tea factory of Malawi, Satemwa, still existing. Tea is exported in large quantities (Malawi is the second largest African exporter after Kenya) and the quality ranges from simple varieties for blending to very pleasant single estate teas. In Satemwa, every color of tea except yellow is produced, even the first post-fermented is offered (in Shu-style), but I was not yet tempted to get to the bottom of it. The Satemwa tea factory also processes material from surrounding plots of land such as Thyolo or Zomba, which can easily be found in international trade.

It has been a long time since I tried black teas from Malawi, they did not knock me dead, but I had not been looking for top quality then either. Still, what I always keep in stock at home are some exquisite white teas from Malawi.

SATEMWA ANTLERS

The stems (called antlers), which were sorted out during the production of white tea and are offered separately, are particularly appealing to me. Thankfully, they lack any tannin and look a bit like the Japanese green Kukicha.

Satemwa Antlers

In terms of taste, I notice some marzipan, or rather persipan, with a touch of apricot or peach. The Antlers are impossible to prepare the wrong way. 100°C hot water with any infusion time will always result in a drink with a pleasant sweetness. I like letting the third or fourth infusion steep overnight and then enjoy it at room temperature in the morning, sober and immediately after getting up.

BVUMBWE PEONY

The Bvumbwe Peony's name already puts it on a par with the Bai Mudan, the popular Chinese white. In sophistication and complexity it does not quite reach the Chinese tea, but it can certainly proudly raise its head on the world's tea stage. The smell of the dry leaf alone makes you think of champagne and promises a lot, which this tea does not fail to deliver.

Bvumbwe Peony

ZOMBA PEARLS

This hand-rolled, high-quality white tea is less reminiscent of pearls than of the cocoons of caterpillars. When dry, it smells a little like a mixture of Antlers and Peony, the tea tastes delicately creamy and floral.

Zomba Pearls

Malawi will most likely remain my supplier of pleasant alternative white teas for a long time to come, and if its other tea types turn out to be as carefully produced and tasty, then a trip into the full color palette might be a very enjoyable journey...

RWANDA

The last African country I recently let flow through my throat once more was Rwanda. It is a long time ago that I last drank tea from this brave country, which is now prospering again. It was about time, especially since a Fairtrade coffee from Rwanda had recently appealed to me. So I bought one green and one black tea each from the tea factory Sorwathe. The factory is located in the highlands, near the northern provincial capital Byumba and, according to its own information, accounts for almost one seventh of the small country's tea production.

Black

The leaves of the OP black tea smelled pleasantly spicy and fruity, but unfortunately very little of this ended up in the cup. The green tea was quite idiosyncratic, grassy, bitter and clearly sour. All in all a little bit unusual, but not without charm, although quite acceptable for a change.

Green

AUSTRALIA AND NEW ZEALAND

Unfortunately, not many teas from this part of the world have found their way into my cup, only two of them I consider worth mentioning.

ARAKAI SUMMER GREEN

This green tea originates from the east coast of Australia at an altitude of about 500 meters, in the area of the Bellthorpe National Park in Queensland, north of Brisbane. The very young Arakai farm relies exclusively on Japanese cultivars, which they process using Taiwanese methods. Handcrafted very thoroughly, this tea offers an interesting mix of flavors, but without being reminiscent of Korean green teas, which often lie between China and Japan in terms of taste. The Summer Green uses material from Yabukita and Sayama Kaori, tastes mild and delicately sweet and reminds of buttered vegetables. Arakai also offers a premium version with material from other cultivars, which I intend to taste soon.

ZEALONG

The New Zealand teas from the northern island, which are sold under the Zealong brand, are pretty much the only teas that can easily be obtained in my home country, but I cannot help but feeling that every second tea dealer has it on offer. It is not my place to judge all Zealong teas, as I have not tasted either green or black so far. I have tried the rather high-priced Zealong oolong in organic quality, which was quite acceptable, but could not justify its price by any means. It was without fault, but in terms of taste it was nothing special to me.

COLOMBIA

As I have never been able to get anything out of yerba mate, which is endemic to South America, and I cannot remember ever having drunk Argentinean or Brazilian tea, I was at least able to find an organic highland black tea from Colombia, which left me quite bewildered.

The first infusion was delicate and yet full-bodied and rich with a pleasant bitterness, the second infusion, on the other hand, was very weak. A desperate third infusion came out well again - I guess I still have to figure out the proper time and temperature for infusing.

Black tea from Colombia

I know of another highland plantation that also produces green tea, and I intend to taste it on site soon. However, I would guess that it may take a few more decades, like in other emerging tea countries, before world-class teas will be available from there.

Alternatively, I appreciate two other drinks from this wonderful country, on the one hand the delicious coffee and on the other hand a tasty herb that relieves altitude sickness and pain, and which I accept even in a bag for once. Unfortunately, its name has just slipped my mind... ;-)

As an indigenous product it is legally allowed to be sold and consumed in some Latin American countries because of its very low content of active substances which can hardly be turned into anything illegal, at least not with the tiny amounts in teabags.

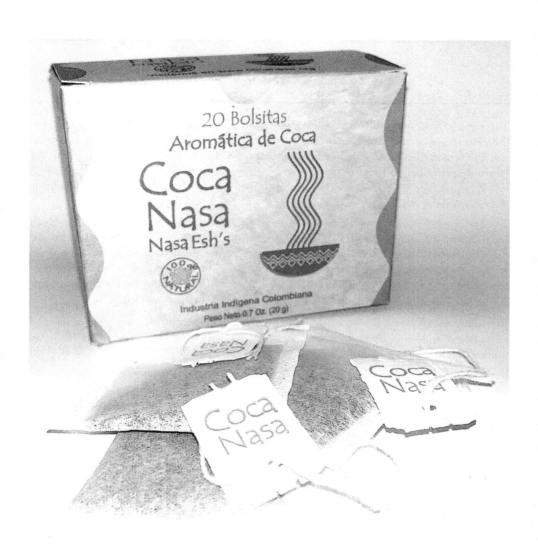

Don't try this at home!

EPILOGUE

Time and again I stand in front of my tea collection and ask myself, how could it come to this? Hundreds of different teas of all origins are waiting to be consumed more or less often. But which teas have really touched my heart, which ones would I take with me to the famed desert island, if I had to limit myself to the proverbial ten best? Oh, that is hard to tell. Why not take 20 or 30 teas? Fortunately, this is just a mind game. So I keep enjoying them, day in, day out.

To conclude, I would like to emphasize that any assessment or evaluation of teas, regions or tea countries etc. only reflects my personal opinion. It is far from my intention to disparage the performance of individual farmers, pickers, tea masters or traders, they all contribute to an outstanding range of teas and they all gave me the chance to develop my personal preferences in the first place. This is also what I tried to convey, suggestions for tasting and studying, which might accompany you on your personal tea journey or Cha Dao 茶道.

According to "chacun à son goût" as the French would nicely put "to each his own taste", I think everyone should drink what they like best. We have complete freedom of choice in teaology, so let us pluck wisely!

I appreciate your attention and the generous support of the lovely people mentioned in the credits.

REFERENCES

As mentioned in the beginning, this is a very personal book, in which I paid little to no attention regarding exact references, as one would do in scientific publications. Nevertheless I would not want to miss out on mentioning some websites and books.

INTERNET

For more in-depth information, I suggest various websites, e.g. of governmental organizations, associations or esteemed bloggers, however, I cannot assume any responsibility for external content.

Organisation or blog	URL
Babelcarp	www.babelcarp.org
China Tea	www.chinatea.com.cn/en
Institute of Fruit Tree and Tea Science (NARO)	www.naro.affrc.go.jp/english/laboratory/nifts/index.html
International Tea Database	www.teadatabase.com
Luyu Standard Rating Center	www.luyubz.com
Mineral calculator (Gerolsteiner)	www.gerolsteiner.de/en/water-knowledge/the-mineral-calculator
Sri Lanka Tea Board	www.srilankateaboard.lk
Tea Board of India	www.teaboard.gov.in
Tea DB	www.teadb.org
Tea Exporters Association Sri Lanka	www.teasrilanka.org
Tea in the ancient world	teaintheancientworld.blogspot.com
Teapedia	www.teapedia.org
Tea Research and Extension Station (TRES)	www.tres.gov.tw/en/index.php
The daily tealegraph	www.instagram.com/thedailytealegraph
The Leaf	www.the-leaf.org

I struggle to recommend any further areas in the so-called "social"[183] networks, even though many decent people do good deeds there. Sadly, misinformation, half-truths, more or less well-hidden advertisement and witticism often undermine this good work. Why not first take a look at the table above?

BOOKS

I would like to share a list of some of the works that have made an impression on me or from which I have been able to obtain educational facts:

- A Glossary of Chinese Puerh Tea; Chan Kam Pong
- China: A History; John Keay
- Chinese Art of Tea; John Blofeld
- Chinese Calligraphy: From Pictograph to Ideogram: The History of 214 Essential Chinese/Japanese Characters; Edoardo Fazzioli
- First Step to Chinese Puerh Tea; Chan Kam Pong
- Puer Tea: Ancient Caravans and Urban Chic; Jinghong Zhang
- Tea Classified: A Tealover's Companion; Jane Pettigrew
- Tea Dictionary; James Norwood Pratt
- Tea: History, Terroirs, Varieties; Kevin Gascoyne et al
- Tea Nation; Rong Xinyu
- Tea Lover's Treasury; James Norwood Pratt
- The Ancient Art of Tea; Warren Peltier
- The Book of Tea; Kakuzo Okakura
- The Classic of Tea; Lu Yu
- The Stonewares of Yixing: From the Ming Period to the present Day; K.S. Lo
- The Tea Enthusiast's Handbook: A Guide to Enjoying the World's Best Teas; Mary Lou & Robert J. Heiss
- The Tea Companion (Connoisseur's Guides); Jane Pettigrew

No books about tea, but crime novels set in Shanghai and all over China are written by Qiu Xiaolong, who resides in the USA. His series of novels about Inspector Chen features ten volumes to date:

- Death of a Red Heroine
- A Loyal Character Dancer
- When Red is Black
- A Case of Two Cities
- Red Mandarin Dress
- The Mao Case
- Don't Cry, Tai Lake
- The Enigma of China
- Shanghai Redemption
- Hold Your Breath, China

Apart from the very cleverly written crime stories, Qiu Xiaolong's books offer insightful literary and personal insights into Chinese history and people's minds, yet I especially like the frequent references to tea and the conversations about and during tea drinking, especially so in The Mao Case. The author also translates classical Chinese poems into English and also writes wonderful poetry himself.

CREDITS

Kudos to the following individuals for their tremendous help:

- Carmen Dennig for intensive proofreading and Isabel Dennig for checking the Japanese.
- Siegfried Spirek, Claudine Bollinger and Ralph Rauschert of our Munich based TeaNuts group for further proofreading and joint drinking.
- Gabriele Messina and Michael 迈克 Ellenrieder as well as Yu Bai 玉摆 and William 威廉 Osmont for their home visits, joint tastings, knowledge transfer and other support.

Any remaining errors are my own. Anyone who kindly provides me with suggestions for corrections also deserves my thanks. I am looking forward to constructive feedback sent to my e-mail address jens@dennig.it.

PHOTO CREDITS

Initially it was my intention to create a text-only volume, but as more and more photos accumulated I decided not to withhold them from you. Nevertheless some supporters also contributed helpfully.

Cover photo, Tea trees, Pang Xie Jiao, Production of Shu, Tea landscape in Yunnan: Copyright © **Farmerleaf**[184]

Matcha qualities, CHADO Mark 1 Matcha Dispenser:
Copyright © **KEIKO** - Shimodozono International GmbH[185]

Yellow tea production, Young leaves of Anji Bai Cha, Tea dealer:
Copyright © **Nannuoshan** - Messina und Hüttig GbR[186]

Huang Jin Ya: Copyright © Ralph Rauschert

All other photos, illustrations and cover design: Copyright © Jens Dennig

Attentive readers will have noticed that the photos in this volume do not always meet the highest standards. Many of them were taken spontaneously on the road or are from olden days, so they were not available in professional studio quality. However, the purpose of this volume never was to produce a coffee table book.[187]

END MARKS

[1] Let's get the brewing temperature right from the start! ;-)

[2] Chádào qīng yùn. To be interpreted as tea ceremony - or even an entire short poem.

[3] Pu'er is officially written as Puer without an apostrophe, but according to Chinese governmental regulations one may also type Pu'er or Pu-Erh. Since I mostly encounter the former spelling, I have selected it. Especially in the Americas Pu-Erh seems to be more common.

[4] Yellow pieces (leaves), which are normally sorted out, but have their own charm. You can read more about this later in the section on Pu'er.

[5] I will still allow myself some deviations, more about that later.

[6] This is something one can live well with, but a rosé or even a "blanc de noir" can certainly make a wine cellar more interesting.

[7] Commonly used transcription method for the Chinese language in Latin letters.

[8] The color of tea in a cup can obviously vary a lot, but a green tea is still a green tea, even if its cup is light and clear or rather yellowish. Relevant for the color classification is only the production process and hence the degree of oxidation.

[9] An oolong cup does not actually look blue, of course. However, the words Lan 蓝 and Qing 清 mean blue or dark green or blue-green. This results from the different perception and naming of colors historically, which not only differs between Asia and the other regions of the world, but also diverges in European languages and cultures.
Personally, I once lived in a house that I would describe as light-mint-colored. Other people, however, sometimes called it green or even blue with conviction. Not only are people's tastes different, but also their perceptions of color.

[10] No rules without exception - more about to follow later in the section on yellow tea.

[11] The tea leaves intended for white tea production are neither kneaded nor fixed, which means that most of the white hairs on the leaves are retained.

[12] This is especially beautiful to observe in Tai Ping Hou Kui. Its tea leaves are rolled or pressed in elaborate manual work and special baskets/grids.

[13] This process called Hong Bei 烘焙 is often repeated after several months or years. If the oolong is left to mature for a long time, it develops special aromas and is then called aged oolong.

[14] Sometimes red tea is confused with the South African rooibos, which is not a tea.

[15] As long as it is not Chinese tea, I will use the internationally accepted term black tea.

[16] Mostly from Darjeeling.

17 Blending is the targeted mixing of different teas in order to achieve a consistent end product for the mass market or to achieve a particularly high quality.

18 This unfinished green tea is called Mao Cha 毛茶. Only further steps like roasting or processing into heicha yield the final, intended aroma. The equivalent Japanese tea over there is called Aracha 荒茶.

19 If you are still not entirely sure what the best tea is, try it again on another day, with different weather conditions or air pressure, with different water or in a different mood. Even small changes can make a big difference.

20 Autumn pickings are often not as valued as the spring ones, which are considered to be of much higher quality, but as it often happens, this is a matter of taste. Autumn harvest is usually cheaper, but due to climatic reasons it might not take place at all and the autumn material is accordingly rare. Therefore, the price differences are not always as big as one might think. Personal taste should be the most important factor in the purchase decision.

21 More about this in the chapter on Tea tasting.

22 For the sake of completeness: the species Camellia sinensis belongs to the genus Camellia in the tea shrub family (Theaceae).

23 It is said to have been brought to the east centuries ago by immigrants.

24 Which actually only applies to the animal kingdom, I am merely putting forward an unsubstantiated hypothesis here.

25 Botanists are trying to put Formosensis at the same level as Sinensis and Assamica based on genetic evidence, as mentioned above. At present, there is still a great deal of disagreement as to whether, when, and if so, to what extent Formosensis is merely a wild cross between Sinensis and Assamica or even a mutation of one or the other variety.

26 I am and always will stay a vegetarian, but I have a dark past.

27 A terroir is essentially determined by its soil characteristics, local climate, altitude, regional cultivars and weather factors such as frequent fog or rainfall.

28 Jin Xuan is also well known and popular under the name Milk(y) Oolong. It is also occasionally used for red tea production.

29 Sometimes also used for red tea.

30 Often used for Pouchong (Bao Zhong).

31 Also used for white tea.

32 Widely used for Long Jing imitations.

33 Qing Xing is genetically very similar to the original Ruan Zhi, so these terms are often used synonymously.

34 TTES #18 is based on a wild endemic form crossed with a Burmese Assamica and developed as a cultivar for red teas. It is reminiscent of cinnamon and fresh mint and very popular.

35 As a cultivar for red tea bred from Keemun (Qimen) and an Assamica from Nepal.

[36] An endangered freshwater salmon species endemic to Taiwan.

[37] Fuding Da Bai is one of the first cultivars mentioned scientifically, also known as Hua Cha #1 or China Tea #1, and many later ones derive from it. It was very popular in the 1960s, but had difficulty coping with periods of drought and lost a lot of popularity among farmers in its native region. In other areas it continues to be a leading white tea cultivar.

[38] Fuding Da Hao (also Hua Cha #2 or China Tea #2) is sometimes mistaken for Fuding Da Bai, but has been bred specifically for drought resistance and has become the trademark of Fuding white teas due to its larger and more productive buds.

[39] Fun Yun #6 is a fine example of a cultivar developed with a focus on yield and uniform development. Harvests are both larger and not as limited by seasons, but it is considered to be rather mediocre in taste.

[40] Xiao Cai Cha (side dish tea) is not well-suited to making the noble Yinzhen (Silver Needles) because of its particularly small leaves and buds. It does not look pretty and cannot be sorted well. Furthermore, its yield after the first spring picking is rather modest and therefore it is also not ideal for Shou Mei. However, since it tastes quite appetizing, it is used for Gong Mei in which buds are still expected.

[41] Zhenghe Da Bai and Fuding Da Bai are the preferred cultivars for the popular Yinzhen. Other qualities such as Bai Mudan or Shou Mei are also derived from it after sorting.

[42] Not to be confused with Pouchong (Bao Zhong).

[43] The proper Chinese name is Zheng Shan Xiao Zhong. But Europeans used to pronounce and spell it incorrectly and so the trading name Lapsang Souchong stuck.

[44] Despite its name, Bai Ye is a cultivar of green tea from which Anji Bai Cha is produced, among others.

[45] Jiu Keng (pigeon nest) is used for Long Jing imitations.

[46] This is a particularly large-leaved cultivar, which is used in particular for Tai Ping Hou Kui.

[47] The date of official registration should not be confused with the age of a cultivar. In 1953, Japan merely began registration, whereas Yabukita, for example, has been known at least since 1908.

[48] In this context Souchong refers to the fourth leaf after the bud, not to be confused with the Chinese meaning in the previous table.

[49] The traditional hand picking and processing is also called the orthodox method of tea production.

[50] The rolling of CTC should not be confused with the rolling of whole leaves in the production of high-quality oolong. Here, the aim is to support the shredding process, not to gently finish premium class tea.

[51] Particles of about one millimeter in size.

[52] The exception proves the rule. Herbata or Garbata was derived from the Latin "herba thea". Herba means herb, grass, green. There are further exceptions in small countries or lesser known languages.

⁵³ Smartphones come in handy here, enabling translating from Chinese or Japanese into foreign languages even in a live camera view. By choosing English instead of other languages as the target language, you might get more precise results.

⁵⁴ They also look quite aesthetic.

⁵⁵ This applies to Mandarin, and in Cantonese there are even nine different ways of accentuation.

⁵⁶ Popular with learners of Mandarin is a rather meaningless, but otherwise correctly formed sentence. In it, only the syllable ma is spoken six times, but with different accentuation. It is exactly this that often causes the greatest problems for students.
According to Pinyin, the sentence 妈妈骂麻马吗 is written and pronounced mā-mamàmámǎma.

⁵⁷ Exception: Japan still uses the traditional Chinese characters for Korea 韓国.

⁵⁸ Strictly speaking, Qing stands for pure, clear, but in the tea context, blue-green is meant. That is why the blue tea or oolong is also called Qing Cha.

⁵⁹ This applies both to purchases made online or in retail stores. However, a Taiwanese tea merchant has asked me to communicate the following advice:
If you are an independent traveller in China or Taiwan and you have been invited by tea farmers or dealers or you are allowed to taste tea in extensive sessions, you have two options. Either you do not buy anything, because the tea is not what you are looking for. That is completely acceptable. Otherwise you have to buy at least 75 grams. Why? Because that is the smallest customary amount of tea. In fact, it corresponds to one eighth of a catty 斤 (600 grams in Taiwan, Thailand and Japan, 604 grams in Hong Kong, Singapore and Malaysia). Open foods are often traded over the counter in catty (in China rather called Jin or Shijin 市斤 and weighing 500 grams). This should not be confused with the metric Catty or Gongjin 公斤, which in China corresponds to the western kilogram.

A purchase of quantities below 75 grams is considered extremely rude, even though Asians usually would not let the implicit insult be noticed. However, this is not likely to generate affection for the western buyer. It is therefore advisable to rather buy 300 grams (half a catty) of the best tea, instead of asking for 25 grams of different teas each.

⁶⁰ In trade and on the bings themselves you will also find the alternative spelling beeng. Internationally, however, the predominant spelling is bing, so this is what I am going with.

⁶¹ 1 Euro was roughly 1.10 US$ at the time of writing

⁶² Artificial word combining tea and education, i.e. the transfer of knowledge about tea.

⁶³ Tea does not always have to be fresh, some of them actually only become truly delicious as they mature. More about that later.

⁶⁴ A tea friend of mine makes it a habit to request a proper customs declaration and invoice attached to the outside of the parcel when ordering from a new non-EU supplier. In two direct comparisons (same dealer, content and order value at the same time) he had a trouble-free delivery, while I was asked to go to customs. I guess I like learning the hard way...

⁶⁵ More details are available in the earlier section on picking standards and leaf qualities in the chapter on varieties and cultivars.

⁶⁶ To repeat myself, the LBZ location offers the most prestigious Pu'er, equivalent to Château Pétrus in the wine world. It is the prime standard of Pu'er, but many other prestigious teas come very close to it and are more affordable.

⁶⁷ A light tobacco or smoked scent can be perfectly appropriate and appreciated in some teas. However, this always only applies to the natural aroma of the plant or what is intentionally applied in the production process. The smell or taste of cigarette smoke or ash is never acceptable.

⁶⁸ A container that can be controlled for humidity or a walk-in room where the temperature can also be controlled.

⁶⁹ Artificial word created from Pu'er and humidor.

⁷⁰ Tea that is no longer fresh but not yet aged may rather be called rested to be more distinct. This typically applies to white teas around five or seven years.

⁷¹ I once used to possess two Long Jing which were almost five years old and which were more than well rested. They had certainly not improved, but were still quite drinkable.

⁷² Now to be called rested.

⁷³ These kettles are called Tetsubin 鉄瓶 in Japan and are used especially during the tea ceremony to provide hot water in style. Large teapots with wooden or rattan handles are called Dobin 土瓶.

⁷⁴ Scale in cm, 2,54 cm equal 1 inch.

⁷⁵ Sometimes you can find pots from Yixing (and elsewhere) under the name Zisha 紫沙. This means purple sand and refers to the corresponding clay quality.

⁷⁶ Instead of clay, sometimes the term ore is used alternatively. This is quite logical, as the iron and mineral content has a decisive influence on the material's quality.

⁷⁷ In fact, the gaiwan is historically derived from rice bowls.

⁷⁸ Barista may sound more exotic, but this is not about coffee, so...

⁷⁹ Zisha 紫沙 or purple sand: generic term for many reddish clay types such as Duanni, Hongni, Luni, Zini or Zhuni.

⁸⁰ Porous clay emits more minerals and softens the stronger Pu'er and heavily roasted Yancha. In contrast, Zhuni is regarded a less porous clay.

⁸¹ Because of their rather smooth and less porous walls, as these teas should not be influenced much by the clay.

⁸² Gaiwan 盖碗: Small Chinese tea bowl (brewing vessel) with lid and saucer, may also be used as a drinking vessel.

⁸³ Typical for the brewing style in Chaozhou, where particularly tiny pots and cups are used, but rarely a strainer.

84 For example, I like to brew Genmaicha in the gaiwan in grandpa style and open the lid just enough so I can drink while the rice and tea remain in the gaiwan.

85 They sometimes also speak of the Matchawan or Senchawan.

86 Occasionally also found in the trade as Cha Zhui 茶锥.

87 The Chinese version of the Japanese word Chasen is Chaxian (Hanzi and Kanji are identical) and may also refer to other forms or purposes, e.g. for cleaning tea utensils.

88 Water vendors are well aware that consumers are conscious of this, and some are already promising improvements, such as the swift introduction of 100% recyclable PET. Whether this can save the planet remains to be seen.

89 Tea can also have an intended and pleasantly bitter taste, for more information see the section on dark tea in the main chapter on China.

90 Of course, all types of tea preparation basically originate in China and "western" brewing is also done there. However, since these terms have become established internationally, I am using them here as well.

91 Known as Chado or Senchado in Japan.

92 I consciously do not quote verbatim here, because it is not my intention to dupe an individual vendor but only to make a point.

93 On the other hand, some experts believe that top-quality teas should be brewed at 100°C, because only then does the tea release all its ingredients. Even if I can somewhat agree with this logic (every now and then I personally inflict the most severe scalding on Long Jing), it should be noted that all ingredients also include those which one would rather not drink or taste.

94 Gong Fu 工夫 stands for work, effort and skill.

95 I go to extremes using gender neutral terms wherever possible but I just never ran into the term grandma style in the tea realm. The name probably derives from elderly men hanging out in the open, sipping their poison whilst playing games with their buddies and such. Meanwhile, back at the ranch, the Chinese women would do all the work, as it still befits some, ahem, rather conservative societies.

96 Without rinsing the first infusion should be made a little longer so that the leaves are allowed to open.

97 I also call it compost heap.

98 Except if one would like to increase astringency by force and extract more catechins and caffeine.

99 This step is optional, but since I often save myself the trouble of sifting the powder, this way I can ensure that no lumps remain in the resulting tea.

100 Please do not let us talk about battery powered milk frothers. Matcha can be easily whipped up manually by any non-handicapped person from age three upwards. It does not make me a snob when I say that anything but the bamboo broom is a break in style, especially since it is so quick and easy to use.

[101] Matcha experts nevertheless recommend beating for at least one minute to maximize quality. The more air is whipped under, the tastier the outcome.

[102] Of particular interest are the aromatic Shincha and medium to heavily steamed Sencha like Chumushi or Fukamushi.

[103] Pun not intended at first, just happened by chance.

[104] A positive side effect of cold infusion: the water quality is not as much a factor as with hot tea. I was usually quite satisfied with ready-to-use ice cubes from the supermarket.

[105] Called Hui Gan 回甘 or returning sweetness. Many tea drinkers rate a beautiful, long-lasting Hui Gan extremely high when selecting and judging tea. Not to be confused with the finish (e.g. when drinking wine), which is noticeable immediately after swallowing, one can feel the Hui Gan further to the front of the mouth.

[106] Comments:
Vanilla tastes spicy, but smells pleasantly sweet, so it is listed twice.

Although botanically strawberries, raspberries or blackberries are not berries but aggregate fruits, aromatically they fit into the berries section..

Due to the production process, a somewhat fishy smell is quite common among some of the younger heicha, especially Shu Pu'er but it passes with the years. The taste of the finished tea should under no circumstances be affected by this.

[107] The topic of aroma is a bottomless pit, when drinking tea you can detect a new aroma almost every day or eventually learn the name of a familiar aroma you could never put a name on. For example, I would like to mention petrichor, the scent that occurs when rain falls on dry earth. Oils and minerals in the soil will dissolve and meet our olfactory organs. Mineral teas like Yancha sometimes display this scent.

[108] With him, however, it is all about whisky.

[109] Botanically, one speaks of the mesocarp.

[110] This applies to most foods and becomes apparent with varying degrees of intensity, especially when flying.

[111] Those who would like to read more about it should research the Internet for keywords such as Five Elements, Five Tastes, Food, Kitchen and China.

[112] It is more or less similar to espresso or coffee, a cup may contain between 50 and 150 milligrams of caffeine. The difference between the Arabica and Robusta varieties alone is quite remarkable, some Robusta may release twice the amount of caffeine compared to a mild Arabica.

[113] People's Republic of China 中华人民共和国 (in simplified Chinese) or Zhonghua Renmin Gongheguo.

[114] Republic of China 中華民國 (in traditional Chinese) or Zhonghua Minguo.

[115] +/- 1 day on the Gregorian calendar.

¹¹⁶ Two great online services assist nicely when looking up details about Chinese teas. At www.babelcarp.org you can search for names and terms in English as well as in Hanzi and get a short and mostly correct definition. If there is a QS code on a tea package, you can also use this code to find out the relevant details provided by the manufacturer online. Although www.qsxuke.com is in Chinese, many browsers already provide automatic translation.

¹¹⁷ Should you ever try to order Ya Bao in China, remember to be extremely accurate in pronouncing it, or even better, ask for Ya Bao Cha right away. An incorrect pronunciation of Ya Bao may also mean Duckburg. Laughter would be guaranteed.

¹¹⁸ The homonymous movie "The Color Purple" is of course an undisputed masterpiece in the fight against discrimination and for liberation.

¹¹⁹ The Chinese green tea En Shi 恩施 is a well known exception, being steamed in the Japanese way rather than pan-fried.

¹²⁰ Anji Bai Cha belongs into the category of Zhen Xing Cha 针形茶 or needle-shaped teas. Needle-shaped can refer to mere, still unopened, buds or to needle-shaped rolled leaves. Loose Guzhu Zi Sun may also be put into this category.

¹²¹ In order to create an authentic taste, however, fresh Nana mint (Mentha spicata var. crispa 'Nane') must be added before serving.

¹²² "It's the teaconomy, stupid!"

¹²³ Gao Shan oolong 高山乌龙 in Chinese. Beware, however, not every oolong from Taiwan is from high altitude, even at sea level there are delightful bushes growing.

¹²⁴ Delicate or well-trained noses recognize the Chinese perfume plant, botanically Aglaia Odorata, in the dry leaf.

¹²⁵ Often also spelled Ti Kuan Yin.

¹²⁶ It has been so long since I last drank Mao Xie that I do not have it listed individually here, because I have no memory of any special features.

¹²⁷ At present there are officially more than 260.

¹²⁸ Admittedly, a number of teas in this chapter bear the syllable Bai for white in their names. But that does not make them white teas, they are and will continue to be oolongs. Likewise, a Bordeaux does not always have to be a red wine, even if this is predominantly the case.

¹²⁹ Taiwan oolong is mainly produced in full ball shape, called Quan Qiu Xing 全球形. This form has also found its way to Anxi on the mainland, where the semi- or loosely rolled shape called Ban Qiu Xing 半球形 used to predominate. Even today the latter can still be found in Tie Guan Yin produced the traditional way.

¹³⁰ The grasshoppers or cicadas go by many different names in China, Taiwan and Japan, depending on the region, thus these shall not be listed here in full detail. Apart from that, current studies show that the scientific name may also have been attributed incorrectly, hence no mention is made here either. If you want to talk about this speciality in English, it might be best to speak of "bug-bitten tea".

[131] Located between Shuangjiang and Yongde, Lincang, in western Yunnan. Also known for excellent Pu'er.

[132] This kind of tea, Wuyi small leaf, was one of the first and most original teas that the English got to know and brought back to Europe. At that time, Wuyi was called Bohea in the West and every now and then this term still appears in writings about red tea or oolong from Wuyi.

[133] Liu Bao and Liu'an are only lightly pressed into baskets, but it is not really "loose" after finishing. Loose (dark) tea is called San Cha 散茶, pressed tea is called Jincha 紧茶.

[134] Most common shape. Usually seven bings are combined into one Tong 筒 (tube). A tong typically contains seven (sometimes only five) bings wrapped in bamboo. Seven bings of 357 grams each make 2.5 kilograms of tea.

[135] With more than a thousand years of tradition one of the oldest shapes of pressed tea. It is noteworthy that bricks are the only form of pressed tea where the syllable Cha comes before the shape. Hence Cha Zhuan instead of Zhuan Cha.

[136] Often written Shou by mistake. In the context of tea, Shou can either mean hand 手 or longevity 寿. In this instance the translation is ripe or cooked and spelled Shu 熟 in Chinese.

[137] For some time now, certain producers have been inoculating their raw tea with a microbial acceleration cocktail which is supposed to aid control of the production process and guarantee uniform quality.

[138] In most cases the date is easy to recognize thanks to Arabic numerals.

[139] www.qsxuke.com

[140] For more details and terms see the chapter Deciphering tea names.

[141] Material from Lincang is said to be used predominantly in the Xiaguan factory.

[142] For the sake of simplicity, the suffix Shan 山 (mountain) has been removed from many location names in this table.

[143] 6FTM for short. Not to be confused with the tea factory of the same name.

[144] A #7 is not known.

[145] Chinese businesspeople are known to be rather creative when it comes to trademarks and copyrights. Especially the digit 4 (factory number) is by far not always correct, as the table after the next illustrates, using the 0821 for example. Also, many leading factories nowadays only trade under the brand names CNNP or Dayi.

[146] Not used for Pu'er, but for many ordinary heicha from other regions.

[147] Also known as Lao Huang Pian 老黄片.

[148] Hence also advertised as Liu'an basket tea.

[149] Su You Cha 酥油茶

[150] Momordica charantia in Latin

151 Also the name of a Yancha

152 As much as I admire Jean-Luc Picard, I just cannot share his passion for this drink.

153 These are the official tea harvest periods. Depending on the geographical, topological and climatic situation, entire regions or individual farms may deviate as needed.

Sometimes no exact distinction is made between the fourth and fifth period in which case this quality is called autumn/winter tea or Akifuyubancha.

For regions with as few as three harvests, the last one is also known as Shutobancha and may take place in autumn or winter.

154 The syllable Ban 番 means order or turn as in shift. So Ichiban is (harvest) #1, Niban is #2, etc.

155 Literally first harvest of the season

156 The equivalent Chinese tea is called Mao Cha 毛茶.

157 Fun fact: Koreans enjoy the roasted brown rice taste so much, they even drink it without actual tea (just steeped in hot water), then called brown rice tea (again: no tea in there) or Hyeonmi Cha 현미차. The Korean equivalent to Genmaicha is Hyeonmi-Nokcha (brown rice green tea).

158 Like Demono, Genmaicha can not only be produced from Bancha, but also from Sencha, Gyokuro and even Hojicha. Genmaicha is also sold spiked with Matcha.

159 Genmai 玄米 means brown rice. However, this refers to the color of the puffed rice. The raw material mostly is peeled white rice.

160 A good 80% of the UV light is filtered, whereas with the Kabusecha it is only blocked about 50%.

161 The special mats used for this are called Kabuse. These block approx. 50% of the sun's rays, while with Gyokuro a different type of covering blocks approx. 80% of UV light.

162 Kabusecha, however, is often only categorized as a variant of Sencha.

163 Kama means kettle or iron pot, thus Kamairicha is kettle (pan) roasted tea.

164 The method of roasting green tea originates in China, which is why Kamairicha is also called Chinese green tea in Japan.

165 When the source material for Konacha is not Sencha but Gyokuro, it is called Gyokuro-ko 玉露粉.

166 The euphemism Micro Cha is also used in trade.

167 There is a trend towards Kokeicha, an even cheaper instant tea.

168 Powdered tea is also available as white tea, black tea and more. Until now I was not tempted to conduct extensive tastings in this area.

169 Bocha is not only visually reminiscent of the Malawi specialty Antlers, but also in terms of taste.

170 Also かりがね

171 Also しらおれ

172 Perfectionists use different whisks (Chasen 茶筅) depending on the intended type of Matcha. For the thick Koicha they tend to prefer a version with about 80 bristles, for Usucha it can be up to 120, thus allowing for more air to make it into the foam.

173 Lesser qualities are offered at reasonable prices for cooking and baking purposes. In the best case this results in a pleasant Matcha taste of the finished product or at least a green coloring. Not a big fan of such pastries myself, I can get a lot out of a Matcha ice cream, especially if it has not been overly sweetened. I also like fresh mochi with Matcha or Matcha chocolate, but I prefer to drink plain water with it. Anybody who enjoys drinking cocoa along with chocolate cake might feel differently.

174 Sometimes romanized as Koucha.

175 Because in the tea business there is no explicit mention of South Korean tea, I will also simply stick to the name Korea, even if the two Korean states have not yet been allowed to experience the joy of reunification like Germany or Vietnam did. Tea from North Korea is only known to me from hearsay, it simply does not matter in this context.

176 Also called Sha Qing 杀青, as detailed in the chapter Types of tea.

177 Assam and southern China are the only two regions in the world where tea plants were once native, still recognizable today by the distinction between the large-leaved and more bitter Assamica and the small-leaved and more subtle Sinensis.

178 Essential traditional ingredients printed in bold.

179 Gaijin 外人 in Japanese.

By the way, I am fully aware of the fact that the term Lao Wai may sometimes be used as a pejorative, too, as it exactly means old foreigner and that more correct terms do exist. Nevertheless, Lao Wai appears to be one of the most common terms understood around non-chinese people and thus I am using it. Also, I am kind of attributing it to myself here, so it should well be politically correct.

180 After all, these coffees are so impressive that Java was at times considered almost a synonym for coffee in the western USA.

181 Ottoman is actually more accurate than Turkish. Virtually everywhere in the former Ottoman Empire tea is still enjoyed in similar form today.

182 Kuding is also grown inChina and Japan.

183 In the so-called social media, many people seem to have nothing better to do but navel-gazing and talking about others and those who look, think or live differently.

184 www.farmer-leaf.com

185 www.keiko.de

186 www.nannuoshan.org

187 Pun intended. More about this at en.wikipedia.org/wiki/Coffee_Table_Book

Made in the USA
Middletown, DE
14 June 2020